Frédérique Lebelley

WALKING THE PATH

Narrative of an experience
with Gurudev Sri Sri Ravi Shankar

Sri Sri Publications Trust, India

Walking the Path
Original title: Célébrez la vie – Leçon de sagesse de Gurudev Sri Sri Ravi Shankar
Author: Frédérique Lebelley

1st Edition 2010

Published by:

THE ART OF LIVING

Sri Sri Publications Trust
The Art of Living International Centre,
21st KM, Kanakapura Road, Udayapura, Bangalore – 560082.
Email: info@srisripublications.com
Website: www.sattvastore.com
Toll Free: 1800-258-8888

ISBN: 978-938059223 7

Translated into English by: Benoite Lavallard,
Alexandra Georgeon-Colin,
Laurence Brian and Sandra Parret.
Edited by Benoite Lavallard

Layout by: Sri Sri Publications Trust
Printed by: Pentaplus Printers Pvt. Ltd., Bangalore

To my Master
and to all
without any distinction of race,
nationality
or religion.

"Without you, where would I be?"

TABLE OF CONTENTS

"I am nothing.
I want nothing.
I am just here to serve you."

Prayer within breath
is silence.
Love within Infinity
is silence
Wisdom without word
is silence.
Compassion without aim
is silence.
Action without a doer
is silence.
Smiling at all existence
is silence!

Your life is writing. It is a sacred book.
Life is the Holy Scripture.
The key is Divine Love, when we feel a lump in our throat.
Life is the expression of the inexpressible.

Gurudev Sri Sri Ravi Shankar

1

THE FACE OF EVIDENCE

OUTSIDE IS THE BLACK FOREST. The only thing that is still black in this area is the epithet, underlined by rows of dark fir trees, the torn earth made up with greenery and the long natural gullies always in darkness, where one could imagine – if memory hasn't disarmed – the tracks of fugitives ending, in the fear-inspired silence, under the hatred of a fatal hail of fire.

Strasbourg is only thirty-eight kilometers away. For a long time, it was too far for me, I who could not face up to the idea of entering the German soil without wavering, and even less to be able to wipe the slate clean one day.

Brandishing this past of war in my dogged determination to prevent the wound from healing would today be like arriving at a compromise. For to tell the truth, of this vow, all the more fervent as I believed it to be my duty, there remains today no anger, no pain, not even repulsion; only the energy to act, with the tools that destiny has attributed to me, to ensure it never happens again.

So, outside is the imposing yet charming landscape of the Black Forest. The scenery remains virtually the same as before, but is now seen through the lens of my peaceful mind.

My bedroom window, as if it were at the end of a trench, looks out on to a vegetable garden, which clings to a very steep slope. A few vegetables among some flowers: you can tell the plot is different from its neighbours by a rather crazy design, obviously made by people from not around here.

It is cold, even in summer, on this side of the huge building, but I always feel good here. I've seen it rain non-stop for a whole stay here; I've seen winters so harsh that the waterfalls stayed hanging, frozen in ice. Beauty, in all its forms, got the upper hand. In the building itself, the mark of the bad old days has been erased.

In former years, the style-less old carcass of a building had been used as a shelter for all sorts of wanderers. Refugees, it was said. Their disastrous squats had left a horrendous smell which, years after huge clean-ups, still soaked one's clothes.

Now life is so gentle within these walls. I no longer count how many trips I've made – two or three each year for the last eight years. Neither the country – that I had struck off the world map – nor the language – that I could not bear hearing – nor the people – whom I hated, taking all generations together – all these are no longer something special for me.

What is the identity of this man, of this woman, or of this child, among the five hundred people around me who have come from all over the world to spend a week or two in this part of Baden-Württemberg? Who is German, who is not? Who cares? From now on, nobody will ever be for me their nationality first, their culture first, their religion first, their social status first, their opinions first, their physical and other characteristics first... I am through with this mind which judges, which sets up partitions, which chooses to see walls where there are in fact only slight differences. I can see the poetical diversity of a world where opposites are complementary, where what is vital can also kill, where what is dangerous can also save. A world that is impossible to define clearly.

The pains and sorrows that I seemed to be made up of, however persistent they were, have metamorphosed into joys of living. As the years have passed, this blessed state endures, without bragging, simply confident in its soundness; aware, anyway, that if it happened to flag, it's got the spirit to come out victorious.

First difficult steps, taken oh, so late. In the end, with no regrets; it had to be this way. But still... so much ignorance, so much conceitedness, so much evil done and suffered, so many denied deeds, so many useless hardships, so much stress accumulated and spread around oneself, so much thoughtlessness... There was already a lot of love, a lot of tenderness, not an ounce of evil, but the main thing was missing for all this to work moving upwards: wisdom was missing.

Is there in France one being alone about whom one could say: he has all the highest qualities required to impart wisdom, because he is himself the embodiment of this knowledge? If there is such a man, it's a very well kept secret.

Anyway, I did not have to search for him. Life had the most unexpected present in store for me: the teaching of Gurudev Sri Sri Ravi Shankar Narayana.

There was hardly a feeling of it being a far-off culture. I hardly had the time to ask myself: "Beyond the form, what is it really all about?" The feeling of strangeness had disappeared. The knowledge taught by Gurudev Sri Sri Ravi Shankar – inspired by the Bhagavad-Gita, the Upanishads and other sacred scriptures inherited from the ancient Rishis – was already familiar to me. Not through its cultural aspect, which was slight indeed and meant nothing to me, but because it brought me back to the universe I had perceived in my childhood, before I could read. The whole substance lay in-between the words. It spread beyond the intellect, in a paradise of silence that I had always felt had been stolen from me.

♦

In Sanskrit, 'initiation' is called *diksha*. *Di* meaning 'intellect' and *ksha*, 'the horizon of the end'. *Diksha* means: to go to the end of the intellect, to transcend the intellect.

Education is called *shiksha*, 'the horizon of discipline' – total discipline.

A teacher brings *shiksha*, 'education'. A spiritual master – a *guru* – brings *diksha*: he takes you beyond the intellect towards the kingdom of Being. It is a journey from head to heart.

The whole discipline is *shiksha*; the whole intelligence is *diksha*.

I always liked to learn, more than to know. So much so that I appreciated the state of ignorance which is the prelude to studying. What I absorbed with passion always seemed to me a bit like a late addition. Just one more piece of knowledge, which cannot be assimilated, to tell the truth; besides it did not fill me. Most of the information that I had accumulated sooner or later made themselves scarce, leaving behind the poor satisfaction of being possessed for a short while. Nothing that I've intellectually learnt has ever really allowed me to live better than the illiterate I could have been. The vast majority of problems or sorrows in my life have originated from words. Isn't that the way it is most of the time? Words used as weapons. Verbal ease is a murderer...

Everywhere, words used to hide unsightly things, concepts drawn like iron curtains: a blockade of the mind which thinks it knows it all, simmers in words, cooks them, seasons them, and even crams you with them in order to praise its own views, its ideas and feelings... Unceasing chattering, to seek recognition in the other's language.

Culture did not bring me the peace of mind, without which there can be no depth; it did not shunt me less around my emotions, did not make me no less a slave of my fears and desires, nor more free, more brotherly, more conscious of my true responsibilities... And I never noticed that becoming cultured was ever sufficient to bring about miracles in civilization, reduce conflicts, reinforce human values and selfless service to others, and develop a real art of living, still pious hope. So, had I been the most accomplished scholar, it would not have freed me of unbearable feverishness, nor let me understand the essential question: who am I apart from my usual identifications?

Basically, all I had ever learnt was through suffering; misfortunes have been a cradle of good luck for me. They did their usual job: they destroyed meanness, brought serenity and maturity. They mercilessly highlighted the illusion that I was the creator of my life; they made me trust in love. Yes, every upheaval has been a blessing, but if destiny had not sent me significant help to save me from this confusion, I would have thrown in the towel a long time ago...

To suffer is to be stuck in the same mechanism and not be able to get out of it. Then, illness takes hold. That is what happened to me. Lungs of course, suffocation, worrying diagnosis, the inability of science to understand it. But that was nothing! Just a matter of utmost emergency: to breathe without any constraint. Who had been preventing me from doing it? Since my childhood spent within the confines of an orphanage, I'd thought myself very clever at detecting confinement in its most cunning forms... I had spotted society's flaws, the vices in human relationships, the monstrosities of the world a long time before. Analysis and criticism were flying around, identical since 1968... One thing had escaped my sharp perception: I was my own jailer.

What was my life worth? Success, failure; that didn't count. The right assessment was: to what point can I make people around me smile? Are those whom I claim to love really happy? Do people feel lighter or heavier in my company? Is my innermost request "What can you do for me?" or "What can I do for you?"

It is said that when the disciple is ready, the master comes...

When I had reached the ultimate in self-tiredness, anger about driving others mad with my blind behaviour, Gurudev Sri Sri Ravi Shankar appeared in my life, most unexpectedly, when I was possessed by nothing, absolutely nothing else than to want nothing. I had no expectations, no quest, no ideal, and no credo. Certainly not the need for an intellectual guide. No more thinking, just some air! Three hundred and sixty degrees around!

And fresh air is exactly what this Indian wise man was bringing to the West through his whole personality, an example of beauty, and through his teaching of an art of living that is both light and demanding.

"Being is a fact, living is an art", he says. And this art, like all other arts, can be learnt, whatever one's personal aptitude.

There is a lot to do in this respect in the West, where we have creative genius for refining material comfort, but are at a loss to build lasting happiness. The most surprising thing is that we persist, trying hard to stick with our mistakes.

♦

Gurudev Sri Sri Ravi Shankar is no missionary of Hinduism, out to conquer the West. Besides, that does not exist. He personally no longer needs anything. He is a fully realised master, freed from all desire, including the desire to gain followers. He is there to take care of those who ask for his help, knowing that they are only a tiny part of those who need it. But he does not force anything. He says, *"Some seeds take longer to germinate than others, and some never germinate; the world is not uniform..."* He does not show off, and yet he is taking on the most difficult function on earth. Most often he says his job involves putting a smile on every face. Just that. To replace grey with colour.

One day, he said to a lady who confided to him she was an interior decorator, *"Ah! So we do the same job!"*

No bombastic message to establish peace in the world, although he works so hard for it. His life is that of a saint entirely dedicated to others, to their spiritual evolution, but he does not try to pull the wool over your eyes:

"This world has always been the same: many incarnations have taken place, many saints have come, yet the universe is still the same. Year after year, the same things happen in the world; you won't change that. Forget about it!"

It does not mean that nothing should be done. Gurudev Sri Sri Ravi Shankar's humanitarian organization is at the moment the second largest, after the International Red Cross, for the number of volunteers. But he discourages this fever from the desire to revolutionize everything, when nothing is ready for it; it would only mean more worries. He says,

"This desire is an illusion. You want to change everything, except yourself, except your mind, except your vision; it is silly to crave for freedom, for enlightenment... Relax and just be! [...] What we need most is to be ourselves."

To be... A whole programme of conscious action... from which the world would not suffer.

To be requires not to let oneself be overwhelmed, dominated by what is not. And to see clearly what is, it is imperative to get rid of stress. There is no art of living with stress. The highest refinement is just antics.

Human nature drives towards evolution, whereas the nature of this world is to pull you downwards. The nature of this world is to cause irritation. It's up to each one to see if they want to let themselves get caught out. Frustration triggers anger... Flattery induces contentment... Can one claim to be free when we accept to be used just like machines whose buttons just have to be pressed?

There's nothing to beat breath for fighting stress. The first priority is to learn how to breathe. Unbelievable as it may seem to me today, I knew nothing about the vital importance of my own breath, like many people in the West. Who learns this? Who competently emphasizes this primordial necessity?

Gurudev Sri Sri Ravi Shankar is *Yoga Shiromani*, supreme Teacher on the path of the union with the Self. This very ancient science of breathing is one of life's big secrets. It is well-known that harmony between body, mind and breath brings stability and well-being. The three are linked.

Throughout the ages, one has always tried hard to manipulate and master the mind to obtain this peace. But the mind is something very abstract. One cannot force it to stay still. How to calm it down? It is easier to use the breath, the natural link between body and mind.

Every emotion corresponds to a certain breathing rhythm. When we are angry, our breath is different from when we are serene or happy. Setting the breath to a particular rhythm, the usual patterns of the mind are broken: the tensions and mental blocks which are their painful memory melt away. Feverishness, anxiety, fear, anger, tiredness, can all be controlled. The mind manages to reach a deep state of peace thanks to the breath.

Breathing problems, nervous tension and state of consciousness all improve when freed from the effects of stress. The immediate benefits have transformed my daily practice into pure pleasure. Each day, discipline guarantees its reward; the breath becomes both the tool and the nectar. To the delight of feeling it working to repair disorders is added the further delight, itself divine, of experiencing, if only for a few seconds, a feeling of total bliss.

Slipping into meditation happened in the same movement. When the mind settles, meditation comes. Rest in oneself, sinking deep into this inner emptiness where the Self lies. The big meeting with 'I don't know', the threshold of knowledge where I had been standing for so long.

Impossible to enter alone. Despair would without doubt have won. There must have been more casualties standing in front of this door than on all the battlefields put together. Alone, you could mope, become embittered, lose your taste for life, and become dull and conceited. You cannot do without a guide to lead you through the dark and unknown areas of consciousness. No more than you can operate on yourself – you need a surgeon. Even to learn how to drive, you need someone's help... So how could you imagine embarking on such an abstract journey on your own, as a self-taught person? The spiritual master is essential. Jesus said it, *"There is no other way to the Father than through Me."* Buddha said it, Krishna said it, and all the other masters throughout the ages... The same Me in each of us. In India, the *guru* is the highest on the pyramid of masters. No one is higher. *Guru* means 'the one who releases from ignorance' through the knowledge of ignorance.

This is not another form of indoctrination, it is less knowledge. It has been shown that through losing, a lot is to be gained.

Gurudev Sri Sri Ravi Shankar says,

"Life is a mystery, love is a mystery, and God is a mystery. You can live it fully, you can never understand it. Your understanding is like putting the ocean in a cup.

You can merge in God, but you can never know Him. You can get the knowledge of the world, of what is relative: you will know the impermanent. But, you can only feel the permanent. Truth can never be known, permanence can be felt and proven, impermanence can only be known."

The ancient masters used to say that the only thing one might say is, 'perhaps'.

♦

I was not curious to meet Gurudev Sri Sri Ravi Shankar, in spite of owing him so much already. He was living in India and was not expected to travel to the West for some months. It was not even sure that he would stop over in Paris. Compared with other countries, France is lagging behind in the spiritual field.

I was reading the knowledge sheets that he sends every week to the one hundred and forty countries where he has disciples. I was also listening to the recordings of his public talks. The Master answered the common preoccupations in a simple, clear, funny and profound way, showing excellent teaching skills. Knowledge was starting to infiltrate into my life and into each of my cells, as when you fall in love... I was under the spell of what was opening up in front of me: the unknown, as familiar as my own nature, without any separation. And this wealth was endless; it would feed me for the rest of my life. There was no more reason to worry: all that I ever wanted was already here, all the knowledge, abiding in me. I had it in myself, just like everybody else. The feeling of loneliness receded. Just by reaching the Master and listening to him, I had come home. The rest, my progress, was his responsibility, and a little bit mine. It was the beginning of a real expansion. At age forty-seven, I was no early starter. I had by no means conquered it by my own merits. Although I had done nothing to deserve it, I was enjoying the pleasure of feeling at peace with myself.

I had drawn a line under past mistakes. My own, and those I could not quite forgive. Gurudev Sri Sri Ravi Shankar has the knack of making us drop them just like that! Guilt, bitterness, criticism... No more complaining; the past is over! It is all like a dream... Wake up!

He said,

"Drop the past; don't even try to analyse it. It is as if you knocked over the dustbin and sorted through the contents: this is from yesterday, and that is from the day before yesterday...

Free up your mind. The Art of Living is about how to gain this skill in life. Very simple, just a skill: to be able to free your mind from the past, to free your mind from fears of the future and to be able to make a game out of every situation you find yourself in."

The Master encouraged a positive attitude, making growth easier, but actively discouraged any signs of a goody-goody spirituality, stuffy attitudes, upstarts' illusions, the quests for the absolute: *"All the problems in the world come from those who want perfection!"*

With him, peace would not be a bed of roses. I was grateful to him for it.

"In a few years time, your head will be under the mud, don't fill it with mud while you are still alive!"

He made of his disciples sincere and enthusiastic seekers. Happy above all. Otherwise, what was the use?

He said,

"Knowledge is a burden if it robs you of your innocence.
Knowledge is a burden if it makes you think you are special.
Knowledge is a burden if it gives you the impression you are wise.
Knowledge is a burden if it is not integrated into your life.
Knowledge is a burden if it doesn't bring you joy.
Knowledge is a burden if it doesn't make you free."

♦

The first time I saw Gurudev Sri Sri Ravi Shankar, it was in a photograph. A slim silhouette, always in white, with unusually long black hair for a man, even in India. It was especially a very thick beard that showed he is a man. I did not feel this new image, which disturbed me somehow, had anything to do with me. Yet the appropriateness of his teachings did not escape me: beyond the genuine smile and the light in the eyes – which forbade any confusion – the brilliance of the soul shone through!

I had put the picture in my office. It triggered a cataclysm in my family; endless suspicion and even demonization. They all agreed to condemn my choice and talk me into giving it up. The photo had not really become part of me, so I put it away.

It was unpleasant. But it strengthened my decision never to let my life get caught up in the prejudice of others, however loving they are, knowing well enough how many fears and personal doubts they are facing themselves. I will no longer be – as Gurudev Sri Sri Ravi Shankar puts it – *"a football of others' opinion"*.

But here again, their hostility was a plus for me. It played the part of a *guru*, as it sharpened my judgment, in parallel with what the teaching of the Master required. Recognizing, instead of complaining about, how any person – no matter how unfair, hostile, ferocious their behavior – is just playing their role to help us to grow, was itself a revelation to me, whose biggest problem was a deep-rooted disgust with human kind.

From the moment I accepted their lack of understanding, it only had advantages. First of all, it safeguarded the intimate experience in which I was becoming involved. It also justified secrecy, even if the absence of communication could bring up more questions. I was protected, well-inspired, first, because there was not much to say about it, no more than about a very precious love story; and above all because I mostly did not know myself how and why things would develop. The effect on my health was huge. The improvement in my nervous state was hardly believable. My joie de vivre stood up better and better to any assaults. It was very mysterious though. How could the system be healed without drugs? How could this knowledge give you solid nourishment without real intellectual implication? What was the nature of this master who met my most essential needs without an obvious 'relationship'?

To declare that I did not understand, but that it was fine for me, would have made my near ones call the emergency services!

To speak about something you know nothing about is very common; the intellectual mechanism has no hang-ups about doing this! But as consciousness awakes, we can then better evaluate the weaknesses of its assertions and develop a keener sense of observation. Observing one's thoughts, sensations, feelings... Noticing how they change all the time, again and again. One's growth near a Master is increased tenfold. The feelings I had yesterday aren't the same as today any longer, which means a lot of idle talk avoided.

♦

Gurudev Sri Sri Ravi Shankar says,

"Love, beauty and truth are all beyond proof. Nobody can prove them. And nobody can prove God. One who tries to prove the existence of God walks a thorny path. Everything that can be proved can also be disproved. God is beyond proof and counter proof. God is an experience."

The name of God used to scare me. What I knew about it was heavy. All this sadness associated with it... And all the joy: it was even worse. God, plus a master, when you have been raised to believe, "no God, no master"... In the beginning, the teachings of Gurudev Sri Sri Ravi Shankar did not amalgamate in this respect... In spite of the attraction of its formulation, the idea of God sent shivers down my spine... I had never understood what was meant by 'God', and I was in no hurry to understand. I was learning how to live well on this earth, and had no desire to have my head in the clouds...

My reservations started to be damaged by something mysterious which I welcomed as the most tangible reality. In the very beginning, every time I took refuge in meditation to try and go through one of the hardest periods in my life, the memory of the hidden photograph would come back to me. The banished image seemed to be supporting me. In fact, the image of the Master, behind my closed eyelids, was helping to calm me. And although none of my worries had started being solved yet, I felt I was being pulled through.

I did not feel particularly inclined towards devotion, but I grabbed hold of the line thrown to me, quite happy with this present that my unconscious was giving up. Did I really need to shake up my reserve even further, when it was in fact ready to yield? In this respect, one day stood out. As I rested in a state of deep meditation, I could feel the ethereal presence of the saint in his white dhoti, with the precision of reality or of its illusion. He was there, as if standing beside me, surrounding me with his white veil. Feeling the protection of this *'sweet home'*, I wept and was thankful for such a profound relief.

Once the emotion was over, I could have closed the file on the phenomenon as a beneficial invention of despair hadn't it triggered a revelation pregnant with consequences.

For the first time, I had recognized, at the core of my existence, the Presence that had always been with me, as far as I could remember, even when I hadn't been able to identify it. It had been there in the best and worst of times. Even in the hell of my childhood, it had already been there. Without its support, how could that little girl, locked up in an institution where barbarity seemed to be the only language known, have overcome so much ill-treatment, with the feeling of not having really suffered through it? Faith in its protection had helped me to grow even though I hadn't been able to give it a name.

This Divine presence that can make you cry with gratitude had shown itself every second of my life, in all sorts of equally recognisable guises. I had never been aware of it before. This unknown Master made me 'see' it in its transparency, before it gradually brought me to feel it everywhere, in everything, in everybody, without barriers.

♦

We probably only hear what we are willing to hear. Gurudev Sri Sri Ravi Shankar's words always came to me at exactly the right moment, exactly the words that I needed. He would light the way for me, step by step. I know today that each of his disciples feels the same personal care, so perfect is the concordance between their needs and the solution. Every time, the Master pushes the chess piece a little further in the direction where he knows it will be received, now or later.

He said,

"This whole universe is made up of God, nothing exists outside God. The self and the unconscious are God; you just need some skill to see it in its different aspects, like the waves and the ocean.

If God is all-pervading and almighty, Satan also is part of God: God is good and evil."

Long before I met him, Gurudev Sri Sri Ravi Shankar had become the *very face of Evidence* for me.

2

THE ATTRACTION OF THE NATURAL

IT IS SAID THAT THE IMMEMORIAL WISDOM which emanates from a living Spiritual Leader is more powerful than all the scriptures in the world put together.

I had not the slightest idea of the benefit of being the disciple of a Spiritual Leader you could actually approach. I had never even heard of the existence, very rare as it turns out, of fully realised human beings. Except maybe in the Bible, where it is written that thirty-six just men, present at any period of time, will prevent the planet from sinking into chaos.

I knew a lot about the worst that Man can do to Mankind, beyond the intelligible. But about the best, beyond reasonable sensibility. I knew absolutely nothing. A few worthy Christian figures sprung to mind, more often for their creating a faux-pas rather than for some distinguished newsworthy acts. Mother Theresa's testimony made front-page news on the day when Lady Di was pictured by her side. And the dalai-lama's wisdom was used as entertainment to his political visits.

At a time when the Media is all-intrusive, the good and upright people of our time don't easily rise from anonymity. Perhaps a bit of cocaine, sex and the lure of money would help their cause. Putting a high profile on the goodness of people is not the 'cup of tea' of the average news writer.

"If you observe the nature of doubt, Gurudev Sri Sri Ravi Shankar says, you will notice that it always concerns what is positive. You never doubt the negative. You know it from experience: you doubt someone's honesty, never their dishonesty. You doubt someone's good qualities, never their bad points..."

In my mind, a saint could only be dead, a messiah could only be awaited and an enlightened being could only be enlightened. As for gurus, no need to expand... I didn't doubt however that my preconceived perception was soundly based. But I discovered how much it also went beyond the bounds of honesty and integrity.

I was therefore a long way from imagining what Gurudev Sri Sri Ravi Shankar would be like.

♦

In spring 1995, the Master had come to Paris to deliver a big public conference at the Guimet museum. I had missed it. However, I had made up my mind to follow the advanced course that would take place in his presence, the day after. I knew I would have to force myself a little, integrating into a group of two hundred people. In theory I knew the advantages of it: sharing is an important element of progression. But in practice, I felt more comfortable with my spirituality in the confines of my home. Community life? Okay let's give it a go for a few days! The programme was attractive – meditations guided by Gurudev Sri Sri Ravi Shankar – and every evening would take place in his company. I did not fully appreciate how lucky I was. The difference between the master I had heard about and the master before my eyes still left me in a state of high expectation.

My first sighting would then take place at the festive time of a *satsang*.[1]

Meditating among people was already not easy for me, but chanting *mantras* in Sanskrit was well outside my comfort zone for exotic entertainments. In those days, I was quite happy to sunbathe in the nude face up or face down; on the other hand, closing my eyes in public, or worse, starting singing anything, even Claude François, I found deeply disturbing.

The people themselves sang without any reservation or self-consciousness. They repeated *'Om nama Shivaya... Om Namo*

1 A meeting during which knowledge has a place of honour through sacred chants and the Master's comments.

Baghavate Vasudevaya...' with the passion we feel when singing old popular tunes. They continued boldly, relaxed, joyful and passionate. Even this enviable naturalness could not make me feel at ease. However, I noticed that the purity of the litany was able to establish peace in my mind, without me having to join in with my voice.

A sudden commotion in the crowd announced the entry of the Master. Everybody stood up spontaneously forming a guard of honour. I did not feel at ease then either. Previous to that day, I had only stood when the *Marseillaise* was played, begrudgingly, when members of the prosecution entered court. This time, I did not move. Some of my friends, whom I estimated had all their faculties, bowed down on their knees as the Master passed by. I had missed something... Gurudev Sri Sri Ravi Shankar made a show of not responding to the acts of devotion; they passed by him, sent unhindered towards their celestial destination. However he discouraged them on occasions with a wave of his hand.

Draped in splendid but sober silks, in the Indian way, the Master advanced with the grace of an angel. His bare feet seemed to hardly brush the floor... Some people were dying to touch him, but stepped aside in front of this apparition... His lightness reminded me of a feather, a musical note in material terms...

On the flower strewn platform, presents decorated with ribbons, toys and stuffed animals created a rather distasteful display but which was undoubtedly intended to please and amuse him. The link with what I knew about the Sage, through his writings, was not immediately made, although humour was present in everything, as well as the feeling of unpretentious spirituality.

The dusky angel sat down in the lotus position on a couch covered with white linen, just as a butterfly settles on a petal.

His eyes welcomed each person in the congregation. The power of this moment, immensely deep but gentle, coming from outside. The song of infinite wisdom drifted over the heads... The first blessing. From time to time, the hint of a smile emerged from his dark beard, so divine a smile that those who had not received it felt compelled to want it...

The lighting in the room wasn't quite right. The Master waved for it to be changed: switching off a certain bulb that annoyed him and switching on another elsewhere. The lighting controls were a complete and utter shambles. He commented patiently: "*Making light... this is a most delicate task! But all you need to do is find the right switch...*" There followed a general outbreak of laughter. The connection was made.

With a quick look round the place, he showed he appreciated people's full attention. In English, translated simultaneously, he was concerned to know if anyone was lacking anything, if everybody was satisfied with their accommodation and food (vegetarian, of course)... He wanted an honest answer: "*Don't hesitate to tell me if there is anything bothering you, otherwise you'll brood over it and you will not get the best out of your stay. These are precious moments you have come to spend here. To stop everything for a week once a year and rest profoundly, yes, we need it...*" This 'we' was expressed so delicately... "*Good, good, good... How many of you have travelled a long way to come here?*" A few hands went up. Happily, the Master repeated the names of the countries mentioned: "*United States... Colombia... Lithuania... by bus!... Slovenia... China... Iran? Yes? Oh... Mongolia... South Africa... Twenty-four countries are represented here! How many of you are tired?... Nobody!*" He laughs: "*We will all go to bed early, anyway, won't we? Tomorrow at 6 o'clock, we can meet here for the yoga session... no, let's say 6.30... 7 o'clock? What suits you best? You want 7 o'clock? OK. But from then on we will start at 5.30. And we will also remain in silence three or four days...You talk, talk talk...When you start a discussion, you are fresh and in good form, and at the end you are worn out. You exhaust yourself using words. We usually fall silent when we are shocked by something; a bereavement and we fall silent... Here, we experience silence as an expression of profound joy, of peace. We are more used to demonstrating our joy noisily... You are afraid of getting bored while remaining silent? But if you are bored in your own company, can you imagine how boring you must be for others? Is that how we get on together? Two boredoms being exchanged? We must learn how to feel good within ourselves... Silence is the mother of all talents. What do you talk about? You chew over the past like an old piece of chewing-gum. Who is interested in it? Do you know how much you bore people? You have no idea.*

Do you know this story? Four disciples were put into silence by the Master. So, there they were sitting without saying anything looking out at the sunset. A passer-by stops and asks them the time. The first one answers "I'm sorry, I'm in silence." The second remarks, "Oh! You've just spoken..." Then the third one says, "You both have broken silence; I'll tell the Master." And the fourth utters, "I am the only one who has kept silence!" Your silence must be of good quality and depth... What shall we do now?"

Glowing smiles in response. Most of the disciples present have known the Master's mischievous tricks over a long time. No suggestions were necessary; he was constantly coming up with something new. But he said, "*Hum?*", as if expecting an idea. There would be no lengthy discussions.

The Master waited for any volunteer in the audience to come forward, and meanwhile he perused the objects around him. Two pieces of wood intrigued him. He was trying to understand their function. They were castanets. Someone mimicked how to use them. A few seconds to look at them closely... and he began improvising a piece of lively flamenco. He added,

"Don't take life seriously. If you take life very seriously, then you will definitely be disturbed. The only way to keep your balance of mind is to take it as a game, and not to take anything too seriously."

He had picked up a stuffed animal by its ears and was pulling them down over its nose. He was examining it in detail... Some mechanism hidden in the fur suddenly triggered off a crummy rock'n'roll number. He kept pressing the button: *on, off, on, off,* recreating a mock version of a swing number. His gestures, his expressions, everything in his manner made this nothing moment full of appeal. He said,

"Scientists have recently established that children smile about four hundred times a day. Teenagers only about fifteen times. Adults smile once at the most. Laughter and smiling have big beneficial effects on your health. My job is to make you all children again.

Spirituality is what makes you simple, natural, like a child. Being intelligent and keeping one's innocence is the most precious thing in the world. The more someone develops his intelligence, the more they tend to become complicated. The innocence of one who is ignorant has no value. But if you can develop both, the value of the heart and the value of the brain – and it is possible – then the conditions can be considered as perfect."

Being used to speaking in public, he put the mike closer, corrected its height and tapped it to indicate that it was not on. Then:

"You often happen not to clearly see what you want because you have never looked within yourself. You are governed by fleeting thoughts, fleeting emotions, fleeting desires. Wake up and realise that this is all made up of thoughts, only thoughts, only thoughts. Your appreciation of beauty is a thought; your aversion for an ugly object is a thought. Just a thought dropping into your mind... Realise that it is just a thought and you will be free. Recognizing that a thought is a thought brings liberty. When you see a thought as a reality, it's then that you are stuck."

The intonation of his voice, seeking no special effect, easily navigated through his words and pauses. Things follow a regular pacifying rhythm as natural as breathing itself once any inner agitation has dispersed.

The Master made no effort to make an impression. Yet, his authority was impressive. There was his weight of knowledge, of course, but above all there was his ever imperturbable personality. Absolutely nothing on this earth could unsettle him. I was discovering in my very bones the intoxicating power of his stillness.

♦

"There are two parts in our brain: the musical side and the logical side. The two parts of the brain, right and left, must work equally. We must take care of ourselves, emotionally and intellectually. When we speak, or think, only one part of the mind is active. Satsang *involves both.* Satsang *is the totality. When we sing together, cohesion is reached among all the minds that are involved with the song. Singing is essential in life; it allows us to bring the mind "home": peace comes from within."*

Someone asked, "What is the point of singing mantras in Sanskrit? Not understanding the meaning bothers me."

Gurudev Sri Sri Ravi Shankar:

"The meaning is not important. You know, singing in very ancient words, Gregorian chants just as much as songs in ancient Sanskrit, has a deep impact on the consciousness. In satsang, what you sing is not important. You can sing bhajans about Allah, bhajans about Buddha, songs from films: the act of singing keeps you in contact with the most subtle aspects of your own consciousness. Your difficulty comes from singing 'Narayana, Shiva...' and you think: "Oh, it is against my religion." It is a narrow religious understanding. These names are all attributed to only one divinity, only one consciousness: the innocent benevolent consciousness. What does 'Narayana' mean? This consciousness which lives in the nervous system... Jesus was called 'Eesha'. 'Eesha' means the Lord, le Seigneur. You feel comfortable when you say 'Seigneur' in French, 'Lord' in English, but not 'Eesha' in Sanskrit. It is because you have been bombarded with narrow concepts and ideas since your childhood. Recognize that all the cultures of the world are a part of you. Go and sing Christmas carols. This is what we do for the end of year celebrations. It does not imply that everybody is forced to celebrate Christmas! Celebration is part of life: choose any excuse to celebrate, it is not important... And the consequences? You will not stop being a Hindu if you celebrate Christmas; you will not stop being a Christian if you sing 'Govinda hare, Gopala Hare'. Spirituality broadens your consciousness. If you do not want to sing bhajans, well! Find something else; sing 'Halleluja'... But singing is essential. In Sanskrit, it is better than nothing! In the beginning we use mantras, and then we advance towards meditation, practices, etc. In the end, we just need silence to reach the Divine. Silence is the sound of the soul. Singing is a part of our silence. The mind becomes calm. When the mind is quiet, then even music is no longer wanted."

Another person in the audience asks, "Some music lovers say that for them music is equivalent to meditation..."

Gurudev Sri Sri Ravi Shankar: *"Music colours the mind. Some colours correspond to some emotions. Music has to do with men. The ancient* Rishis *made lots of melodies, even invented instruments... But music is not an 'excuse'; it is not the same dimension as meditation."*

He started singing, an impromptu effort... A hundred per cent. On the verge, sometimes, of being off-key, but the pure sound always rose from the heart... In the room, voices, proud of their tones, tried to break through the rest to be appreciated... Superb chorus, to tell the truth. So many real talents astonished me. Maybe the good effect of a healthy life, without any tobacco, alcohol, or drugs of all sorts...

I found myself singing.

The Master was looking at me. When our eyes met, we both burst out laughing. One same beautiful laugh. An explosion of joy which seemed to mean: "That's it. You've got it."

The followers continued *bhajans* in front of him. He had closed his eyes and just plunged into deep meditation, his face smooth, radiant, detached... His head was progressively leaning towards his chest as if he was sleeping. He was far away... He slowly came back. But once his eyes were opened, the mind was clear, ready to answer questions...

Dozens of scraps of paper, dropped into a basket at his feet, were expecting his answers. He started going through them, classifying them according to some sort of random order which he never maintained. For sure their organization would follow no logic. Gurudev Sri Sri Ravi Shankar enjoyed the informal, ephemeral, paradoxical, and only used that which can be dismantled for structuring the mind. Light, flexible, anti-seismic material. *"Do not depend on logic, he said. What is supposed to be is not all that is. This creation is so mysterious. Logic can take you from one point to the other. Logic is to say, for example: "A half closed door is a half open door." So, logically, if a door is totally closed, it is totally open... Logic is a small portion of our existence. The whole universe can't be put in a little teaspoon we call logic – which is predictable."*

Awaiting what he would say next, I was desirous of listening to him, and passionless at the same time... The evening could just as well go by without a word. This did actually happen sometimes. Gurudev Sri Sri Ravi Shankar's presence alone was itself knowledge.

"All the problems with which you are confronted in life come from the fact that you attach too much importance to events. Events grow whereas you become smaller... Knowledge is not in the event, it is beyond it. It is only when you go beyond the event that the truth is born.

A particular event taken by itself just brings you an erroneous notion. You have to consider the whole events, the whole of all events, indefinitely. Beyond the event is knowledge.

A personality, a body, a mind, a set of behaviours, everything changes constantly. Love, in itself, does not change. Beyond the person, there's love. When you lose your personality, you become love. If you can't lose yourself, you will not be able to find yourself. So, lose your personality: you will find your real Self.

Behind each object, there's the infinite. An object is limited. Take an object and reduce it, reduce it, reduce it again, you get an atom. The atom is the infinite; each atom contains an infinite space.

The object beyond the object is infinity. The person beyond the person is love.

Maya, illusion, is being ensnared in the event, the personality, the object. Knowledge, love, divine consciousness, is seeing beyond the event, the personality, the object. Do you see? It's just a little shift in perspective...

You are not limited, you are the universe. You grow outside the event."

Silence...

"See what is happening in the mind at the present moment: 'Yes, yes' or 'No, no', 'How can this be?' Are you fully aware of this phenomenon? It is happening now... When you become aware of your own dialogue, then your consciousness is fully awake. What I am saying does not matter; you can agree or not; but if you are aware of what your mind tells you, then you have a mature state of mind."

Back to the bits of paper... He had put aside the questions written in English to read them aloud himself, and he threw the others, without ceremony, to a young woman, an improvised translator, according to imprecise criteria: maybe her competence, maybe just her shyness, or something else... each one could also, any moment, directly question the Master; however, few felt like it.

Question: "Is it helpful to heal old emotional wounds concerning events dating back to childhood?"

Gurudev Sri Sri Ravi Shankar: *"First of all, believing they are all deeply present inside you is an illusion. When you believe that you have lots of 'old wounds', of 'childhood emotions' and you want to heal them, you are doing something impossible. It is like trying to catch a cat which is not here. Or like saying: "OK, I want to forget this, I want to forget this." How can you forget something wanting to forget something? Can you do it? Each time you remember: "Oh, I had these childhood emotions and I want to be cured of them", you reinforce these experiences. You can ask for assistance for fifteen or twenty years and you will still find that you have not been cured, that something is still there... You will feel momentary relief and the same thing will be repeated again. It is not the way to get rid of negative emotions. You must turn your attention to the cause, the root.*

What is it? An emotion creates a sensation in the body. Disconnect it from the event observing the sensation and breathing. Through breathing, you can overcome the problem, and healing comes, spontaneous, natural. Know before everything that deep inside you, not one of these emotions, not one of these events damaged you. Your Being, your soul, are immortal. Your soul is light. Can anything damage light? Can darkness ever diminish light? This has never happened and will not happen. Whatever the impression, it was just peripheral. It is not a fact, it is not reality. Do you see what I mean? Understanding this is a beautiful thing.

It is the function of meditation to put you directly in contact with yourself. 'Yoga' means 'to come back to one's nature, to establish oneself in one's own nature, to come back to oneself, to the Self'... The goal is just where you are. There where you are, you are invincible... There is no wound at all in you. A scar can come up, but it is only peripheral. And the periphery perfectly heals by itself, as long as you recognize it as simple. So, please, don't go on thinking: "these are my childhood days, and my mother said this, my father did that." Don't go on making this link all the time. Do your practices, meditation, pranayamas, and you will see that you are wonderfully fit.

– What is the idea of resorting to psychotherapy?

– All psychologists should study Buddha. Otherwise, their research can't be complete. Buddha very methodically exposed the knowledge of the mind and its functions. [...] Wisdom is to disconnect the event from the emotion and the emotion from the sensation. Ignorance is to connect a sensation – sadness, or any other feeling – to an event. This makes you unhappy. And this starts the cycle up again and again. [...]

There may be some value in traditional psychotherapy; I don't exclude it totally. It has some value, but I say that it presents serious flaws and that it is high time this was recognized. I think some are already aware of it and add the value of meditation, the value of silence, the value of observation.

Unfortunately, none of the psychologists who developed their profession had an interest in Buddha or any enlightened being of the past. They have written volumes and volumes without feeling depth, without knowing what meditation, the very source of the mind, is.

What do you do if your mother is cruel?

After a pause, he answered rather seriously, aware of touching a wound still open: "A mother cannot be cruel. If some behave this way, it is due to stress... Help her get rid of stress and find her love.

– What is the origin of stress?

– Being engaged in activities above one's own capacities. If you do more, this brings stress about. If you conscience is so big that you must manage something bigger, this brings stress about. When you don't realise your potential, it is also stress.

– How can I be always happy?

– Forget 'always' and then you will be happy. Wanting comfort all the time, you become lazy. Wanting perfection, you become quick-tempered. If you always want to be rich, you become greedy.

Fear comes when you don't realise that only life goes on forever. This projection of the nature of the Self – which is 'always' – on what is temporal – which can never be 'always' – is called maya, illusion. There aren't several paths; there is only one, which guides you. If you erase 'always' from your dictionary, then everything is 'alright'. Drop 'always' and everything will be alright. That is intelligence.

– I find that the more money we earn, the less happiness there is. Why?

– It is not money, but your desire and greed which don't allow you to be happy.

– What is good and what is bad?

– What can bring discomfort in the short term, but give joy in the long term is good. The opposite, what gives joy in the short term and makes you miserable in the long term, is bad.

– Why does the mind go on judging, analysing? This is good, this is bad... I am too analytical. How do I change this?

– There should be limits to the analytical part of the mind. Leave space for innocence. The mind needs to analyse, to show its maturity. Keep a balance. When you listen to music, love talks; you don't analyse... You made your first step realising it. Now, sing, dance, and leave everybody their freedom of thought. Meditate and you will start seeing changes... But it is already better, isn't it?

– Why does judgment arise?

– Why wouldn't it arise?

– How do you stop feeling anxious in society?

– One, consider everybody as fools; two, consider yourself as a fool. Three, consider yourself as a student.

– How do I get rid of the anger raging in my mind?

– Through observation, through knowledge, through practice. There are two ways of being angry. The first one is to lose one's temper

without being able to stop... The other one is to show one's anger. When you can feel anger in you, just show it, as you do with children. You are not really angry; when you get angry with them, you quickly recover your smile. But if you are furious with someone else, your friend, your cousin or your neighbour, for two days, this anger grows in your mind. For two days it torments you, sometimes even for several weeks, perhaps even months. This kind of anger makes your mind boil, puts your mind upside down. This is not good. But if you just show your anger, it is Okay.

– If we live in the present moment, do we get rid of anger?

– Yes. And the practices help you to live in the present moment, deeply. You have to get rid of the anger which is already there, in the cells of your body. Children are in the present. Tears well up in their eyes, they cry, but they can smile the next moment. It does not take long to cajole them. They come back almost instantly. Sometimes, they get irritated, they refuse to wear what you force them to and they scream. And then, everything is alright. Parents totally succeed in diverting them because children are in the present moment. Show them a toy, a sweet, some toffee, and their attention is diverted. They are fine again. They totally forget their anger. They don't go on harping on about: "Mum, you combed my hair too hard" or "You made me put this coat on"... What is, is. They have forgotten. And yet, they were really mad. Their anger was so intense! Even a six-month-old baby... He has something in his hand and you take it away from him. See how worked up he gets! Have you observed that? He may become red in the face, but this intense anger vanishes very quickly. All emotion is sound if it lasts no longer than a line drawn on the surface of the water... If your emotions only last that long, then it is sound. It is wonderful.

– Offering your left cheek when the right cheek has been slapped, is that the right way?

– If the other person is sensitive, offer the other cheek. If they are dull and indifferent, then face up. As the Indian saying goes, "If it is a buffalo, take the big stick; if it is a cow, the shadow of a stick is enough."

– How do you suggest correcting children's bad manners?

– Tell them, teach them, talk to them, show them. Children understand it is necessary. They totally agree. They can be moulded.

We must first make sure we are stable. We must listen to our emotions. We must clean within ourselves. During sleep, we simply get rid of tiredness, weariness. But the stress and emotions in the body are so deep... they enter each cell. So we must do practices: meditation, kriya, breathing exercises can clean the whole system. Then, we get better centred. Nothing can affect us. Otherwise, our balance, our peace can be upset by the slightest little thing. Someone tells you something trivial and you lose your temper; your whole sleep is disturbed... These practices are essential.

When can you solve a problem? When you can consider it as a challenge. What is the difference between a problem and a challenge? When you see something as a problem, you are part of the problem, and not of the solution. When you consider something as a challenge, then you are part of the solution rather than of the problem. You can consider it as an adventure. Now is the time for being enterprising, for pursuing lots of adventures.

– Is there a limit to meditation?

– Meditate as much as you are told to. It is the same as for a bath: do you spend twenty-four hours over a bath?

– How do you fight against laziness and lack of discipline?

– Never *mind, be rebellious. And be rebellious to your rebellion.*

– How do you console a loved one?

– You need more than words. Simply being with them. Time will heal and later, after a few months... six months or a year, if they are in the same mood, you will be able to tell them "Wake up!", simply "Come on, wake up!"

– What do you think about suicidal tendencies?

– Suicide is like taking off your coat when you are cold. Why do people commit suicide? To be free, not to feel miserable any longer... Suicide is such an ignorant act! A lack of understanding of oneself. It comes from the fact that no one explained how to get rid of the stress. Honour life. It is useless to commit suicide.

– What can you tell us about life after death?

– *Take an interest in this life first. There's enough to do... You will surely know what it is all about when you are over there! It will be impossible for you to miss the experience! When you are alive, you try to understand and you are curious to know what comes after death. And after death, the same is repeated in the other world; you wonder, you say "What is life like? Let's come back to earth to see what it is like!"*

– And what about AIDS?

– AIDS *calls out to your conscience because it reminds you that you will have to leave this world, and earlier than expected. Normally, we live our life as if we were going to remain on earth forever. Nobody imagines that they will have to leave some day: maybe we think we will stay here! But we will have to leave one day. This knowledge is missing.*

AIDS *has made life shorter: we were not born for our body, even if we enjoy it; this enjoyment will also disappear. Whether you accept this idea or not, everybody will leave this world. The people affected with* AIDS *had a shock. They were suddenly aware: "What will happen to me?" But you must not wallow in self-pity. Just remember that the most important thing is not to know if we will live long, it is to live one's life to the full. You can live your life asleep, on drugs, drunk, miserable, for a hundred and twenty years. So what? Some persons live in a coma for seven years: what's the purpose? Their family also live in a seven-year coma. Even their nearest loved ones will ask to allow them to die.*

Live your life to the full and have people around you live twice as much.

– How can we overcome the fear of death?

– *Only in two ways: the first is dying; the second, meditating.*

– What is the purpose of life?

– *Those who know the answer will not tell you and those who tell you don't know! What is the true meaning of life? Ah... It is better to discover this by yourself. Don't ask me. It is like asking me to chew your candy for you. It is not possible. I can put the candy into your mouth, but I can't chew it for you. Live with this thought in mind. I can tell you one thing: you are very fortunate that this questioning comes to your mind. One in a million people wonders what the purpose of life is. It is a very sincere question. It means that you have stopped just existing and have started your way on the wonderful path. Live with this question and do not be eager to get a ready-made answer from just anybody. Go deep inside yourself and you will discover it.*

– How do you know what is one's mission in life?

– If you lose the sense of time when you are doing something, when you feel like doing something again and again, and when you feel happy doing it, allow this to be your mission in life.

– Does destiny exist and if so what is free will?

– What is not destiny is free will. Do you know what you call 'destiny' or 'free will'? When your thought coincides with what happens, what do you say? "I wanted it to happen and it happened." When your thought does not coincide with what happens, you call that destiny.

– How is it possible not to expect anything from someone you love unreservedly and to whom you gave everything you have? It is really difficult...

– How is it possible not to expect? Okay, then keep expecting! Lots of people tell me "It is so difficult to forgive"... I say, "Don't forgive." Or "It is so difficult to forget..." I say, "Don't forget." Why do something which is so difficult to do? Is it easy not to forget, to go on judging someone? Do it if it is easy. Thus, if not to expect is difficult, then expect! If it is easy to expect, go on expecting. And if what you expect does not come, if you don't get anything, you will be disappointed. And if being disappointed is easy, be disappointed. If it is easy, do it. Do what is easy!

– How can I have faith?

– Do not struggle. Forget it. Have you got faith in the fact that you don't have faith?

– What is knowledge?

– *What do you want to know? What you want to know is knowledge.*

– What is the origin of ignorance?

– *The wise used to answer "It is asking too much; do not ask this." Life is ignorance. This question can't be answered.*

– Our nature is to be joyful. Why don't we simply appreciate it?

– *Go on asking yourself these questions. Go on marvelling.*

– What is the infinite? What is the Creation?

– *Look at the sky and you will understand.*

– What is the art of living?

– *What is art? Art is appreciating what is. Have you started appreciating life itself, not the accessories of life? Since that moment, you've learnt the art of living...*

– I am attracted to people of my own sex...

– *Love is not an act; it is the state of our being. We are love. You just know love as an act. Go beyond that. The nature of consciousness is love. We are much more than a body. Jai Guru Dev.*

Then he said, "*You are constituted both of your father and of your mother. So, inside you, you have two characteristics, male and female. Lots of men have maternal qualities in them, feminine qualities. In the same way, some women have more masculine qualities in them. Love is beyond qualities; love is beyond the male/female distinction. It is not limited to the body or to emotions. It is something which transcends all these identifications.*"

– What do you do when spirituality starts interfering with social life?

– *How would spirituality interfere with social life? You just need to organize your time cleverly.*

– Do you believe in astrological influences?

– *Each thing in the universe affects another thing. How far it affects you, it depends... Astrology is to put the blame on the cosmos. Your anger turns to the stars...*

– Do miracles infringe the laws of science?

– *Miracles are exceptions to the rules for which science has not found any logical answer or explanation. A phenomenon such as a flower opening is also a miracle.*

– I am very ambitious, but the advanced course teaches me to be spiritual.

– *They are not non-complementary. It is like asking the question: "Should I watch TV first or refer to the programme first?" You can do both!*

– What is most important to follow and to assume, what we feel as fair, or to do one's duty, for example assume one's responsibility towards your family?

– *Both. Sometimes one, sometimes the other.*

What is the significance and importance of fasting?

– *Fasting is giving rest to your system. Your system must work continuously. It doesn't have annual paid leave... Give it a holiday! But fasting must be observed cautiously, under a qualified person's supervision.*

– What is the difference between devotion, fanaticism and dependence?

– *Love in its fullness, at its pinnacle, is called devotion. Fanaticism is to refuse to listen to the others. In devotion, there is compassion, so opening. Fanaticism is closing, absence of belongingness. There is anger, hatred. In devotion, there are no bitter feelings. Dependence is this thing which brings you no joy, which makes you miserable.*

– I lack devotion for you.

– *Never mind. Anyway, there is no need for it. Simply feel at home, be happy, smile. Do seva. Never force yourself to devotion. Do not compare. You can be inspired by that, but do not compare. Be patient. Do not worry. Who cares about knowing if there is devotion or not in you? Do not feel separate from me. Sense a true feeling of belonging. Feel totally free.*

– What is truth?

– *It is that which does not change with time. What changes is not real. Let's suppose you say: "There are flowers on the table."*

This statement will not be true tomorrow. What is not affected by time is absolute truth and relative truth is what is here today and will not be here tomorrow.

– I do not feel the need to have a master. What do you think of someone like me?

– *Do not follow my advice!*

– How can you distinguish between a good *guru* and a 'trickster'?

– *Rather than asking this question, ask yourself if you are sincere seeker. Go deep into yourself. See if you are really true to yourself. You find me when you are true.*

– Who is your *guru*?

– *Each child. They were all born with this divine nature. You have lost it somewhere and I don't have it. Your nature is divine, vices are just superimposed.*

– Is it necessary to have a guru for the realisation of oneself?

– *Is it necessary to answer the question! It is like asking someone if they are sleeping... If they say 'yes', it means... If they say "no", it means... It's like saying: "I will prescribe the medicine for you, but do not call me doctor." The word guru means the one who sheds light on what you do not know... The one who takes darkness away. The mother is the first guru because she teaches the child the language... Your teacher, at school, is also your guru... A guru is what a teacher is, in a deeper sense... A teacher who brings transformation in your life is a guru.*

– People blindly love their *guru*; is that good? Shouldn't they adore only the Divine?

– *Why does one person adore another? At school, rock stars, film stars, sportsmen are worshipped. This adulation is part of human nature. Deep inside is your ability to appreciate and honour good qualities. This adulation of gurus goes back to the beginning of time. In the East, people are proud of their gurus. We know that giving up your ego to a guru, you get in touch with God.*

When your life is full, you feel gratitude. You start with the guru and you finally love everything in life. The guru is just a beginning.

In India, in October, there is a festival where people worship everything, cars, scooters, etc. Everything is worshipped. The Divine lies in each molecule. It is tradition that before cutting a tree, you plant five... An innocent mind sees life everywhere. Life must be honoured, adored. If you can't do this, then what else is left? It is so arid... just eating, drinking and sleeping. When you praise, it goes to the Divine. If you praise your guru, it goes to the Divine. When you praise someone, your own consciousness expands. So, for your own good, love and worship others.

– Apart from you, it is difficult for me to love others. I would like to get rid of my pride.

– Do not judge yourself too much... Love is always here, that's fine, don't have doubts about it. Just keep going. Do not compare. Some express themselves, others don't. Everything is Okay! Do as a horse does, move forward with blinkers to follow a straight path. Not everybody is the same... You have your own talents. The ability to love is the same for everybody.

– What is the link between truth and love? What is love?

– Love is something each one has experienced. There is no one in the world who does not know what love is, has never felt it profoundly. You already know this. Sit down and think about it. Observe it, be more aware and more will be revealed to you. You don't need to read books about love... It just reinforces the concepts in the mind.

When we are full of stress and tensions, we are unable to perceive love in its purest form; you come from this pure space of love. Do you see what I mean?

Now, how can we overcome one's tensions? Look at them closely... Don't they come from what happened yesterday, the day before or ten years ago? You cling to the past, which is over. All your anger comes from the past. Can you bring the past back? Each moment, look at what your mind does. It goes back to the past, it gets angry because of the past, or it is afraid of the future, doesn't it? Do you remember what happened ten years ago? Look back and see. Weren't you worried? "What is going to happen?" But you went through life, didn't you? If you observe your own life, you can note how useless this worry about the future was; a waste of time and energy. "What is going to happen?" "What is going to happen?" When this fluctuation of the mind stops, you get in contact with the source of energy which is inside you. Live the present moment. Now!

– What do you do when you have negative thoughts?

– *Welcome them with open arms. Welcome them. But do not act on them. You are worrying? Do worry! What will happen in Bali in five thousand years?*

– Talk more about love, your favourite subject.

– *When you love someone, don't express it with too many words. Love is like a seed: if you express it too much, it can't germinate in the outside air. It is a problem in the East and in the West. In the East, people don't express love at all. They have love, but don't express it. In the West, it is too much expressed with words. So, in either case, love does not grow; it is not deep, powerful, strong enough. If a seed is buried too deep in the soil, it can't germinate. If it remains on the surface of the soil, it doesn't germinate. It needs to be somewhere in between. When you tell someone, "Oh, I love you so much, I love you so much, I love you so much!", it is all wasted in words. Just live. Act, but use fewer words. You will see that love finds its way into your actions, the way you look, and your life. It becomes very active. Do you see what I mean? A person can feel this real love within you. You don't need to say "Oh, I love you so much!" Do you see?*

– I am with someone, but our relationship is not going well. Should I change partner?

– *If you can row, you can row any boat. If you can't row at all, then changing boats will not help you.*

– What is your biggest responsibility?

– *My biggest responsibility is to make you responsible.*

– But how do I bring my dearest love to this teaching?

– *Use a bit of craft.*

– Did you bring us here that way?

– *You need some special craft when something does not turn you on. [Applause] That's enough for tonight, isn't it?"*

♦

The Master's attention turned towards one of the presents put next to him. He examined it, turned it over and over, shook it close to his ear... He tried his best to open it ever so carefully, without tearing the wrapping paper: "*What is it? Well? Life is a surprise parcel for you... The world is a beautiful parcel, the world is not bad. A wonderful gift is given to you, wrapped in beautiful paper. But if you stay stuck in the wrapping paper, you won't even open the present; you won't see what you have been given. This is what most people do... All the pleasures of the senses in the world are like wrapping paper: true bliss is the present inside. Unpack the present. Stop struggling with the wrapping paper. The whole world is there for you to appreciate it.*"

A glittery plastic salad bowl emerged from the parcel. *Ooooooh...* Gurudev Sri Sri Ravi Shankar put it on his head and started singing *bhajans* again, in the most natural possible way, unwrapping his presents: little somethings, just for fun most of the time, which he will give to children or to grown-ups on their birthday. Water pistols, squeaky toys... amused and impassive, the Master discovered more and more things; children's drawings, poems and... big pink rabbit-headed slippers! It does not matter! He put the bowl down and put the slippers on. And Gurudev Sri Sri Ravi Shankar Narayana, more informally known as 'Guruji' or 'Gurudev', walked off like an angel, with these awful things on his feet... totally unaffected.

Another day, someone asked him why he wanted to get involved in the big balagan of the world, he who had all that anyone could want. His answer was: "*What had to be reached is reached. Now, nothing seems tiring to me. For me, all this is a game. And games can never be tiring...*"

3

UNCONDITIONAL LOVE

AGAIN, THE NEXT DAY, the Master kept looking at me insistently. It could be noticed. "Hey, he is taking your picture!" someone whispered. Others emphasized in turn how lucky I was to receive what they called "the *Guru's* grace"...

Whatever possessed me to feel that I was special? The moment a faint smile of euphoria wormed its way into me, I knew I was completely off track. From that moment on, anyway, I became totally invisible to the Master!

His apparent disinterest did not greatly affect me. There was no risk anyway of being left behind. A genuine Master, like Gurudev Sri Sri Ravi Shankar does not act in reaction, neither for nor against. He has no personal moods. No "I like, I don't like"... Everything suits him. Everything that has happened has happened, nothing more! It's enough for him to point out the mistake. He won't preach, nor criticise, nor even give advice: to influence does not help. The Master will simply tell the direction it is 'preferable' to take to avoid going down blind alleys. He very subtly undoes the mechanisms of repetitive patterns wherein we continue to make the same mistakes over and over again.

The light he shines on our behaviour comes at unexpected moments. It can be just as things happen to be said during *satsang*, or in the question/answer game. It can be the topic chosen for the week's knowledge sheet, to be meditated upon... Or just a fleeting indication during a personal conversation with the Master, to be caught on the spot, because it won't be referred to again: an expression on his face, an attitude, a gesture, whatever comes up spontaneously. It is up to everyone to decode what is suggested, and to hear, or not, what is being said to them. Whether it becomes clear or not does not matter. Gurudev Sri Sri Ravi Shankar continues, without giving more explanations, to look after people's needs, no matter what stage they have reached, in his own way, unfathomable of course in its totality. Sooner or later, the person will get over the obstacle, nobody knows how...

"*Any mistake,* he says, *happens through ignorance only, not intentionally.*"

Having got rid of guilt, Gurudev is an exacting teacher. He does not compromise over the sacredness of the knowledge. This demand remains a mere principle in fact, as he asks no conditions and doesn't penalise any fault. He says,

"*Ignorance is never, ever to be forgiven! But the person is innocent...*"

The Master is magnanimous with shortcomings, but tough when faced with inertia. To raise your level of consciousness, he can give you a real shake up, or let you stew through a tricky situation, even if it means making your ego suffer. Gurudev calls it, 'a little passing discomfort.' It is very useful in allowing the disciple to discern how deeply he is established in the knowledge. If he does not appreciate all the beauty of this path, if it is not a priority for him, if he does not realise how lucky he is to be on it, he may soon find himself out of breath! Because the path to progress is made up of steep climbs followed by inevitable falls.

"*The knowledge is not for chickens...*" Gurudev warns us forcefully! In other words: let the cowards afraid of their own shadows, in a hurry to peck at their subsistence, not waste their time with him: "*Don't take on this additional burden in your life, you have more than enough already!*" He will say it is high time to be 'lions', strong, courageous and fiery...These are his tricks to boost that part of a person which always longs to improve.

"*You can spend your whole life worrying, grumbling, brooding and being miserable, when that same energy could be used to lift you up to unbelievable heights.*"

Somebody once asked him, "If there was one question you never wanted to hear, what would it be?"

Gurudev Sri Sri Ravi Shankar, pensive, repeated the somewhat disconcerting question aloud:

"*Hmm... I had never thought about that...*"

Then, laughing: *"Don't ask me where ignorance comes from, because... I don't know! Ask me rather how to get rid of it."*

How can ignorance take pleasure in being lethargic when the tracks are actually there to help us move forward? How can the initial enthusiasm sometimes fall flat, the desire for self-discovery fall by the wayside? It is a mystery...

"When you said 'mystery', you put a full stop. It is a question without a question mark, but with a full stop!" And Gurudev adds: "You cannot go backwards in spirituality. You move ten steps forwards, go back five, and move forward again..."

The slope may seem steep, but the ever-present Master is the handrail. It amuses him to see how we can make a mountain out of a molehill. He laughs! Because he can see how it will turn out. And if you lose confidence, he will give you just the right boost.

♦

Days went by... The Master had not changed his attitude towards me. He would turn his head conspicuously when I walked by, pretended not to notice my presence in public. I still would not believe he was really keeping me at a distance. Small details constantly betrayed his thoughtfulness. But just as his presence was probably starting to work on me, sadness overwhelmed my faith.

When Gurudev glanced round the hall, his smile failed for a minute at the sight of my red eyes.

The *satsang* was taking place normally. Singing, dancing, laughter... And dissolved into the course of the day's lesson he was already delivering, he spelt it out: *"How could the Master ignore you, he who does not ignore even a wrapping paper or the flower in a vase? How could he ignore a human being, walking, talking, breathing and who is connected? If he seems to ignore you, know that it requires a lot of effort on his part... It is a sign that you are very dear to him. When you understand this, you should feel immediately close to him."*

Were these words addressed to everyone? Yes, of course. Anyway, it put new heart into me, even if the skilled teacher went back to his facade of indifference...

"You can only be hurt when you love... There are only two states of being in love, and the second is indifference. You can live like a stone, indifferent, or be in love. Then different emotions can come; you feel the wound. If a person whom you love deeply doesn't smile at you, it can affect you. On public transport, in airports, many people don't smile at you, but you don't care..."

He says,

"When does the ego show itself?
When you don't get attention.
When you seem to lose attention.
When you do get attention."

Of course, I was laughing...

"Attention is not love. In fact, when there is a lot of love, there will be no attention."

Happy when he looked at me, unhappy when he did not... Was I going to subject everything to this kind of pettiness? To try to reproduce near Gurudev Sri Sri Ravi Shankar the small problems of the ordinary world, would be to expose oneself to frustration. Because there was no chance at all of managing to communicate with him on this wavelength. The waves were definitely too short. Any thought of getting there through some feminine wiles was doomed. It would be pure foolishness too, because his love promised much more than the mere satisfaction of simple whims or desires.

Finally, the 'closet and dry bread and water' cure was speeding up the growth of some form of detachment. Deprived of his concern, I realised how useless it was, how thoughtlessly pretentious it would be to legitimise it, and especially, what small-mindedness it would be to expect, or even worse, claim that concern. It was still far from being enough to erase all the ambitions of attraction. But there was the example of the Master and his Divine love to avoid the mess.

I had always thought that in matters of love, I had been remarkably lucky. But in listening to Gurudev Sri Sri Ravi Shankar, and particularly in observing him, I perceived better how these beautiful love-stories I had lived, without trying to go back on them, had nevertheless had their shackles.

The Master's love was above all friction. He never imposed any conditions: "If you behave like this, I will love you; if you don't, then I won't"... He never demanded anything. Still, everything was within his reach. He could easily take without asking, and would even be thanked for it. But he said, "*The most beautiful gift is no gift!*"

Often people think he has more love for certain people close to him. In fact, he only has more to do with them. They are the figurehead of the ship that must lead the knowledge as far as possible. But the Master's love for all is unconditional, and his task is to make it contagious.

"Sometimes, I can hear: 'Love everybody'. How can you do that? Can you? Can you create love inside you? It's not possible. Love is a happening, an event...

There are many sorts of love: the love of a mother, of a father, of a brother, of a sister, of a spouse, of a husband, of children, of animals, of trees, etc. All these types of love are different. Each is unique and marvellous. But is it loving the person as they are? The love of a fully realised Master accepts you as you are. No conditions; as you are in your entirety.

– Do you love everybody equally?

– *No, I love everybody uniquely."*

I never heard of a disciple doubting this truth, and not feeling deeply loved. Such confidence may not be felt quite so clearly with one's own family.

Gurudev Sri Sri Ravi Shankar says,

"You want love, you demand love, but what have you given unconditionally? Having expectations destroys love. If a father has expectations of his child, he destroys the child's love. If a spouse has expectations of the other, they destroy the other's love.

In the same way, if a child has expectations of his father, mother, brother, sister, friends, love will wither. Love is a pure unconditional gift. No matter how you are and where you're at, I am with you, I support you, I am you. This is what love is. But we gradually turn love into possessiveness and business. We want to possess love, but in doing so, we destroy love. Then you demand love, you destroy love. Love is not taking, it is giving. Giving and giving and giving again; this is how love grows in you...

If you are looking for security, love, comfort in your partner, you become weak, you are in a state of receiving. And when you are weak, all the negative emotions rise in you; you have demands. Just become aware of this simple fact: expectation destroys love, and then you will save it from decaying."

♦

You will never see Gurudev Sri Sri Ravi Shankar read his papers or consult his notes while teaching. He doesn't prepare his talks. An ancient text is often placed before him. It simulates the long river of enlightened masters who have preceded him since Shankara. His words flow from those waters, their colour changed each day by the latest mood created by the audience whose individual and collective needs Gurudev picks up with an intuition that never stops amazing people.

Throughout his whole stay in France, Gurudev Sri Sri Ravi Shankar spoke a lot about love and ego. He was untangling our misperceptions: ego and temperament, love and seduction, because the confusion is common. It was a very good thing he went back to square one.

"Ego means 'I am. I am somebody'. But beyond the ego is Being. What is ego? It is a limited identification, an idea about yourself: I am this, I am not that; I can't do this, I can do that... Ego means keeping up a distance from others, building walls, trying to impress. Thus stress and tension are created in your nervous system. Feeling separation, feeling you have a separate identity from being, this is what ego is. This is the first characteristic. The second is identifying

with some ideology. Through the ego, we justify our actions, and always want to be right, to be good, to be the best among the best, we try to be somebody, we don't have a feeling of 'belongingness'." A state of non-relaxation is also ego: when you don't feel at ease, when you are uncomfortable, not natural. The opposite of ego is being totally natural.

Have a look at ego. Ego causes heaviness and discomfort. It does not allow love to flow... Often, the attitude you adopt with people with a big ego is contempt or jealousy. But you should rather have compassion or even pity for them, shouldn't you?

When you think good about yourself, in a subtle way, you think bad about others. Then anger, hatred, jealousy, all sorts of emotions come in.

When you think well of yourself, in a very subtle way, you think ill of others. When you think ill of yourself, you feel inferior, and again you get angry and feel hatred for others; if you think well of yourself, you are in trouble; if you think ill of yourself, you are in bigger trouble! So forget about your self-image!"

– Don't you have any ego left yourself?

– It is ego that makes me brush my teeth every day! There is also a positive aspect to ego. It urges you to realise something. A human being carries out a work urged on by compassion or by their ego. Most achievements in society come from an inflated ego. But in satsang, work is done through love. Ego is wanting to prove and wanting to possess. But when you wake up and see that there is nothing to prove and nothing to possess, ego dissolves. This dissolution of our 'I, I, I, I' is great happiness, great joy. It is divine love. For a moment, let it melt away. Say: "Okay, I let go"...

– Should I eliminate ego totally to love unconditionally?

– Who could eliminate ego? If you think, you have dropped your ego, that is a bigger ego. "Oh, I got rid of my ego!" It's like saying: "I am the humblest person in the whole world..." But don't worry about it; don't try to get rid of your ego; that would only cause you more problems. If you think there is an ego, put it in your pocket; let it be...

– Why do I need to be or feel important?

– Because you just don't know how important you are! Once you know, then you don't need to feel so important. You are so unique. Each of you is so unique in this Creation... People who are not important make important people important! So, who is the most powerful, the king or those who make the king?"

I ask him: "We have an expression in French which says, 'Chase your nature, it will come galloping back'; it seems it is rather the opposite: once it is chased out, it is difficult to gain the naturalness again..."

He answers,

"This sentence is out of its context... If you turn a candle upside down it is still the nature of the flame to go up... It is true too that if you chase your naturalness away, it creates problems..."

Another question: *"Why is it simpler to be complicated?"*

He laughs:

"Why does it seem simpler to be complicated! It seems so to everybody in the beginning... You are so used to being complicated! But with a little bit of effort, you will discover truth, real joy, and eliminate tensions. It is like asking, when you cannot sleep, why it is so difficult to sleep... An old saying has it that the path of love is very narrow. There is no room for two! It is love, or you. Love is about forgetting the 'what about me?' and dissolving. You look up at the huge sky: so many stars, the moon, the sun, but if you have just a little speck of dust in your eye, and everything is concealed. In the same way, the little 'me, me, me' covers your infinite nature, the love without hindrance that you are."

♦

One evening, as he entered the hall, Gurudev Sri Sri Ravi Shankar saw that his seat was occupied by a huge stuffed toy. Everybody was watching how he would react. In the middle of taken aback laughter, the Master went and sat down at the end of the hall, on the only available chair. So people had turned around to face him. *Satsang* started like that, backwards, the luckiest ones finding themselves sitting next to him. However, those left their seats one after the other, and the Master went on in the middle of an empty row of seats... After *satsang*, they all explained: they could not stand the powerful radiance of all those eyes focused on Gurudev Sri Sri Ravi Shankar. They felt they were on tenterhooks!

Some of these *satsangs* had been filmed in the past, to keep a record of the entirely oral teaching. The camera is of course focused on the Master, but sometimes, for a few moments, it focused on such and such participant. Every time I had had the chance to watch these videos, I had been struck by the magnificent expression on peoples' faces. Nowhere else had I experienced such a feeling of perfection, of real beauty, in spite of my well-honed sense of aesthetics. There is a sacred word which we often sing in the *bhajans* that expresses it: '*Shambo*!', simply meaning 'Oh, how beautiful it is!'

During these natural moments, in the presence of the Master, when what is not necessary is abandoned, this palette of faces sublimated by the peace of the soul, it seems to me, testified to the inherent beauty of humanity. Knowing how deeply it can be buried in garbage could do nothing to lessen the frankness of this revelation.

Gurudev Sri Sri Ravi Shankar welcomes this love that seems intended for him with undisguised joy, because he knows its nature. He gives it his respectful and patient care: he shelters it, nourishes it, helps it to rise, to overcome dependency to become autonomous and fulfilled. This love may cling on to him, but the Master takes care of showing you this is not the way to go. He is not the end in itself:

"Love is neither an emotion nor a feeling, it is our veritable existence. It is your natural state of being."

So in a way Gurudev Sri Sri Ravi Shankar's teaching exploits the wonder that he himself causes. He is simply the mirror in which the disciple sees only his own reflection.

The *Guru* is nobody. He is an energy, an entity. He is at the same time familiar and inaccessible. For the faithful who come to him, he is the springboard they need to reach God. They need to love someone tangible to be able to love the abstract; the 'form' in order to love the 'formless'. As there is no personal connection with God, then love may not come. Through the *guru*, they find the bridge between the personal and the infinite. So far, for most of the disciples, love had only meant personal contact. The *guru* breaks this pattern. He puts you in a situation where you live love, and at the same time cannot hold on to it. Through his intimate closeness, the *guru* is no idol; through his spiritual dimension, the *guru* can't be possessed.

Gurudev Sri Sri Ravi Shankar says,

"In our lives, love has a high mortality rate! Love dies young! A few days, a few weeks, a few months, a few years, and it is dead! [...]

If you sit and look back in your life, no doubt you have loved people, but it did not last long. Why not?

You haven't understood or experienced the sources of love, or the feelings, or the emotions linked with love – or to sum up, what love is. You never went to the bottom of it. This is what you learn with a master. [...]

There are three different kinds of love: the love born from charm, the one coming from comfort, and finally, divine love.

The love born out of charm doesn't last long, it feeds itself on the attraction of something new, but when the power of attraction weakens, boredom sets in, like in most love marriages! This love may decline and bring you fear, uncertainty, insecurity and sadness.

The love born out of comfort and familiarity grows, but doesn't bring you any thrill, enthusiasm or joy, no more than it sets you on fire.

Divine love outshines the other two by far. It renews itself continually. The closer you get, the more you discover charm and depth in it. Divine love offers at the same time comfort, enthusiasm and familiarity. You are never bored and it keeps everyone on their toes.

In divine love, you cease to exist; you dissolve like a pinch of salt in water, just allowing the divinity to be there. Unless you reach this ultimate love – imperishable – the real core, the centre of your existence will not be satisfied. You may try this or that technique, you may well try all kinds of meditations and spiritual 'trips', you may go on meeting many, many saints, receive their blessings, visit many astrologers, get their interpretations, know everything about your future... you will go on repeating all these things, there won't be any fulfilment.

When love is born out of exaltation, attraction, it is short-lived, superficial. You see, in the world, everybody wants love. Who doesn't want love? Even a dog wants love. When you are back at home, even the plants in your garden can feel your presence. Everybody wants love. Everybody loves something or somebody. And yet, there are so many problems in the world, why?

If you really look at the problems in the world, the main culprit is love! Because of love, there is jealousy; because of love comes anger; because of love come many other things too. Do you see?

Here again, we can distinguish three categories: first, the love for objects, then the love for people, and finally, the love for existence. How much do we value these three? Objects, people, or the Self-life itself. This indicates the level of our existence. To what do we give the utmost value? It is very interesting to examine our value system. What is the most useful? Gold or iron? Which of the two is more essential to life? Iron of course; without iron, you can't live; it is present in blood itself. Gold is not at all necessary. You can live without gold! And yet we give the utmost importance to gold, because it is more rare than iron. If gold was as common a metal as iron, nobody would give it importance, would they? These are two value systems, one based on rarity – if something is not available, then it has more value for you – the other, based on its usefulness for life – if something is more useful, so you give it more value.

Now, a person who loves objects too much will end up forgetting to love people. Their preference goes to things first, and then only they are interested in people. If they have some time left, they will also like life, good qualities, the Divine, God... You see? What do you appreciate most? When a person becomes richer on the level of the knowledge, of wisdom, they respect people more than money. Objects have less importance, human beings are more precious. It is the very purpose of civilisation and of culture. When you forget it, it is the beginning of violence. Why are people violent? Because they don't value people more than objects.

The next step is when you love people so much that you become obsessed with their positive and negative qualities. You get stuck in the relationship and end up quarrelling. This happens in practically all relationships. When you love someone, you start expecting that he – or she – will behave the way you would like them to behave. And when the people you love make a small mistake, even unintentionally, you feel hurt. Have you already experienced this? You love somebody and this somebody surrounds you with so much attention that you feel suffocated. They get angry for nothing: you decide to go and see a movie with somebody else, they get upset. You were supposed to pick them up at six o'clock, and can only come at eight, they are perturbed. They expect you to be absolutely perfect. You have got to get it right. It is as if they were binding your hands with golden chains. Because of that, what happens? Then comes possessiveness; and jealousy; and danger... Desires intensify, and you start quarrelling with the person you loved so much! In the end, people think it safer to love objects, because objects don't react. They prefer to love a dog or a cat because they don't have the same faculty to react as human beings. When you love a dog or a cat, they don't demand anything from you.

From then on, either you slip back into the love of objects, or you go beyond the human love experience to move further up and become conscious of this ruling principle, this superior Mind which drives the world and encompasses all the small individual minds. This happens when you come to understand the way the mind functions. The 'small mind' gives you the illusion of individuality, yet, it is ruled by a more global sphere, the 'universal Mind', the 'Big Mind'. This Big Mind, in which everybody merges, you can call it God, you can call it the Supreme Power, or the ultimate creative energy, it doesn't matter what you call it. When the small mind is relaxed, it merges with the Big Mind, and experiences happiness. Happiness is the 'expansion of the Mind'. The small limitations dissolve and you relax. Have you noticed that?

When you are happy, what happens? What do you feel? When you are happy, you feel you are expanding... And when you are unhappy, what feeling is prevailing? A feeling of being crushed, as if your mind contracted. Isn't it so? When love grows from the love of things to the love of people, it is called generosity. Greed conversely, is saying,

"All that only for me; I love that more than people". You can see that beyond people, beyond individualities, beyond the 'small minds', there exists a divine Intelligence; it's then you become 'unconditional love', and you reach a state of inextinguishable joy, which nothing in the world can shake. To accomplish this in your life is worthwhile. And it is possible! Look: you are smiling, happy, calm and composed; but a tiny thing is enough to make you wild with rage; isn't it true? Be centred in this inner space; it is worth it! Then all you have longed for in life will come to you naturally."

♦

All his disciples fall in love with Gurudev Sri Sri Ravi Shankar. Women and men, young and old. If there need be reasons for love, to their eyes, they are all present: good qualities, appearance, and wisdom. According to him, "*a spark of beauty, just a spark of beauty in the unconscious creates desire.*" That just shows how many hearts are broken by the number of sparks he radiates. There is naïve sentimentality sometimes, but often also feverish desire. Our senses work on instinct... The secret extravagance of passion... Dreaming of a caress from his hand... Head spinning if it comes... Rare... Never if one wants it...

Gurudev Sri Sri Ravi Shankar belongs to all, but he cannot be owned.

"When you see beauty somewhere, when you fall in love with something, the next impulse that comes to you is to possess it, to have it; and once you have it, it loses all its significance."

Crowds worship him as a pop-star, and Gurudev doesn't teach them to be reasonable, but to be more crazy, to make something beautiful out of this frenzied love, something that will not be tied to his own person, but spread without any limits. And out of their desire for his own person, this 'brain fever' he has no use for, he wants them to attain a much fiercer desire that would be a 'cry from the heart'.

"Set the world on fire." When Jesus said that, explains Gurudev Sri Sri Ravi Shankar, he meant he would start a fire in people, because their relationships had become stale and cold. 'Fire' means 'life'.

Jesus came to set the world on fire, which means to bring life back. This is what we have to do."

Enthusiasm rather than intoxication, that is what he advocates, in order for the true self to shine through: love not attached to a face or a name.

"Don't fall in love, grow in love! It is this limited consciousness of ourselves, this limited experience of love which confines us in a narrow and tiny compartment, where you are starting to suffocate. And you want to live free. Love can suffocate you if it is lacking in depth. That is what we see today: so many people fall in love and then separate, don't they? We cannot even handle what we are asking for, what we want. Because we have never probed into the depth of our own psyche, of our mind, of our own consciousness.

There is a deep need for contact in each human being. This need urges us to seek for a relationship. And then we get caught up in a spiral. Once the relationship is established, we want it to last forever. When somebody tells us: "I love you so much", we ask: "Will you always love me?" This present moment, when we love somebody or when somebody loves us, is not enough for us, we want guarantees, and we want love to last forever. We are not in the present moment as long as we are not sure of the next moment.

Just observe this: if your relationship is based on personal need, it will not last for long. Once the desire is satisfied on the physical or emotional level, the mind will seek elsewhere, something else. If the relationship is based on an exchange, then it can last longer.

All relationships in the world go through upheavals. You build a relationship, then you break it. Any relationship can be broken or restored, then broken again. You feel desire, then aversion. This is the world. This is samsara.

But the Master is not a relationship; the Master is the Presence. To feel the presence of the Master, it is necessary not to make a relationship of it. Don't make the Master an element of your world.

Our relationships are very limited, and limitation is always a problem. So don't expect the guru/disciple relationship to be just like any other, such as mother, father, brother, sister, husband, wife, friends.

If you try to make it like your other relationships, you will adopt that same attitude of wanting to possess and rule.

Just let love be! Don't give it a name. When you give love a name, it becomes a relationship. And to impose a relationship on love restricts it. What is your relationship to yourself? Are you your wife, brother, husband, guru? There is love between you and me. Just let it be.

In the guru, *you cannot but see this love; however, you cannot cling to it. Your mind has the old habit of trying to possess love. So, in the process of letting go, it can feel some tension, a pain, a little frustration. And this concept enters your mind: "Oh, this is not the path for me; I don't want this..." You came to swim, but you only wet your feet, and go away. You have to learn a new way of loving and always stay centred.*

First, comes attraction. When the object of your attraction becomes a little bit difficult to attain, then you start loving it more. Have you noticed this? If you simply get what attracts you – just like that, in a second – you don't develop love for it. First you must be overcome by a languor – an ardent desire for life, for something more. This will lead you to love. And when this love blossoms, it becomes bliss. When love becomes a bit difficult to attain, then devotion starts happening. Just think about it!"

♦

Somebody once had asked Gurudev Sri Sri Ravi Shankar what he thought of *gurus* who had sex with their disciples. He had answered not to judge them. But what he explained about the positive role of a master implied that those missed their goal and lost a great part of their credibility.

"The Master is a unique opportunity in your life to experience love without being possessive. There is no other. There is no likelihood you will possess him. Absolutely none! Every time you seem to be possessive or dictating the terms of the relationship, he will turn you in the other direction!"

Fortunately, this is the way he is. Otherwise, as he puts it himself, "*There's no use in having a Master then... Say good-bye to him and forget about it.*"

What would Gurudev Sri Sri Ravi Shankar be if he grabbed hold of anything he fancies? For me anyway, the slightest divergence between his words and his actions would have been totally unacceptable. Conformity is the first test of the authenticity of a *guru*. A pact needing no signature and without any moral obligation; a pact meaning peace and not deal. But this clarity is essential to the spiritual growth of the disciple and represents no sacrifice for the Master. *He* lives in bliss, an ecstasy much more powerful than any pleasures the senses can bring. What more could he seek? "*A fulfilled desire brings frustration; an unfulfilled desire brings frustration*", he says.

His lack of interest in the joys of the flesh still bothers people. "How do you resist temptation?" he is often asked.

He answers,

"By having a bigger temptation. When you have the highest temptation, nothing else matters! When the flame is burning, no need of a spark, what could it do? If you live in an apartment flooded with sunlight, there is no need to light a candle, is there?"

They want to know more: "Is *Brahmacharya*, celibacy, a must for a spiritual person?

– *Brahmacharya is something which happens spontaneously. When a person finds this ecstasy in their own Self, the need for a physical relationship ends.*

– But... but... but, haven't you ever thought of getting married, of being settled, of having a family?"

To intrigue people so amuses him greatly:

"I don't think I am grown up enough to get married... Children are not allowed to marry! I will have to think about it when I am a grown-up! Now, do you need to get married to start a family? See everybody as your family! What do you think of that?"

The audience burst into huge applause, even if it stops there.

During each meeting there always comes a time when the Master is asked to play the part of a marriage counsellor, or give personal or even sexual guidance. With a laugh he denies being the right person for that: "*I have no experience in these matters!*" And most of the time, he tackles the problems submitted to him in a joking tone. One must admit that the questions lend themselves to this:

– "Guruji, can you help me find somebody?

– An old saint whom I met recently told me the story of an angel arriving on a donkey's back, to visit a man who had hoped and prayed for him to come. The angel asked, "What do you want as a reward for your charity and prayers?" The man asked for a horse. The angel answered, "If I had a horse, why would I come on a donkey?"

– No, no, Gurudev... Please, be more precise!"

But the Master goes on: "*First I have to find somebody for myself!*" And amidst a roar of laughter, he adds: "I think we should open a marriage centre!"

If it existed, the marriage centre would probably come in useful... In a discreet way some couples do get together during these mixed courses. The atmosphere of tenderness fosters the impulses of the heart, which remain, however very discreet. You will never see couples kissing or hugging, maybe just holding hands... and certainly not in the presence of the Master. Simple instinctive feeling of respect: Gurudev is no censor, but lovemaking does not belong here. Besides, abstinence is recommended during this short period of self-development. Even married couples cannot share the same room. A break which couples usually come to terms with: they are generally very happy to totally belong to themselves for a while.

Every year, everywhere in the world, Gurudev Sri Sri Ravi Shankar celebrates weddings. The newly-weds come to ask him for his blessings and recommendations:

"Don't question the love of your spouse; don't ask them to prove it to you! A lot of time is wasted trying to verify the love of the other. If someone asked you to prove it, it would be difficult for you, wouldn't it? So don't impose on others what would be difficult for you.

"Everything you want me to do, I will do it", this is what real marriage is about. "Whatever you want, I will give it to you. I will support you. I will stand behind you all my life." But we demand: "You are my spouse; you must do this or that..." And gradually love dies."

There are no limits to the questions that people ask him, about all types of subjects, nor even to the personal secrets revealed to him. In the realm of sexuality, people's confusion is often immense, and the ability to change their behaviour is often poor. The skill of the Master lies in being able to answer the present needs of the disciple questioning him, according to a present necessity and within the perspective of a solution that the Master alone foresees. With the passing of time, the person concerned realises that Gurudev had in effect foreseen exactly how things would turn out, and never stopped giving him or her his support all the way.

This long-term clairvoyance can give Gurudev's comments a seeming inconsistency. Answering a similar problem, to one person he will say, "*Stop, you're wasting your time*", and to another, "*Go on, don't worry*"... To this young man very much in love who asks him, "Am I right to want to settle down with this girl?" he will answer: "*Leave things as they are, don't change anything. Single life is good for you.*" The relationship will prove to be short-lived. To another complaining of being plagued by uncontrollable lust, he will answer: "*Don't worry! It means you have good mechanics!*", and in fact his body will soon prove to be less of a tyrant.

Although Gurudev knows everything about the desiderata of the senses, people's total subjection to preoccupations – sex in particular – seems to have, for the wise man, an irreducible part of unintelligibility. About the industry of sex, he says, "*How can one want this? These people are so heavy, without joy, their intellect doesn't function... I am not saying sex is bad, but see: you eat, and after having eaten, you don't go on thinking about what you ate... It should be the same for sex. You have sex, and... finished! Then, you shouldn't carry it on in your head forever.*

Sex is not considered a sin or a bad thing in the East. This body came to existence through sex. Life comes out of it. It is the most basic memory, the animal instinct. You just need a balance, and you have it. Don't think you have to acquire it.

Teenagers have a sexuality of the body, like people who are not very aware. Like an eagle, they only look at a piece of skin. They don't focus on the organ, but on the flesh.

Above that, riper people are more interested in the vibrations on the level of the mind, the sense of touch, of the person. One is looking for a person; one is more selective; the mind is involved.

Conscious people seek the union of the souls with the All. When the desire is mature, the form is refined. Then sexuality permeates life and even the whole creation. The ultimate form of sexuality is the union between the mind, the soul and the Being. It is called love, which leads to divine love. [...]

But you are obsessed with sex. You are given a silver tray and you still hand out your small bowl...

You want enjoyment, but cannot experience Joy. This is the whole problem. [...]

What is it that makes you weak, dull? Your desire – stupid little desire. [...]

Something is giving you great joy, so the craving for this great joy doesn't leave you in peace. [...]

You are always hankering after pleasures, one after the other. This hankering for pleasure will lead you nowhere. Something that gives you a lot of pleasure also gives you a lot of suffering. Don't waste your time. Don't drop the divine one second for these petty details. [...]

There is no end in going from one scene to another scene, from one person to another person, from one thing to another thing... You could spend your whole life doing it. [...]

Your mind is tired, reduced to ashes running from desire to desire. It is all so exhausting! Look back and see all your desires that have been fulfilled; have they given you rest? No, they only created more craving in you. [...]

Desire and misery go together. With each desire, misery is only postponed. [...]

Your desire for pleasure or happiness makes you unhappy. You can see it by yourself: every time you are miserable or unhappy, you will find a will to be happy behind it. [...]

Now, I am not saying you should not desire. Desire comes, and if it comes, it is fine! You have no control at all over that.

Even if you say: "I should not desire", it is still a desire! Asking: "When shall I be freed from desires?" is yet another desire! When they come up, recognise them and let them go. Offer everything as they manifest and come up in you. And remain centred. When you are able to do that, to stay centred, then nothing can shake you, nothing can take that state away from you. But craving for the fulfilment of your desires, thinking that when they do get fulfilled, only then, things will become possible; thinking "only then shall I be happy" is an illusion. [...]

This is what we see in the world today: everybody is drawn to joy, but people are not happy. Quite the opposite, they are dull, because they cling to the objects of senses instead of to the source of joy. [...]

This is absolutely natural: your mind is not satisfied with limited joy. It wants unlimited joy. The desire of every mind is to go to the source where it is unlimited joy. [...]

Each of the senses takes you to a deep point inside you which is the fountain of joy. Whether it be touch, sex, sight or music, smell, taste: the joy dawning in you comes from a source deep within you.

You are the source of joy.

Joy is there, every moment. No need to make exercises with somebody. It is a natural state of total bliss. Move inside this vastness. [...]

For a few moments, repose in the Self. Say: "I want nothing!" Be without desire. These moments are very precious in your life. These moments strengthen your inner self, and they will be with you forever.

Every pleasure leaves you exactly where you are. It doesn't lead you anywhere. Pleasure only makes you tired.

A very beautiful thing, how long can you contemplate it? Your lids will drop off, you will have to stop. The delicious smell of a perfume, how far can you appreciate it? When you are wearing it, after a while, you don't smell it any longer. Can you stay with your nose in the perfume bottle? If you like doughnuts, how many can you gulp down? How many scoops of ice-cream can you enjoy? How many chocolates can you appreciate before feeling sick?

The capacity to have a say over your senses is a wealth. They don't carry you along, and you don't let yourself be taken away by them. You must be able to say yes or no to your senses.

When you look for amusement, suffering runs behind you.

When you look for knowledge, life is only amusement."

4

AN *ASHRAM* IN THE BLACK FOREST

LISTENED, BREATHED, MEDITATED... The 'small I' was keeping still in front of the revival which was taking place without it. Answer quickly followed answer without any further questions being asked. The 'small I' was excluded, but it was delighted to see its questioning simply clear away as fog lifts when the right conditions prevail.

At the beginning, it was very eager to share its discovery. It sang the praises of Gurudev Sri Sri Ravi Shankar Narayana, this jewel of humanity who came as a simple pilgrim to tell a limited audience what a whole population would have been better off hearing.

The 'small I' was indignant about this marginality. It regretted the years lost in the passive dependence on philosophies of life which had not been worth the detour. But the Sage's teaching had convinced it to keep its efforts for that which could be changed, and to accept that which could not be changed any more. The 'small I' was then thinking: 'Thy will be done.'

♦

Traditionally, at the end of the courses, Gurudev Sri Sri Ravi Shankar receives the groups of participants by nationality. It was the turn of the French. I had come first into the meeting room. The Master had put his stern look on. Some asked their questions and answered his... I kept quiet. He asked me, "*Have you a question*?" – "No, no question."

Those private meetings remain printed on memories. They are the high points of the stay through the powerful impact of the physical closeness of the Master, always intimidating in spite of his humour; through the fear of not knowing how to ask for his thoughts which will have a dramatic 'seven-league boots' effect on the future; through the feeling of relief that you now feel loved, protected, cared for when you are discouraged by difficulties...

Sometimes there are some who leave the meeting perplexed: "What did he want to tell me?"... But nobody leaves with the feeling that they have been left without prospect, in spite of the little time afforded them.

So, on that last day, each one came out with what preoccupied them... A young man wanted to quit his job to become a psychotherapist... The Master firmly discouraged rushing ahead. A woman was worried for her nephew whom she judged schizophrenic. He did not listen. Another one was waiting for him to give her his advice before she had a child or not. He answered, *"You decide."* A self-confessed egotist wanted to fight against his defect. He smiled, *"You are fine like that... Are you happy?"* – "Yes, very happy." – *"And you?"* The Master moved on to no-one in particular. "I am not", came the answer. *"What can we do for you?"* – "I don't know. I've got the feeling that nothing works..." – *"Be patient... Do your practices regularly. Sing 'Om Nama Shivaya."* A disciple approached him to discuss privately his personal problem in a low voice. *"I'll take care of it"*, Gurudev reassured. Someone in the group needed him badly; he didn't dare to come forward, but this had not escaped the attention of the Master, who told him, *"Come."* After exchanging a few words, the middle-aged man put his head on the Master's lap. And, as he was weeping, Gurudev took a tissue and dried his tears.

Then he turned towards me: *"Where do you live?"* – "In Paris." – *"How's life with you?"* – "Fine." Not to leave it at that, without thinking, just as detachedly as someone who has nothing special to expect from it, I added, "I would just like to say this: before following your teaching, I was desperate, personal problems mounted one after another and I thought: one more and I will have to end it all." The Master was looking elsewhere... I ended, "Today I don't look forward to problems, but I am not afraid of them anymore. I feel I have been saved."

He did not say anything. Besides, I did not care about his reaction which I prejudged in line with the previous ones. However, I felt a change in his mood. Like a tap left on, I continued letting flow my gratitude for these inestimable lessons of life... I thought I could feel some embarrassment around me. Never mind, I added with the same emotion-free tone, "For me, you are a gift from heaven." He did not say one word, maybe did not even smile. Everybody was standing up to go out. I followed, with neither any needs nor desires.

Some days later, I went to Zurich, where Gurudev Sri Sri Ravi Shankar was giving a public conference. He had been offered a basket of apples and he wanted to distribute them. So he invited the people to come one by one to receive their gift. When he saw me coming towards him, he looked pleased... He put a piece of fruit in my hands and held them in his. What I had felt imperceptible in his recent words about love was now taking life:

"From the very moment when you let go of passion, there's only love left. There's only intimacy left. 'Two' does not exist anymore. You stop existing... And just allow the Divine to be here."

For the first time, he hugged me. The Master's arms are like the wings of a bird which clutch you to a cloud. He smells of roses.

♦

The next step was very difficult for me to take. I was not sure I could bear it. But, in spite of external pressure, it was decided: for New Year celebrations, I was to go and meet my Master in his European *ashram* in Germany. At that time, no one in the world, not even a lover, could have succeeded in making me cross the cursed frontier. I was not then aware how ridiculous it was.

Since I had met other disciples, I had known to what extent each one came to the Master with their Gordian knot. Stunning life stories; traumas never overcome: so many unexpected tales of incest, rapes, and other sexual offences.

The Shoah remained my wound.

So, Bad Antogast?

♦

Gurudev just adores the Black Forest covered in snow. In autumn, he prefers to stay in the Canadian ashram, whose red maple forest he loves... In winter, he rather comes here, with followers from India, for them to experience the extreme feeling of being away from home. The temperature is currently fifty degrees lower than in the country they have just left. But they swear they have never seen a place closer to paradise... The snow, the mountains, the seclusion, the damp cold, the cabbage soup... Everything is idyllic.

Personally, I clench my teeth a little. I took the unwise step to go down to the village on my own on a sausage fair day: I remained huddled in a corner, almost faint from breathing in the smoke coming from the barbecue chimneys!

Back at the ashram, I wrote to the Master.

♦

A crush in the stairs and Gurudev's voice ringed with laughter, whatever he says, indicate the departure for the walk. I am going too.

The Master is wearing sandals and his white cotton *dhoti,* as usual, but his shoulders are wrapped in a very warm shawl, and despite its extreme thinness, an old *shatosh,* the ultimate in rarity. He walks fast to stave off the cold, the crowds of followers on his heels. He would have really liked a respite, in silence with nature, but the people won't leave him alone. They fight over the space next to him, just to be there, to ask him... a question! Any question. He is so squashed from every direction that he loses a sandal; every now and then, he looks back to see who is behind him. I follow on a short way behind. He makes a small gesture to me... stops and turns round. I find myself facing him. He senses that everything is not totally Okay. He says in French: "*What do you want?*" – "I want to talk to you..." – "*Okay, later...*" and he grabs my arm, and, leaning on someone else at the same time, enjoys himself sliding along patches of ice...

♦

Some have travelled up to five days in demanding conditions, to come here to see Gurudev. Although the stay is not very expensive, for lots of foreigners the financial cost is a sacrifice which will not allow them to afford other holidays. It is often the case for Africans, people from the Middle East (Turks, Jordanians, and Israelis), ex-Soviets. The Master promised to go and meet the Siberians who clamour after him... and to various parts of the world where the long journey brings up insurmountable problems...

When the finances are all right, it is often time which is lacking. Employees or self-employed, company directors, chairmen of multinational companies, managing directors, newspaper editors, lawyers, ambassadors, deputies or ministers have to juggle with their commitments in order to free themselves up. Now that they are here, each hour is precious. Most of them don't let the Master out of their sight.

Wherever he goes, whatever he does, Gurudev is hounded. He sometimes sneaks away, or nips off to give a conference in Berlin, Frankfurt, Stuttgart or the European Parliament in Strasburg. But the signs of his imminent escape are quickly spotted. The signal is given and jam-packed cars shoot off after him. So the Master seizes the chance to escape when people are collectively busy, at meal time for example. On this occasion he will be pursued by a reasonable number of vehicles... When he comes back some hours later, the whole welcoming committee will be there, waiting for him. And he will be hassled all the way to his room door.

"Guruji, can I do two advanced courses back to back?

– Yes, if you eat well.

– Guruji, can I see you?

– You are seeing me...

– Gurudev, I have a headache.

– It's purification: the stress is going away. Don't bother about it. Drink more water; go and have an ayurvedic treatment...

– Guruji, can I come to India in February?

– Just wait a little, you can come later."

The Master does not protest. He takes whatever comes and lets people do as they want. Even when he is exhausted, he still grants time to those who think they need some. And also to the others, to please them.

He says,

"The ability to receive sincere love comes with the ability to give love. The more centred you are and the more you know by experience that you are love, the more you feel at ease with any quantity of love expressed in any way, because deep in yourself, you know that...love is not an emotion, but a state of being!"

♦

The *ashram* is full. Extra spare rooms in the refurbished attic were sufficient for only one season. For each new course, it is necessary to call on the availability of surrounding hotels and guest houses, which in the end are also full, to accommodate all those who want to enjoy Gurudev Sri Sri Ravi Shankar's presence in his European ashram.

The Master now has millions of followers spread over one hundred and forty countries, mostly through his foundation, the Art of Living. Lots of other people have received the basis of his teaching, delivered by the teachers he has trained (of whom I am now one). But not everybody feels the need to meet the *guru*. Some are not interested in a spiritual approach; others confine themselves to their own religions, although there are definite links. They are content with practising at home the techniques learnt for life, and enjoying the outcome. Multi-levelled benefits which affect the people around them. Getting so far suits them. They do not yet feel the need to go any further.

Gurudev, for his part, has made it tougher to access the teaching he gives personally: to get this far, you must have followed up the basic course with an advanced course. Feeling ready before taking up his time is a minimum requirement...

♦

Not having extendable walls – although we sometimes wonder – the five hundred initiated in the Christmas week had to pack up and go to make way for the fortunate guests arriving at New Year. So, yet another five hundred participants now get together spontaneously, bound by the value they give to the knowledge and to the Master's love. Hearts are opened trustingly. Sharing what each one has been immersed in, what they really enjoyed and have chosen to deepen, creates a fraternal bond which far exceeds a mere feeling of brotherhood...

In the Master's house – a translation of the Indian word ashram – Nature lives on, under its roof, in full bloom. The disciples feel very much at home here, perhaps even more relaxed and cheerful. No shouting, even at the children! No dramas, or rarely any. And from the first hour to the last, as standard issue, bursts of laughter and even tears: the consumption of tissues breaks records here...

Garments symbolising social standing are left in the cloakroom. What use would they be? Whether rich or poor, is there any difference in the way we all breathe? Whether a leader or one of the masses, is there any difference in the way we all sing? Whether a celebrity or an unknown, is there any difference in the way we all meditate? They all are followers of the same ideal: learning how to get to know one and serve others. Chief executives or production line workers tackle the same tasks: cooking, cleaning, repairing, transporting, decorating, flower arranging. Two hours a day of *seva*: time dedicated to carrying out a task as the needs of the moment arise, of use to someone or to everyone. Just doing. No particular objectives, no ulterior motives. A golden cure for depression. No 'me, me, me, me' in *seva*. And yet, with the pure enthusiasm of not expecting anything from it immediate reward comes. The whole body feels happy, every living cell tingles... The true simple nature rejoices.

The Master says,

"When you are doing seva, don't think you are doing someone a favour. You get back more from your seva than what you put into it, for sure. If you expect pay-back, then your seva becomes labour."

Even if the reward is not perceived in seva, there is no moaning. On the other hand, even if the reward is significant in labour, there will still be moaning.

Service is neither action – always egocentric – nor self-satisfaction. Merely a response to necessity. Gurudev Sri Sri Ravi Shankar, a servant to servants, puts service as high as knowledge. Seva is the very core of it: the inner attitude. It is a personal disposition for saying, "If you need me, I am here." Just being able to say it is seva. Who has never expressed or thought these words?

"Observe your state of mind at that moment, Gurudev says; they are the very moments when you have truly lived your life."

When the hands are busy dicing carrots, with people all around you dicing theirs, and once their size has been compared and the standard checked, you've only the rest of the pile of carrots to finish off. The mind is at ease. It could be the right moment for making acquaintances as we do in life. What's your job? What do you enjoy? The last book you read? The last film you saw? As far as I'm concerned, a bit of this and that... Becoming closer by recognising common attributes is not the aim. There are better things to be discovered about others and about oneself.

In those meditative situations, where the personality has no role to play, it appears more clearly to everybody that they are not what they generally say they are. Am I the job I do? Am I my taste for Wagner? Am I my opinion about French politics? Am I my thoughts, my feelings, my memories, my emotions? None of those facets of identity will help answer the question, "Who am I?"

What is exchanged in sharing the tasks, without taking any specific interest in anyone, leads to getting to know one another far deeper than after hours of casual conversation in a cafe or hotel lounge.

The Master says, *"I see people who have stood still at 'What about me?' for such a long time that they become permanently preoccupied. Things don't change. Twenty or thirty years pass by and they are still thinking: 'What about me?' They carry on worrying about it... They don't even have any new concern, only the same old concern!"*

Seva teaches how to distance oneself from the fixed idea of being someone, the futility of which can even be perceived by the megalomaniac himself. He too will go empty-handed into the grave. *Seva* changes priorities. There, evidence becomes the whole, and the landmark, being useful to others.

In the anonymity of work, free from issues, special gifts are fully put into practice on unusual grounds. Unknown talents and forgotten qualities are unearthed. We measure to what extent one limits oneself in one's life, mistreats oneself, and how much this depreciation lacks humility, in fact. Gurudev Sri Sri Ravi Shankar allows no-one to wallow in his own lack of self-esteem. If someone claims not to be capable of achieving something, they might well be confronted to it. And it will be proved, for the Master, for his part, makes no mistake about each one's potential. Inventive, adventurous, non-conformist, he knows how to have all personal skills work to the full: "*What about doing this? Good idea, isn't it*?" At the time, the stroke of inspiration knocks you out. The project seems wild. But finally, it is confirmed to be accurately targeted. Many people have taken off from there. A good many youths who arrived out of their depth, jobless, battling with drugs, managed to perform outside the responsibility driven out at the *ashram*. There, they came up against it with a very patient 'boss'. What other 'boss' than Gurudev would bear the number of mistakes made? Oversights, errors, clumsiness, material breakage of equipment – even cars... All things considered, with little promising school qualifications, they found their vocation: sound engineer, carpenter, florist, educator, caterer. Others, on the contrary, moved towards more modest activities than before. In all cases, self-confidence gives the necessary impetus. To exploit one's talents, honour them, make them brilliant: Gurudev Sri Sri Ravi Shankar makes this ambition bolder. For talents were not given to sing one's own praises, but to be useful to everybody. He says,

"Work in itself does not make you tired as much as the impression of being the doer. All the talents you have are for others. If you have a lovely voice, it is for others. If you are a good cook, it is for others. If you write a good book, it is for others. What do you do? You don't sit and read your own book! If you are a good carpenter, it is for others. [...]

Giving one's life for others is loving. We are the others; they are like a part of ourselves. There is a technique to become depressed – do you want to know it? Just sit down and think: 'What about me? What about me?' I tell you, you will be totally depressed."

Through the menial jobs done at the *ashram*, the automatism to contribute everywhere else gets into its stride in the spirit of *seva*. For Gurudev Sri Sri Ravi Shankar, all the interest of the washing-up or cleaning training, whatever, is there: to adopt a different comportment outside.

He says,

"Place yourself in the service of society. Take this for granted: when you do something for the world, inevitably the world will take care of you. If you are content with just sitting idle, twiddling your thumbs, waiting for society or the world to provide for you, it will not happen...

If you offer yourself, if you put your body, your physical strength, your power, all that you have at your disposal to the service of society – 'I will serve' – then be sure that the world will provide for you. It is a law, as true as fire burns: the world cannot not take care of you. No need to bother, then, or to dwell on that: "What about me? What will become of me?"

The way to go from a state of individual consciousness to a state of universal consciousness is to share other people's sorrows and joys. As you grow up, your consciousness should also grow...

The best way to overcome one's personal miseries is to share universal misery. The way to increase tenfold individual joy consists in sharing universal joy. Instead of weighing up: "What can I take from the world?" think "What can I do for the world?" When everyone comes to take responsibility for their contribution to society, what you get is a divine society.

Service is the expression of love. Serve whichever way you can. Life becomes small if it is not shared."

The Master constantly reminds us of the high value of *seva*. Whatever stage the disciples have come to, it may be useful to repeat it. What he teaches is not perfectly understood all the time. Of course, at the *ashram*, there are Stakhanovites, who get through loads of work and really want to slave away when others are sleeping or enjoying themselves... There are the absent-minded ones who need to be reminded of the forgotten washing up... There are the work-shy, who put their coats on the very moment help is required, and there is over-abundance of volunteers for the least tedious tasks, and shortage of people to accomplish the most unrewarding ones.

The Master always raises the stakes: "*We must be able to be enthusiastic in something we do not like because it makes us pure. Just be enthusiastic. Seeing the objective is no use. A multidimensional opening is coming. Infinite nature is appearing*".

The feeling of being at peace with oneself, felt when you do *seva*, bans fighting against the lazy ones. Each one evolves at their own rhythm... Certainly, some serious minds wave their small manual of the perfect disciple to make the lazy-bones feel guilty. This is immediately demolished by the Master: "*Do not preach. Do not use knowledge as a weapon or it will be resented.*" However, apart from those rare moralistic cutting remarks, judging the way others act, behave or express themselves is not established in the *ashram*. Feelings, emotions, states of mind come and go without giving rise to any comments. Impulsive criticism will come to nothing, and gossip, *a fortiori*, will here fall on deaf ears.

Accepting people as they are is the basis of Gurudev Sri Sri Ravi Shankar's teaching. It is nonetheless striking to note how this aspect of the art of living – which is lacking so much outside, where one wears oneself out trying to make others into replicas of oneself – manages to meet no difficulty to be enforced in this socialization laboratory; it comes by itself. Acceptance is assimilated, nicely and quickly, as an elementary fact of existence which brings comfort in return.

The Master can then go further easily:

"If people don't accept you as you are, you must also accept them not accepting you. Accept it! It is beautiful and simple. Accept them; don't expect them to accept you in return. It is most important for you not to see to it that they accept you. The more you apply yourself to doing it, the less it will work."

♦

A light is left on almost all night long in the Master's room. He sleeps only two or three hours. But he makes up for it with meditations which give him a more recovering rest in a much shorter time. In fact, each instant of his existence is meditation.

At the end of the corridor, a heap of shoes and a permanent crowd indicate unmistakably the place where he is accommodated. A small two-room flat (room and meeting-room) with a bathroom: shambles of love tokens. His private kitchen is elsewhere. There, an Indian devotee cooks cordon-bleu meals in accordance with ritual rules of absolute purity, as for everything related to the *guru*. The same scruples go with the care taken for his linen and housework. Nobody is really accredited to these tasks. Gurudev appoints the worthy among the devotees to this *seva* of honour.

Despite the instruction given to not disturb him, there is a continuous stream of beggars. No notice seems deterrent enough to divert he who wants to come in. At the hall door, the temple guardian protects the Master from anything getting out of hand. Whenever someone knocks, he takes a cursory glance and passes the message through to say who is allowed in and who is not amongst the crushing throng attempting to force their way in.

This duty, striven to get, is shared among those who are in charge of the *ashram* all year long. There are only about twenty of them: the visit of the Master is the occasion to favour them for their work and especially to increase their morale. Living in the *ashram* permanently is no picnic. It is a hard training, but the best to become strong...

Why does the meeting room door open to let in one rather than the other? An enigma about this *guru* who always knows about every individual's concern without having to be informed.

Thus, those who think they hold their pretext to talk to him in private, wait religiously. There are also those who watch out for those occasions when Gurudev totally gives in to all those who happen to be there. Open day event to share a moment with him, talking, watching CNN news or a DVD shot during a recent trip, reading the mail, listening to him telling funny stories or answering the phone to some devotees exerting themselves for the Foundation somewhere at the far side of the world... Dry fruit and sweets distribution won't be forgotten...

♦

Since the episode of the village, circumstances had not yet allowed me to pass my letter on to him. The Master often leaves time do the big work. The time expectancy of all emotion would be of 'two days and a quarter'. Then, the mind perks it up, keeps it warm, but whether you like it or not, it has changed. And the problem which stimulated it has started to settle down. Gurudev, an assistant of nature, then brings his magic touch of wisdom.

The carefree hours spent next to him had largely eased all my tensions. But, being a bit dishonest, I was anxious not to lose the thread... The core question remained nevertheless topical...

One early afternoon when there was nobody waiting in front of the Master's quarters – maybe because he was resting – I had come to slip my message under his door. At the very moment when I was slipping it, *he* opened the door, totally unsurprised to find me there.

He beckoned me into his room – a consideration I would later understand. I had never had a private conversation with him before. I was struck by the impression of light density around him. But I personally felt like a prince crowned in a historic tragedy, the right person to deserve his consideration...

He had gone back to his futon. Sitting on his heels among the sheets, he was smiling, looking towards the white mountains, as marvelled as if he was seeing them for the first time.

– *"Lovely afternoon... How are you feeling in Germany?*

– I can't feel good there.

– *And in this place?*

– Better, yes. Here it is Okay...

– *One day we will have an* ashram *in France; will you be happy?*

–Yes..."

I wanted to come to the point. But *he* was already dismissing me. He took the postcard I was holding out to him as a worthless 'offering'. He stared only at the picture: the blue of the sea, zoom on the abyssal ocean supposed to illustrate my attempt to disappear... He said in English, "*Nice*"... then he cast a distant and neutral eye over what I had written to him... He said again, "*Nice*", before he concluded with a traditional "*Jai Guru Dev*", victory to the greatness in you...

I left the room, feeling a little miffed at not receiving the consoling I expected. To allay my disappointment, he added in the half-open doorway: "*You have a very beautiful shawl*". I was fuming. '*Nice*'! Hundreds of people disturbed him for nothing; I was coming to witness a drama which still concerned millions of victims, and *he* was finding that 'nice'... I headed towards the woods in order to calm down...

With my mind in bitter turmoil, I was making an accusation! But everything dissipated like the mist. What to formulate against the Master that would reach its target? That he had not understood anything of the specific horrors of the Second World War? That he was anti-Semitic? That he did not care about people's misfortune? That he was laughing at me? Nothing held true. How to get through to him, then? Contemplating leaving the *ashram*, maybe? Hoping to upset him? It was like trying to bore the wall through the open window...

I thought of a paper someone had recently put in the 'botheration' basket for the Master: "Guruji, I love you, but at this moment I feel angry with you..." He had answered, "*Even if you are angry with a wise person, you will get something out of it. Even if you love a fool, you will get light from it.*"

♦

How did it happen? I don't know, at least not in any detail. Day followed day at the same pace, in harmonious cosmopolitan life under the same roof... The fact is that after some time, there was nothing left in me of the scars of the past. *Sadhana, seva, satsang* and silence had burnt the roots of my sorrow.

In the department store of experiences, which memory is, some other old items, displayed for a long time in the shop-window, seemed also to have had their day. Phew! Once the inventory was made, nothing could prevent life from being homogeneous any more. A continuum...

Never mind really the precise alchemy which allowed the putting back of memories into their drawers. Appreciating it is enough for me.

"You are curious enough to understand everything. It is not necessary. There are some things which you need to know, others to take for granted. Go ahead, it is very important. [...]

When you eat pizza, you enjoy it without wondering the way it takes in your organism to be digested... How pizza is transformed into bolus by mastication and the action of salivary glands, then how it goes down along the esophagus and into the stomach where it undergoes the action of gastric juices, how hydrochloric acid and pepsin secretions act on pizza... What is it like when it goes through the small intestine, duodenum, then the jejunum, then the ileum where, under the action of new secretions, biliary and pancreatic, pizza is transformed into chyle... Which acids intervene, what enzymes and what bacteria take over in the intestinal wall, what particles pass into blood, into urines, etc. You don't wonder about the dose of peptones produced by the piece of pizza. No, you enjoy it... Full stop! [...]

If you don't feel close to the Master, hold only yourself responsible for that. It is because of your mind, because of your ego concepts. Share with the Master what is important to you or personal. Share it. Don't be ashamed, or shy, don't judge yourself. Unless you express to the Master what is really personal or important to you, the only fact of being in a formal or informal relationship can't bring you a feeling of closeness.

'How are you?' 'Where are you going?'... Stop those formal and superficial conversations with the Master and speak with your heart of what is really important and personal, determining for your life. Avoid talking about the price of orange juice...

Masters don't expect anything from you. They just take care of all that anxiety and of all that rubbish you can't get rid of by yourself. All the realised Masters on this planet are garbage collectors."

So, hundreds of thousands of bags of tears are emptied at his feet. For Gurudev, they are treasures: the more people get rid of them, the less they pollute the world's consciousness.

And miracles happen, those too in silence, at any time.

♦

When Gurudev Sri Sri Ravi Shankar undertook to go all over the world to revive human values, he was a young eighteen-year-old master, already recognized by his senior peers as one of the prophets of his time: "Here is Ganga!... Millions of people will submerge and find salvation", announced Mâ Anandamoyi, a famous saint highly revered in India. The word 'Ganga' – the Ganges – symbolizes knowledge.

The erudition of 'Ravi' – as his parents called him – was prodigious: a year earlier, he was finalising his cycle of studies after reaching the highest level in all disciplines, including mathematics, modern sciences and fine arts which in India include all human sciences.

The assimilation of founding texts had not cost him either: Christianity was as familiar to him as the Hindu writings he seemed to possess innately. The child was three years old when he proved to be able to recite the Bhagavad-gîtâ by heart. The Sanskrit teacher in charge of his religious education – since his prime infancy, according to the tradition of the time – witnessed a gripping demonstration: she read a line of the text and the child gave the following... Today, when Gurudev Sri Sri Ravi Shankar is asked how this could be, he confirms the fact and answers, "*Maybe imprints of the past in my consciousness.*" Later on, it was Gandhi's Sanskrit teacher who provided the lessons. After Mahatma was assassinated, Pandit Sudakar Chatunvedi had pledged to teach no one else, until young Ravi Shankar was introduced to him.

At the beginning of his schooling, he was made to skip three years in the same day... The teachers themselves saw in Ravi more than a child prodigy whose maturity far surpassed that of pupils of his age.

There was in him both a lovely fresh innocence and an intense desire to learn, focused on the Creator and his Creation.

In Papanasam, the village in Tamil Nadu where he spent his earliest childhood with his parents and his sister Bhanu, eighteen months younger than him, the young boy was seen as a miniature mystic with a mystery hanging over him. But it was no surprise: India lives in the company of gods. Moreover, the child was born into a family renowned for its deep piety. Gurudev Sri Sri Ravi Shankar's forefathers were rich and renowned Brahmans – it is to his great grandfather that we owe the façade, streaming with light, of the touristic palace of the maharaja of Mysore, tens of thousands of lights put up at a time before the country had electricity, in 1912. A generation later, all their fortune was distributed to the poor. Since then, the family had met their needs by working. Sometimes they were a little short of food, but the children were taught to always see abundance and, even in front of an almost empty cupboard, the women used to say "Oh! There is still a lot left..." At times, there was enough left to give more to beggars.

Ravi did not play with the other children. He did not avoid them, but he was bored by their games. Had he taken part in football, it would have been a guaranteed fiasco for the team: "*My feet will never be able to kick anything*, he thought, *not even a ball.*" He preferred to sit quietly and meditate. Some warned Amma, his mother: "Don't leave your son in meditation like that for hours, he will become stupid!" But Amma was aware that there was no point in worrying for him.

All sorts of inexplicable events and miracles have happened since his birth in 1956. Acknowledged facts, defying logic and basic physical laws. Like the day when the heavy chains of the garden swing-seat in which the new born baby was lying had suddenly broken. The old iron had collapsed with a loud bang; Amma had passed out through shock. Yet, in an abnormal way, instead of falling inside the swing-seat, the chains had scattered all around and the baby was chortling away, without a scream, not even crying... There was also the day when the car in which Ravi was travelling lost a wheel. The vehicle had kept going, without any stability problem, until someone, two kilometers farther on, pointed out the slight defect...

The parents interpreted the veiled messages sent by destiny as the omens that they would have to bring up a Chosen one. When the question whether it was right to think that these repeated signs were sent to him is asked, Gurudev Sri Sri Ravi Shankar answers, "*For parents, children are always very dear! Miracles occur in everyone's life. Each moment is a miracle – the birds which chirp, flowers which blossom...*"

Anyway, the hypothesis was accepted by oracles. The visit, later, to their house in Bangalore of a very high spiritual authority, His Holiness Shri Shankaracharya from Shivganga, had finished enlightening Ravi's parents about this phenomenon of nature they had: "Your child is divine. You are lucky and blessed to be his parents", the Wise one had confirmed. And he had joined hands in a sign of respect in front of the young master.

The unknowable is the stage of Gurudev Sri Sri Ravi Shankar's life. But he remains modest about it. I don't remember him talking about these miracles which scare the West but to evoke the divine nature of all human beings. And to be surprised that one attaches more credit to the invisible elements exploited by a machine than to those detained by Man who has nevertheless conceived it. Throwing spirits into confusion would be going against his approach. However, from time to time, in front of an informed audience, the Master tackles the existence of irrational phenomena, little by little, as to check the elasticity of the neurons strapped into the Method.

But no fuss is made of the mysterious corrections brought to the painful situations confided to him. Good news doesn't need a legend. Gurudev Sri Sri Ravi Shankar does not stir up the agitation of the one who records his secret weapon. He endeavours to anchor in firm ground those whose feet tend to leave it too often and to give wings to those who walk with lead soles. The happy medium is the rule: coming into the scope of a tangible reality where the irrational, beyond normality concepts, has a choice place.

He says, *"Nature is irrational: why have we got two eyes, only one nose for two nostrils and only one mouth which does two jobs at the same time – speak and eat – while the others only do one? Why not an eye in front and another one at the back of the head which would allow us to see what is going on behind us; it would be more convenient... And why not an ear as a radar on top of your head? Nature lacks rationality!"*

Like all enlightened beings, Gurudev Sri Sri Ravi Shankar possesses extra-ordinary powers, that is to say above the 10% of human potential generally used. Each one can observe in passing how developed the acuity of the *guru*'s senses is. But here too, no abracadabra. He is not interested in pomp and ceremony.

A disciple had one day asked him if he approved of his wishing to meet a Master famous in India for his materialization power. He had answered, *"If you feel like it, do it.*

– *What* are those miracles he works?

– *Miracles are nothing...*

– *I* love seeing miracles!"

Gurudev had laughed, fallen silent for a while and answered, *"If you want to meet him, go for his wisdom, for his love. Do not go for his miracles... That is worthless."*

♦

Gurudev Sri Sri Ravi Shankar likes to think he is just a wise man coming from the East. A humanity lover who can't bear distance, apart from the one necessary for the transmission of knowledge. This act needs the stage to "*flow like water from a higher to a lower level*" and to command respect: "*Ego breaks when there is reverence towards knowledge.*" Otherwise, venerable without height, Gurudev Sri Sri Ravi Shankar is for the masses he addresses a 'fellow man' who shows by his example how high a human can rise.

"I am like you. You are like me", he always says.

People, all over the world, ask him the same question again: "What is the difference between you and me?" He repeats with a tone which forbids doubt:

"There is absolutely no difference. All that I am, you are.

– Are you God?

– *Yes, and you also are."*

Nevertheless, there seems to be light years between the one who still eats his soup with the back of the spoon and this super-human incarnation which he seems to be. But he will not facilitate passive adoration.

"First find the answer to: 'Who am I?' If you know who you are, then you know who I am."

From some angles, Gurudev Sri Sri Ravi Shankar's teaching is in a way the route marked with arrows of this Being searching. For spiritual life has its prerequisites, its inevitable laws. As material life has its own. As sure as a full glass cannot be turned over without losing its contents, as sure as the cart put before the horses cannot plough the land, as sure as Newton's apple did not fall back up to the top of the Pisa Tower, there are *sine qua non* conditions to mind matters. A way to respect so that it works. Without correct use of one's own faculties, one quickly experiences muddle. "*Being happy requires just a little skill*", the Master says. Knowing how to hold one's spoon is not so complicated.

5

THE PRINCIPLES OF SPIRITUAL LIFE

GURUDEV SRI SRI RAVI SHANKAR lists eighteen essential principles for spiritual life.

1. BE CONFIDENT

Confidence is the first step. Self-confidence. Without confidence, self-realisation cannot happen. Doubt undermines confidence. When you discard negativity, you realise the positive has already happened. When doubt disappears, confidence is there. So, to become confident, you must first understand what doubt is.

If you observe the nature of doubt, you will notice it is always about something positive. You never doubt the negative. If someone tells you, "I love you very much." you answer, "Really?" But if somebody tells you, "I hate you." you never ask, "Really?"

You never doubt your anger, your depression, your sadness, your sorrow, but you doubt all your positive qualities; you doubt your capabilities, not your incapabilities. Do you see what I mean? Doubt your incapacities, doubt your weaknesses; then, faith in your capacities will grow.

As soon as you think you are weak, you lose your self-confidence. Be kind to yourself, rest on the things where you are good.

Don't look for perfect action, you will delay it. Even if there are some mistakes, act quickly, be dynamic.

Understand your doubt as a questioning of the positive, as a confidence in the negative, and know that if you have doubts, something good must nevertheless be there. Seen from this angle, doubt will allow you to move on. I am not telling you to drop your doubts, doubt as much as you want! Be with it 100%! It will help you go beyond it. Once the barrier of doubts has been crossed, there will be new progress.

Gurudev Sri Sri Ravi Shankar adds,

Have faith in yourself. You don't have to be too wise. Be confident, don't be so hard. Don't be adamant about having a very structured life. Allow miracles to happen in your life!

Don't think you're lacking confidence. You can only say 'in the past', but not any longer. As soon as you recognize you're not surrendering, you are in a different moment, you change every moment. If you say you are lacking confidence, it becomes a reality.

Doubting is wanting to get rid of something. Doubt is a temporary state where one is standing neither on this side of the river, nor on the other. Hence comes the tension.

You don't have ancient doubts, have you noticed? How do your doubts arise? With somebody new, whom you don't know very well.

Doubt cannot happen when there is a sense of closeness. Doubt needs a distance to arise. You never doubt something that is dear to you, which is close to you. The moment you doubt something, it is no longer dear to you; a distance has been created. You can doubt yourself, but you never doubt what is yours. Self-doubt is a lack of nearness to oneself.

All our fears and doubts arise when we don't want to let go of the joy, the love, or the pleasure we receive from the world. Your doubts are based on fear, and fear has only one form: that is to lose the joy or the pleasure you derive from the world. Your fear is unfounded; it is an extension and expansion of the same love that you experience in life, only a thousand times more intense. Your joy will be higher. No need to be afraid. You don't have to reject or leave whatever.

Fear is an impression from the past reflecting the future of the present...

Because fear is love upside down, everything that can be interpreted with love can be interpreted with fear. A child clinging to its mother can be understood in two ways: it clings to its mother out of love or out of fear. This primitive instinct of fear can be totally transformed through the awareness of divine love.

Total lack of fear is possible only in complete chaos, or in total orderliness. A saint or a fool don't have fear, but fear can be found everywhere in between! Fear is essential to preserve order in the world. It is a primary instinct.

The fear of death protects life.
The fear of evil preserves good.
The fear of illness encourages hygiene.
The fear of suffering makes you virtuous.

Don't try to eliminate fear; just meditate and feel that you are nobody, or that you belong to someone special.

One has to observe fear, as if it happened somewhere else, in somebody else.

You cannot, and shouldn't, eliminate fear totally. Fear helps you be grounded, but it is essential only up to a certain point. It is like salt in the food: if there is too much, it is not edible, but you cannot eat without salt. A little bit of fear is essential in the growing process.

Nature has made you so. You drive on the right hand-side of the road for fear of an accident; you walk on the pavement; you only start when the traffic light is green. These actions are motivated by fear. If you were totally deprived of fear, you could do anything and violate all rules. Laws are always respected with a little pinch of fear, and it is not a bad thing, but too much fear is not useful. You must keep a touch of fear, just like you put a pinch of salt in the food.

Ambition is a sign of a lack of self-confidence. When you know you can achieve something easily, you are not ambitious. Ambition is the sign of a challenge and an uncertainty, which are the opposites of self-confidence. So, somebody who has total self-confidence cannot be ambitious!

In the same time, somebody totally lacking in self-confidence cannot be ambitious either! For ambition to be there need be a little bit of confidence and a total ignorance of the self. It is impossible to have total confidence without self-knowledge.

With the knowledge of the Self, there is nothing left to achieve, because the entire nature of existence is only the play and show of one's own consciousness.

Some people are proud of their ambition. The wise will only smile. Ambition can never be about something you know you can achieve easily. You can only be ambitious about something for which you must put an effort, which is a challenge, and when you are not even certain to succeed or not.

Moreover, it chases away the joy of the moment; in joy, there is neither desire, nor ambition. Ambition promises joy to you somewhere in the future. It creates a mirage of joy, that leaves you with only frustration in your hands.

With the knowledge of the Self, nothing is a challenge for you, nor demands an effort. Nature is ready to fulfil your desires even before they arise, without leaving you a chance to long for or to wish for anything. Nature doesn't allow the wise to have this desire of ambition. The fool must fulfil or get rid of this desire.

Do you still want to be ambitious? Or is your ambition to get rid of ambition?

♦

2. STOP CRITICIZING YOURSELF AND OTHERS

The next step is to stop criticizing yourself and others. The spiritual journey is a journey towards the Self, and when you start reproaching yourself, you stop seeking the Self. You are no longer attracted by this quest. Unless you initiate this movement towards the Self, the Spirit, you are travelling towards the matter. The joy coming from matter tires you, the joy coming from the Self elevates you.

You will find negative qualities in yourself, but don't criticize yourself for them. Every time you blame yourself for it, you come to blame others, because self-criticism cannot last for too long. You find a way out in carrying it over to someone else. This gives rise to hatred. And every time you blame somebody else, you are preparing yourself to blame yourself again. So many criticisms are made today that they permeate the consciousness in the whole world.

Gurudev Sri Sri Ravi Shankar also says,

Putting an end to blaming others and blaming oneself does not mean you should refrain from making comments when it is necessary. You can criticize, but your criticism should not come from the heart, it should be from the lips only.

How do you feel when someone blames you? Do you feel a heaviness? Do you feel hurt, unhappy, sad? All this is because you resist. That's all. Whatever you resist will persist.

When someone blames you, you resist inside. You may resist outside, but when you resist inside, it makes you suffer.

An ignorant person will say, "Don't blame me, because it hurts me!" They warn you, because they will take revenge on you. An enlightened person will also say, "Don't blame me." Do you know why? Because it might hurt you. He will say it out of compassion.

You can ask someone not to blame you either by compassion or by anger.

The assurance for your soul is to have compassion for people's mistakes, otherwise you're bound to be angry with them.

So what! Nothing can touch you. Can the sun become impure, can it be stained? It is the same for you! Nothing can touch you. Put this in your mind, and you will be able to cross the most uncomfortable situations.

You have been told words that are unpleasant? They are just words, like a fish in an aquarium: it opens its mouth... If somebody blames you, just appreciate the expression on their face. Don't take it in yourself. See how little things can irritate you... Your life is much more than that. In your small body, you contain the essence of Creation. This frail body of yours is essence of the universe. We are wasting our forces, our time, aren't we?

You can only achieve freedom from a certain level of consciousness. You cannot be free if you are against something or someone.

Doubt people's compliments, but don't doubt their criticisms. It is more difficult to criticize than to praise, so somebody who blames you has more chances to be sincere. There can be wrong reasons for praising, nevertheless, we expect praising from others. When you become calm and centred from deep within you, praise comes to you naturally.

Only speak about knowledge. Don't repeat what has been told to you, or what So and So said, "So and So said this about you." If somebody comes to you to tell you such things, discourage them. Don't believe them.

If somebody criticizes you directly, know that he is taking your bad karma and let go; don't give them credit. If you are close to the Master you will accept all criticism with a smile.

To criticize somebody binds you to them, glues you to them.

The wise man learns from others' mistakes; less wise is one who learns only from his own mistakes. The fool goes on making the same mistakes over and over again and never learns from them.

Thinking of a mistake made by another puts you in a sort of fever. It destroys the peace in you. It darkens the love in you.

When a mistake has happened, it has happened. What's the use to punish afterwards?

I say, let go of all the walls around you; anybody can make a mistake; even you. Don't justify your mistakes, just accept them and move on. You won't have any more walls around you when you are totally strong.

You can point out a mistake, but also give a solution. If you point out an issue and don't give a solution, you have only done half the job. If you don't find an immediate remedy, work at finding one together.

You are asking, "What am I here for?" I am telling you what you are not here for:

You are not here to blame.
You are not here to cry.
You are not here to sleep.
You are not here to show off.
You are not here to fight.
You are not here to get angry.
You are not here to be unhappy.
You are not here to worry.

♦

3. PRAISING OTHERS AND ONESELF

The third law is to praise oneself and others. Praising others goes beyond not blaming them. To praise enlivens the spirit, and the presence of the spirit elevates you, elevates the other and the whole environment. Praising oneself and others creates a space full of joy in you.

If you are able to congratulate yourself, you won't wait for others' congratulations. We believe that praising oneself is ego, but in fact, ego cannot praise itself, it expects praises from others. Understand that all praise goes to the Divine anyway. If you say you have beautiful eyes, who has created them? Every praise goes to the Divine, to the Creator. The very act of giving praise develops the consciousness. Something opens up in you. Blame narrows the consciousness. As the spiritual dimension is to expand the consciousness, we don't want to counter it with blame. Sincerely offer your praises to the each another and observe what you feel.

Gurudev Sri Sri Ravi Shankar also says,

How to conquer jealousy or envy?

When you feel jealous, tell yourself that everything passes. The object of your jealousy itself won't last. One day or another, it will all be gone, it will be dead.

Know that the person you are jealous of has created some good karma in the past and is harvesting the fruit of it now.

Be inspired from it, to acquire some merit now.

Create a sense of belongingness with this person, and realise they are part of you.

Think of all you have that they don't have, and be grateful for it.

Stretch out your hand to them and make a team together.

What to do if others are jealous of you, or envy you?

Think of all those who envy you, and see that what they envy you for has not given you any great joy.

Go and ask them if they are happy.

Give them a huge compliment.

Be observant.

Know that their feelings are temporary.

The best thing is not to recognize at all their envy or jealousy. If you confer a reality to a feeling, it will only aggravate your ignorance.

Don't display your talents in front of them.

Know that they are just puppets. They will all perish, like apples or tomatoes, even if they have a little longer shelf life.

If nothing of this functions, just go to bed!

Cultivate friendship with people who are happy. In doing so, you can avoid jealousy. Be indifferent to people who do bad things. Be compassionate towards people who are unhappy; be happy for those who do a good job.

♦

4. SINCERITY

Sincerity is the fourth principle. Be sincere in everything. Don't cheat yourself and don't try to cheat others. You are not on this spiritual path for anybody else's interest. Spiritual quest without sincerity is empty. It brings no benefits. With sincerity, it brings a peace, a happiness and a joy you cannot find anywhere else on this planet.

Gurudev Sri Sri Ravi Shankar also says,

Don't be too smart with the Divine. Don't try to fool the Divine. Most of your prayers and rituals don't seek anything else than manipulating the Divine. You are trying to get the most and give the least, and He knows it! But He is a clever partner; He will fool you even more. If you go under the carpet, he will hide under the floor.

Be sincere in your efforts, don't try to outsmart the Divine! The moment you have attained bliss, all the rest is a source of joy. Without this bliss, the joys of the world won't last.

A person who is dear to you and whom you trust lies to you and gets caught. What do you feel? Sorrow, anger, resentment, disappointment, compassion, deception, loss of respect, astonishment, a trauma, embarrassment?

Recently somebody lied to me. I felt happy and even more love for this person, because this person was a bad liar. If they had been a good liar, they wouldn't have been caught. I thought, "This person is so innocent that they cannot even lie properly!" They lie and get caught! If they had not been caught, how would one have known they were lying?"

So one can never identify a good liar.

The one you call a liar is not a good liar, so he is innocent. Isn't he? It is of no use going through all these mental games! Instead of that, just melt and dissolve in love!

♦

5. BEING RESPONSIBLE

A spiritual path does not mean fleeing from one's responsibilities, but taking one's responsibilities with you. It is the number of responsibilities you have taken in your life that will indicate your progress on the path. If you think what has been given to you is too heavy for you, more will be given to you! People imagine that to be spiritual is a way out of hard work. No. The characteristics of a spiritual path are dynamic and efficient activity.

Gurudev Sri Sri Ravi Shankar also says,

Responsibility is the nature of life. A stone doesn't take any responsibilities. It is the nature of consciousness to do so. The more responsibilities it takes, the more powerful it is. If it takes total responsibility, it is almighty.

Question: *What balance should be observed between amusement and responsibility?*

Answer: *They are not opposed to each other. No balance is necessary. When you like your responsibility, it becomes a game.*

Some people say, "Let God provide for everything and surrender to him." Others say, "I must be responsible."

To surrender to the Divine is to say, "Let Thy will be done" and His will for you is to take responsibility of the whole world.

These are the two sides of the same coin. The more you surrender, the more responsible you become. Somebody irresponsible cannot surrender either. Why does one behave in an irresponsible way? Out of laziness, out of fear or both. If you are lazy or a coward, you cannot be in love.

Total responsibility is total surrender. It is a bit hard to chew, but it is the truth. People usually think: either I take responsibility, or I surrender. But both go hand in hand.

When you take responsibility and are facing obstacles, remember: surrender! It gives you the strength to move forward. It frees you from the weight of thinking you are the doer. Responsibility is the dynamic expression of the present moment. When you are shaken, remember that the foundation for responsibility is to surrender to the Divine.

Taking one's responsibilities or surrendering without feeling one is the doer of an action, is the art of the wise.

Total irresponsibility is impossible for you. A limited responsibility makes you weak and is exhausting. Unlimited responsibility endows you with power and brings you joy.

We are totally responsible for our experiences.

♦

6. DROP THE PAST

The sixth spiritual law is the capacity to let go of the past. When you can see the past as a dream, you come back to the present moment. You realise it is not necessary to make an effort to be in the present moment. The moment you drop the past, your mind comes back by itself to the present moment. In the present moment, your mind is fully aware; the smallest spark becomes a glow. When you hang on to the past, the spark is covered with ashes. Be in the present moment, and blow away the ashes of the past.

Gurudev Sri Sri Ravi Shankar also says,

We worship the past. We have only praise for our past, our glorious past... Or else we glorify something that is far away, distant, out of reach. The mind is satisfied when ideals and objectives are far away. Very interesting, isn't it? As man's vision projects itself onto the past or the future, he is unable to recognize the Divine here and now, in the present moment, within his own heart.

Different ways of thinking cross your mind, come and go. You may hold on to one of these thoughts and prevent it from escaping. When a thought is stuck in your mind, like an old gramophone needle is stuck in the record's groove, we call it anxiety; and all anxieties cause sorrow. All sorrows arise when we are stuck in an event, a thought, or a desire from the past.

Why are you sad? Why are you distressed? It is because of your desire; you are hanging on to the past. Sadness is the memory of the past. The memory of a past desire creates grief now.

The memory of the Lord, of the Divine alone can remove obstacles from your path.

All your projects, all your past memories are nothing but a dream, because neither of the two exists at this moment as reality. You are in a constant state of dreaming; this is why you are unhappy – the waking dream and the sleeping reality. An enlightened person lives entirely in the present moment, and yet, they appreciate beauty in its entirety.

Don't ever regret the past. Time used is never wasted. All the past, all we have gone through until now, has built our foundations and erected our walls. Now we are here to put the roof, to finish it up. So you will always have a shelter against storms.

You have to look and cut the past from your mind.

Everything which makes you cry belongs to the past and has no substance. I am the consciousness.

When you hang on to what you like or don't like, you bind yourself to the past.

Chewing the cud of the past is enough to make you miserable. To remember good things makes you as miserable as remembering the bad.

If you hold stones in your hands, they won't be free to take diamonds and gold.

The mind cannot remain in the present; it is frustrated, depressed, rebellious. This very mind exists through illusion. It wants something impossible, constantly. The mind is used to living with desire, frustration.

Our mind vacillates all the time; either it is angry about the past, or anxious about the future. Have you noticed? It is like a pendulum.

♦

7. ACCEPTATION

You must learn to create a harmonious environment around you. You can believe that your environment creates you, but in fact, you create your environment. See that what is is. This acceptation of what is has two aspects.

The first one is the acceptance of the present moment as inevitable. What has happened has happened. If you want things to be different, they can only be different in the next moment. It is only when you accept calmly what is that you can effectively change something.

The second aspect is to accept people as they are. Whatever their attitude is, see that it is the best they can offer in the present moment. Analyse the situation. Look for possible explanations to their actions. Simultaneously, take on your responsibilities. This way, the acceptance becomes dynamic and your environment harmonious.

Gurudev Sri Sri Ravi Shankar also says,

You fight so many battles you become heavy. When you become heavy, you collapse. Ego is the weight. Your weight hurts others. One without weight is wise. Then non-violence happens. A bird flying high is just floating. You must float in life in full acceptation.

There are no problems, there are only solutions; and if there are no solutions, then there are no problems. All you have to do is to accept.

There is a big expectation in each relationship that the other will change. We never think we should change ourselves instead of others, "You have changed for the best!", "You aren't the same anymore!", "I don't know what happened to you!"

What opens us up to this marvellous being that is in us is that we accept others as they are, because then we are able to accept ourselves as we are.

Many people think tolerance is a virtue. Tolerance is a negative term. If you like something, you don't have to tolerate it; tolerance indicates a deep antipathy that can any moment change into hatred. It implies an idea of separativeness, narrowness of mind, limitation of consciousness. To tolerate is a temporary state. Tolerance is a potential volcano. If you tolerate, it means you restrain yourself.

Acceptation also is negative. You accept what is not 'loveable'.

Tolerance and acceptation are the fruit of judgment and separation. We think these terms are positive, I tell you they are not!

Question: *"But aren't we supposed to accept people as they are?"*

Answer: *"If you don't love them, then you have to accept them.*

Don't accept people as they are; just love them as they are."

♦

8. THE CONFIRMATION OF YOUR OWN DEATH

The eighth law of spiritual life is the confirmation of your own death, that you are going to die one day. Because deep in us, there is something that does not die, it is difficult for us to accept totally our death. The confirmation of your death can bring you back to the present moment. It can help you escape all the little temptations that take you away from the present. Once you know you are going to die, the future does not haunt you any longer.

Gurudev Sri Sri Ravi Shankar also says,

Death puts you in contact with reality. Death creates a vacuum, an empty space, and this empty space is a fertile soil for the spirit to manifest. All talents, inventions and creativity appear from this empty space. Creation has a tendency to go back to emptiness. All worshipping places in the world are linked to burial or cremation grounds, because the consciousness of death alone can bring detachment to you and make you grow in the knowledge.

Divinity lies in the emptiness as much as in celebration. There is empty space in you and there is celebration in you.

The knowledge of death will improve the quality of your life.

The knowledge of life brings confidence and the knowledge of death makes you fearless and centred.

Celebrate silence and celebrate noise.

Celebrate life and celebrate death.

Life is very beautiful. It is structured. And to make it more beautiful, death has also been planned.

Death is very complementary to existence. It is in no way opposed to life. It complements life; it makes life new and fresh.

The universe is mysterious, every bud does not open and every wave doesn't rise. You can only wonder about it; don't try to understand it.

The main thing is to experience this 'Something' which does not change, this 'Something' which does not die, and this 'Something' which does not decay in you.

Nobody ever feels that somebody is going to die; do you know why? Because it is Reality!

You pity somebody who died because you feel you are not going to die. And it is true. Something deep in you never dies. This is why you never feel you are old, or are going to die.

You are not going to die. Although you can think, "I am going to die, I am getting old." It is superficial. Deep inside you, you know you're not going to die; you are beyond death.

♦

9. THE IMPERMANENCE OF LIFE

The ninth law is the impermanence of everything that exists, the impermanence of situations, circumstances, emotions, and people around you. Knowing that all that is impermanent elevates the level of the mind. You can then act with more energy, enthusiasm and vigour. We think that recognizing the impermanence of things lowers our enthusiasm and leads to apathy. On the opposite, the correct understanding of impermanence elevates the spirit. When the spirit is awakened, you feel elevated. Enthusiasm and dynamism are there.

Gurudev Sri Sri Ravi Shankar also says,

Everything changes around you. Your body, your mind, your priorities, your friends, your enemies, all are similarly constantly changing. But the deep thirst in us is for something which doesn't change, which remains always the same.

To become conscious of this change, we need a non-changing entity, a reference point. It is your being!

Opinions change, work changes, relationships change, friends change; they last for a moment, a transient moment. Moods come and go, thoughts come and go... Whether we want it or not, things don't stop changing. Everything that is, is subject to change. And you identify yourself with those changing things!

Stick to this thing in you which does not change. Be with it. It is you. Your body has changed, you haven't changed. This central core in you which has not changed is the same principle which underlies the entire existence, which is responsible for this flower's regular pattern, for the colour of its petals, for the shape of its leaves.

When we understand this, a great unification happens in our consciousness; our perception changes. Everything we look at is seen with great keenness of vision. Everything we hear is heard with great keenness of hearing. We dissolve in everything we see and hear. There is an evident difference in the quality of the perception that binds us to everything we perceive. This is why at all times saints have brought up the union with the Ultimate, with the Source, with the Rhythm.

There are two ways of being successful: to make a success of one's life, and be successful in the world. You can be successful in the world without necessarily having a successful life. To lead a successful life is to be attentive to the Source, to live in joy and unconditional love.

♦

10. TO HAVE FAITH

Have faith in the supreme and infinite Intelligence that has formed this whole Creation from the cosmic disposition and interactions between genes, atoms and molecules. Through the simple arrangement of electrons, one thing becomes a flower, another one a stone, one is gold, the other is charcoal. See that there exists a basic substratum, an intelligence underlying it all, a unity in this whole Creation. And see that it is alive. We don't see the Universe as a living thing; we only see matter everywhere. The objects alone are evident to our eyes. We know there exists a magnetic field in the Creation, but we only see it as a dead field. Pure consciousness, which is the foundation of the spirit, and which you are part of, is a field of this nature, and it is alive. Understanding, accepting, and having faith in the Intelligence that creates and maintains all things, this is the tenth law of spiritual life.

Gurudev Sri Sri Ravi Shankar also says,

There are three types of faith:

– Faith in yourself... Without faith in yourself, you think, "I can't do this; this is not for me. I will never find freedom in this world."

– Faith in the world... You must have faith in the world, or you won't move an inch. You deposit your money in the bank having faith it will be given back to you. If you doubt everything, nothing will ever work for you.

– Faith in the Divine... Have faith in the Divine and you will grow.

All these faiths are connected. You must have all three to be strong. If you start doubting one, you will start doubting everything.

Atheists seem to have faith in themselves, and in the world, but not in God. However, they don't really have a complete faith in themselves. And their faith in the world cannot be constant because the world is ever changing. Lacking faith in God, in the world or in yourself brings fear. Faith makes you full; faithful.

Having faith in the world without having faith in God doesn't bring you complete peace. If you have faith and love, you automatically have peace and freedom. People who are very disturbed should simply have faith in God so that He will help them overcome their problems.

If you don't have faith, there is no use asking questions, because then, how could you have faith in the answer? But if you have complete faith, then there are no questions!

If you have faith in God or in yourself, or in your family or friends, then, questions cannot come up. When you know somebody is taking care of you, what is the need for questions? If you have taken the Karnataka Express for Bangalore, it's no use asking at every station, "Where is the train going?" When somebody takes care of your desires, why go see an astrologer?

Faith is your wealth.

Faith gives you instant strength. Faith makes you centred, brings you stability, calmness, and love. Faith is your blessing. But this is a paradox here: if you are lacking faith, you must pray to get faith, yet, to pray, you need faith;

In the realm of science, first you acquire the knowledge, then comes the faith. In the realm of spirituality, faith comes first and knowledge follows.

For example, the idea that pesticides and fertilizers are good for plants came from science. People believed in it and they have been used in the whole world. Then we came to realise they were harmful and faith was transferred to organic farming. Same for antibiotics.

Knowledge had given birth to faith, and when knowledge changed, faith itself was transformed. Knowledge and faith in science arise from the 'event'.

In spirituality, faith comes first, and knowledge comes later... If you do your meditations with awareness, the knowledge of consciousness will follow. Even an illiterate, through faith, attains a deep knowledge.

People put their faith in the world, but the whole world is only a soap bubble. People have faith in themselves, but don't know who they are. People think they have faith in the Divine, but don't really know who is God.

Question: *What is the difference between faith and confidence?*

Answer: *Faith is the first step, confidence is the outcome. Faith in your Self brings freedom. Faith in the world brings peace of mind. Faith in God induces love in you.*

Question: *Can you comment faith and credibility?*

Answer: *Faith is a matter of the heart, credibility a matter of intellect... A good combination of the two makes your life peaceful and easy.*

Faith is necessary when you have reached the limit of your knowledge. Your eagerness to know the unknown is faith.

People speak a lot about God, but if you go into it in detail, you will discover that their faith is shaky. They have no faith in the fact that there exists an infinite organizing energy, a Power residing in the total control of everything; this faith is absent.

Faith is the nature of an undivided mind, of an undivided consciousness. You have faith in God, so, you don't try to know God; you have faith in the Self, so you don't try to know the Self. Don't try to make an object of knowing of what you have faith in. A child has faith in his mother; it doesn't try to know its mother, it simply has faith in her. When the faith is there, what is the use to know? If you try to make an object of knowing of love, it will vanish. God, love, Self and sleep are all beyond knowledge.

If you try to analyse, doubts come up and faith disappears. So don't undertake to know or analyse whatever you want to have faith in. Analysis creates a distance; synthesis brings together. Faith is synthesis, knowledge is analysis.

Consciousness cannot exist without faith. It is like a candle flame. Faith is a relaxed and stable quality of consciousness. Faith is the nature of consciousness.

Have faith in silence.

11. THE UNITY OF CREATION

When the human mind is stressed and tense, it judges, makes choices, likes this, doesn't like that, puts up barriers. In doing so, it cuts itself off from existence. Cutting oneself from existence, from the flow of life, is called 'separation', but this separation is only illusion; it is impossible to separate oneself from existence. If you take out a portion of a circle, there is no more a circle. See that you are part of existence, a fragment of the Supreme Intelligence expression, of the unifying force underlying all creation, all that is.

Gurudev Sri Sri Ravi Shankar also says,

It is the intellect that divides and synthesizes. Some creatures in the world only synthesize and some only divide. Ants only synthesize; they gather things and build anthills. But monkeys cannot synthesize; they only divide. You give them a garland, they tear it to pieces and throw it around. A monkey can only divide and analyse. A beaver synthesizes, he gathers wood and builds a dam. Some birds, like the weavers, also synthesize.

Human beings have both capacities: they analyze and synthesize. You analyze the relative world and synthesize to find the One. The intellect divides to find the truth, and truth, once found, synthesizes everything.

One cell only becomes the whole body. Here, it becomes nail, there nose or tongue, but everything is the manifestation of one cell only. In the same way, the whole universe is made of one cell only.

To remember and feel that everything stems from one thing only cures the body and the mind, and balances the system.

Every atom is like a universe. The smallest molecule is complete. The Rishis found this out ten thousand years ago and modern scientists confirm it today. They have discovered that human DNA *contains the* DNA *of all animals, insects, and of about fifty thousand different living beings' species... From human* DNA*, you can reproduce an elephant or a fly. But from the elephant* DNA*, one cannot give birth to a human being. The human body is special.*

Question: Is there a similarity between you and me and animals?

Answer: The appearance is different, but the existence is the same.

Recognize the unity. If you recognize unity in yourself, in your body, in your heart, you will recognize unity anywhere and everywhere. It is as simple as that.

In the whole creation, there is a tendency to become one, to go back to the One, because two is painful. Creation aims at going from the two to the One. Everything tends to dissolve into something, and this something is called love.

A sign of intelligence is to see the One in the many, and to find the many in the One.

You can only see the waterfall; you cannot see how the ocean becomes the cloud. How the ocean becomes a cloud is a secret but how the cloud becomes the ocean is obvious.

Have you ever sat on a rock thinking you were part of this earth? That this body is coming from the stuff this earth is made of? What is this body? Proteins, amino acids, carbohydrates, minerals, salt. Everything belongs to this earth. And one day, this body will go back to this earth...

Be aware that this body is part of this earth. Ninety percent of your body is made up of water. This water has the same percentage of salinity, the same composition as the ocean. You are a part of the ocean living out of the ocean. And the breath coming in and out of your body is part of the air surrounding the earth. There is no new air; it is ancient air that is being recycled.

You are part of the existence. Your body is just a part of the expression of the Big Cosmic Mind. When this realization takes place, then the small 'I' with which you think 'I, I, I, me, me, me' becomes a 'big I', or a 'no-I'.

When you know everybody is part of you, your cravings disappear, all your aversions disappear. Your cravings come up because you think you don't have. Your aversions appear because you don't want what you think you have. Do you see the irony? When you know that everything belongs to you already, your cravings subside. When you know that everything you hate belongs to you, aversion disappears, and a total synthesis happens. Unity happens.

Even the word 'unity' is not the right word. It also indicates duality. If we can say 'one', it is because 'two' exists. This is why I say that language is inadequate to express any truth about existence. It is better to keep silent.

♦

12. YOUR NATURE IS PEACE AND LOVE

When you understand the unity in Creation, you don't have any more effort to make in order to love others. Love is your nature. Love is what is. Nothing else than love exists. See that love is not an action you accomplish, nor a moral obligation to fulfil. See that you exist in love, and that every single thing exists in love. And know that peace is also your nature. At any time, wherever it is, you can simply sit and let go, knowing that in you, there is a clear, pure, vast and deep space. This inner space is what you are, and when you feel it, you are in contact with your spiritual dimension.

"I come from peace, I am in peace, I will return to peace. Peace is my origin and my goal. I am peace, I am space, I am love." This inner statement, or experience, makes you a researcher. Knowing that your nature is peace and love is the twelfth law.

Gurudev Sri Sri Ravi Shankar also says,

In deep meditation, we observe that everybody is part of us. The flow of love happens then spontaneously. It is not over imposed. It is not an artificial, cultivated love.

Love is no realization, it is a recognition. Peace is not to reach, but simply to conceive.

Once you have known such a peaceful state of mind, simply remembering it will make you experience it again.

Observe: you would like to be friends with a handful of people, you are friendly with them and then you become enemies.

It is like trying to hold a flower roughly. If you hold it too tight, all the petals are going to fall. A person who is indifferent to you will never be your enemy; you will never get into a conflict with a person whom you don't love. All your conflicts happen with a person whom, at a given time, you became friends with. Isn't it surprising?

Learn to become friends with as many people as possible. Be friendly with everybody, then you will see that your being will become such that everybody will like to be with you.

Joy is the love of what is.

Sadness is the love of what is not.

Love is incomplete, and will have to remain incomplete. If it is complete, it comes to an end. Everything that is complete, full, total, means you have set limits, you have found restrictions. For love to be infinite, it has to be incomplete. All that is incomplete is infinite.

God is the cheapest raw material you can find. You may not have fresh air somewhere, but God is there. You may not have sunlight, but God is there. You go to the moon, God is there; you go beyond the atmosphere, God is there. God is unique, so life is unique. Love is in everything. And when you go deeply in this state of love, there is no difference between you and what is.

You want peace, but your need for peace has made you nervous. In wanting to see everybody peaceful around you, you have created restlessness. Peace comes from inside, not from outside. If you are peaceful yourself, your environment becomes peaceful, and people around you become peaceful too. You are the centre of the universe.

Peace is your real nature.
Peace is your innate nature.
This can never leave you.
Conflict is the nature of the world,
Comfort is the nature of the Self.
In the midst of conflict, look for conflict.

When you are tired of comfort, play the games of the world. When you are tired with the games of the world, go back to the comfort of the Self. If you are close to the Master, you will do both simultaneously. Trying to end a conflict extends it. Face the conflict by finding the comfort of the Self.

The moment you accept to be with the conflict, it vanishes.

♦

13. EQUILIBRIUM

The thirteenth law of spiritual life consists in finding a balance between rest and activity, between enjoying the world and going back to the Self, between silence and speech. If you keep silent all your life without ever uttering a single word, it doesn't necessarily mean you have a spiritual life. Speech has been given to you. Talents and abilities have been given to you. Make good use of what has been given to you and balance it with meditation, self observation with awareness.

Gurudev Sri Sri Ravi Shankar also says,

Give priority to yourself for some time; be with yourself for a little while, a few days every year; this will strengthen the energy, the spirit which you are.

You see, there are moments when – for no apparent reason – you don't feel well. Suddenly, you feel completely out of your centre. Sometimes you go and eat out somewhere, and you don't feel well. Sometimes it is a contact with somebody that makes you feel ill at ease. So, what to do?

For a little while, don't seek contact with others. Stay a little bit away from people, don't go and eat at people's places. Five days or a week can be enough.

Just be with yourself; you'll see, it will change. If you are very depressed, it is very efficient: give up all contacts and remain centred on yourself. You can offer presents, but don't accept anything during this period. You will see that all this discomfort and depression will disappear.

The mind becomes centred, focused, sharp. It becomes light and free; calmness sets in and the senses increase in power and strength. You become able to judge by yourself, to feel your soul, your Being.

Stay with yourself. All this will allow you to benefit from the situation. Otherwise, we are constantly exchanging energy with others.

At every moment, we are losing our energy and receiving other people's energy. So, when you feel a lot of confusion, of chaos, when your mind is not clear, put everything aside and just observe. This period of silence does not mean that you cannot speak at all; it is rather like a retreat. This is what religious communities do: they isolate themselves. You don't have to choose a cave for yourself, but stop receiving indistinctly what others send you. If you are a doctor, a nurse, if you are in charge of patients, don't stop working of course. But once you are back at home, take a shower and be with yourself. Postpone all other occupations and social contacts while you are recharging your batteries.

When you observe, what is negative diminishes, disappears; what is evolutionary is enriched, amplified. If you observe love, love grows; if you observe fear, fear falls. If you observe joy, joy grows; if you observe jealousy, jealousy disappears.

Question: "Can anybody in this life succeed in transforming all their possibilities, all their suffering into happiness?"

Answer: Yes, it is possible, very possible.

Question: In a week?

Answer: Even in an instant, it is possible!

Anybody can understand all this intellectually, but it is not enough. You need a few simple techniques to calm the mind down, to come to your centre again.

Although people have all the comfort, they fall into depression and, to escape depression, they fall into drugs, or into activities which are not in accordance with life, or do not go in the direction of evolution.

It is extremely important to spread this knowledge of the breath, of the Being, of the Self. It doesn't belong to one nation only, to one race or community alone. It belongs to the whole world. The whole world needs this knowledge. The telephone and electricity were invented in the West, yet, the rest of the world can use it too Thanks to this beautiful knowledge, our life can gradually be lifted up to a state of unconditional joy.

◆

14. SELF-ENQUIRY

Self-enquiry is the next principle of spiritual life. Start with awareness of the feeling of your own body – your own skin, the feeling of your skin under your garments, and under the skin, your muscles and nerves, and then your bones. Do not be insensitive to life, like an animal that only eats drinks and sleeps. Observe every sensation. Have the keenest awareness. In knowing your own body, you will come to know spirit –which is different from the body.

Gurudev Sri Sri Ravi Shankar also says,

Life permeates every cell of your body – your skin, your hair, your whole body. You can be unaware of yourself, sitting in front of your television, completely absorbed by some event or by your thoughts. But whether you are aware of it or not, life is present in each cell of your body.

I won't say you are always connected to the earth; I would say you are part of this earth. Have you ever thought, when you sit down to eat and take a piece of bread in your hand, "This is my body; this bread I am going to eat is going to become the cells of my body. This bread is my future body; it is just a matter of time"? You have a cup of milk in front of you. Have you ever thought, "This also is a part of my body; this milk is going to become my blood."? When Jesus instituted mass, he said, "This is my flesh, this is my blood." He meant, 'This whole creation is my body.'

Feel you are one with each thing. You are part of the food you eat already. Even before absorbing it, you are part of it. It is already your flesh. Jesus said to his disciples, "Don't lament, do not believe I am only in this body! This bread is my body, and all the food in the world is my body, because this food becomes my body!"

Why do you attach so much importance to the body? When this body leaves, another body will take its place, because there will always be enough to feed it. Food creates the body.

If you absorb food with consciousness, I am you! This consciousness that I am and which you find so extraordinary is in you too! There is no lack in you of what I have.

This body is not my flesh, this bread is my flesh. The flesh is the bread. Recognize the difference between the physical body and the flesh, and the whole world will become your body. This is cosmic Consciousness.

They are all mine, like my own finger is mine. Everybody is part of me.

♦

15. DISPASSION AND MATURITY

Keen awareness comes with maturity, or you could say, with dispassion. Maturity and dispassion come together. You cannot be mature and not also be dispassionate. Dispassion is often wrongly understood to be a flat, dull state of mind or a negative mood. It has the connotation of being aloof and disinterested. This is not true. In dispassion, you are aware; you are intimate with yourself. In maturity there is no feverishness. In maturity there is royalty, there is freedom, there is understanding, there is mystery. This is the fifteenth principle of spiritual life, gaining dispassion and living maturely.

Gurudev Sri Sri Ravi Shankar also says,

Real intimacy is dispassion. Observe your mind. What's going on in it? Likes and dislikes, cravings and aversions, "I want this; no, I don't want that." Constant debates, cynicism, criticism, apathy, discouragement. Are you aware of all these fluctuations happening in your mind? For just a moment, drop everything! Sit down quietly. This is dispassion: to be centered.

Have you noticed that after having laughed a lot, after a lot of bustling about, your mind can no longer bear this restlessness? It becomes too much. You want to get rid of all the excitement and be quiet for a while. What big joy can you hold on to forever? Wisdom starts the day you recognize joy hurts. Dispassion starts the day you discover joy is disturbing.

We have lost this sensitivity. This is why we are hankering so much after joy, after something always greater. "There is probably something better for me, something which would bring me more happiness." This is feverishness. So we keep jumping from one feverishness to another. It is a constant struggle.

Sorrow induces feverishness, joy brings about feverishness. Dispassion is the subtle balance beyond both joy and sadness. In this state, any great joy can happen to you, it will not shake you. Even if you are offered heaven you won't move an inch! This is enlightenment. The secret lies in dispassion.

You can learn how to meditate, you can learn other techniques, but dispassion cannot be learned. It can only blossom in your life, with time, or thanks to the presence of your master. There are no other ways to make it blossom. You cannot attain it through books. Experience alone will teach it to you.

The highest wisdom you can attain on this planet is dispassion. Everything can be shattered, but not dispassion. Everything can be bought, but not dispassion. One who is dispassionate alone is rich.

Dispassion always reveals truth. If you want to know the truth about something, be totally dispassionate, centred, perfectly centred. This is the strength. Real intimacy can only happen in dispassion.

Being dispassionate, you are intimate with yourself. You can then be intimate with everyone. If you are totally in harmony with yourself, you can love and be intimate with all without any difficulty. Then criticism, cynicism and indifference disappear. Indifference is distinct from dispassion. Passion is the cause of your indifference.

Everything that exists belongs to the Divine, so let go of your burden. "I have been insulted, I have been mistreated..." You see intentions behind every action. Just drop all that. Let it be. Follow the flow of the moment and life will become more peaceful by itself.

Dispassion doesn't separate you, in fact, it connects you. It connects you to the present moment so totally that you can be 100% in whatever you do.

The main obstacle slowing down many seekers on the path is their desire to let go. Don't say you want to surrender, know you have already done it.

The desire to surrender becomes an obstacle on the path. It is as if a child were saying to his mother: "I want to love you!" No child will ever say this to his mother; it is evident it loves her already.

Surrender is not an act; it is a state of being. Whether you recognize it or not, it is real. The wise wake up and see; the others take a little longer. Know that you have no choice. Deep in yourself, you have surrendered already.

♦

16. APPRECIATION OF BEAUTY

The sixteenth principle of spiritual life is to acknowledge the beauty in creation, the beauty in every person, the beauty within you, and to know this beauty is the nature of spirit. The mind runs after beauty, appreciates beauty, but there is a difference between appreciating beauty and wanting to possess it. In wanting to possess beauty, we lose our dispassion. Know it is spirit that is beautiful. Wherever you perceive beauty, spirit is there. If someone is beautiful, it is because of the spirit in them. A dead body is never beautiful. Attributing beauty to spirit and differentiating that from matter takes you a long way on the spiritual path.

Gurudev Sri Sri Ravi Shankar also says

Beauty is an inner feeling, an inner awakening. When negativity and stiffness dissolve in you, then, deep inside you, you recognize beauty in the Creation. Waves of beauty, waves of contentment dawn from your entire being.

One of the most precious faculties the human body has is to be able to appreciate beauty. The basis of Creation is beauty.

Truth is a quest of the intellect, but beauty is felt by the heart. The intellect analyses, is curious to know how a flower is made, how it grows, in what season it blooms. The heart doesn't bother with these knowledge details, it simply feels: "Wow! This is so marvellous!" the appreciation of beauty dawns in the heart and carries all your being along.

Beauty is not a judgment. It's not like a beauty contest where judges sit and decide who will be Mr. Universe or Miss America. Judging who is beautiful is ugly. Miss America, Mr. Universe, this is degrading. It is like talking about love for sale. Beauty cannot be sold. Beauty is not to be exhibited. Beauty is a phenomenon. Something that happens, like a tornado. An exclamation, "Oh!" and the mind goes blind, automatically. It is not a mass phenomenon, it is intimate, personal. If it wasn't, it would not be divine. The Divine is always personal.

We say, "Beauty is in the eye of the beholder." When you are full of joy, when you are blossoming in love, only then can you appreciate beauty. A certain level of consciousness is required. When you are stressed and tense, even the most beautiful thing will appear ugly, or you will try to find some fault in it. Somebody who is hungry or sick cannot appreciate beauty. All they want is to be normal. But the simple fact of being normal cannot satisfy them, because it isn't the ultimate. Beauty is the ultimate. It is the final touch.

When you feel wonderful, even stones and thorns will reveal to you the beauty that they are.

Beauty and love go together. One can't help loving what is beautiful. When you love something, you find beauty in it. Do you know the story of Lilah and Majnu? They were in love, like Romeo and Juliet. When Majnu was asked, "If God came to you now, how would you like to see Him appear?" he said, "The best would be that he came to me under Lilah's appearance; only then would I like to speak to Him."

You have never loved something without trying to possess it. It starts from childhood on. When the second baby arrives, the first baby wants its entire mother's attention. "Why did you bring this baby home? Send it back!" Many children say that: "You belong to me, and me alone!" We have this deep impression, this fear to lose our place in the heart of somebody we love.

The love that is afraid to lose doesn't blossom. It pulls you towards other horrible sensations and feelings. Jealousy comes. There is somebody you love very much, a friend, a boyfriend or girlfriend, but their attention is transferred on somebody else. See what happens to your stomach. It is churning! You try all kinds of things to deny what's happening inside you. A lot of ugliness comes up, because you are afraid to lose something. You never love something great, considerable, because you haven't yet become considerable yourself. And as long as you remain very small, I tell you, there is no joy, no happiness, no peace. Joy is expansion, greatness in your heart.

This can only happen in a situation where you are very much in love, but cannot possess what you love.

People live as if they were dead, 90% dead. They sleep, go to work, eat, chatter, and sleep again. The whole day is spent in unconsciousness; they are not present where they are. They are like a frog in a well, thinking the well is the universe, that there is nothing beyond it. Limited consciousness is death. It is a lack of fire, a lack of progress.

Along with the feeling of being unlucky comes jealousy. Somebody else is lucky, but I am unlucky. Along with the feeling of being unlucky, comes greed, anger, hatred; a chain of negativity. I am not telling you that you should never feel jealousy or other negative emotions, no. I observe the mechanism of beauty, and let you see how these feelings are connected to beauty. I am showing you the phenomenon that beauty is. In beauty, there is innocence; in beauty, there is total vitality; in beauty, there is a sense of good fortune.

The history of a tree's life appears in a dead wood log. The beauty of the tree is maintained even in its transformation. The awards in cinema festivals go to the actors who express intense emotions like anger and frustration. When children cry, there is beauty in it too. This beauty is all pervading. All you have to do is wake up and see – this is reality.

In enlightenment, beauty manifests in its glory as wisdom, as knowledge. It is knowledge that gives beauty to an ignorant person. How does it happen? Through consciousness, through the energy in you. When the energy in you is awakened, when you are able to laugh and let go of the past, you start becoming so radiant! The practices we do here enliven this knowledge in you and awaken this beauty in you.

For a poor man, beauty resides in wealth. For a hungry person, beauty is in food; for a lonely person, beauty is in company. And for those who are enlightened, beauty is in enlightenment. They say, "Oh! What have I done all my life? Where was I? I was caught up in so many little things! But now my life is beautiful!" And the gratitude that manifests is the most beautiful thing! Have you seen the face of someone who is crying tears of gratitude? There is no such beauty on the planet!

Shyness adds to your beauty. It is your ornament.

Divinity is nothing else than an expression of beauty.

♦

17. WORSHIPFULNESS AND HONOUR

The appreciation of beauty brings worshipfulness. You worship beauty, you adore it. Adoring and worshiping everything in creation as a reflection of the Creator is the next principle of spiritual life. And honour everything. Honouring is more than an emotional response. It is an attitude. It indicates a balanced understanding of life. When respect and love are both present, that brings honour. When there is honour, the mind is one hundred percent present and a sense of sacredness comes. Love and respect bring honour, and honour brings sacredness. You cannot feel for something and not feel its sacredness. Sacredness brings alertness in the consciousness. Awareness comes.

Gurudev Sri Sri Ravi Shankar also says,

The spirit that rules your life is sacred; honour this life force. When you honour the life force, naturally, all the other virtues become your expression, effortlessly. You become generous, you have a sense of belongingness, and you feel connected to the whole world, and to everything.

Question: What to do if people don't respect you?

Answer: Thank them. They have given you freedom! When people respect you, they have taken away your freedom. They expect you to smile at them, to acknowledge them, and that you behave a certain way with them.

If they don't respect you, you don't have to answer their questions and you can drop all formalities.

When you gain respect, it is often to the detriment of your freedom. Wisdom is to place freedom first and not to bother about respect.

And when real love is there, respect follows you, simply.

Respect everybody as you respect me, but don't expect from others what you expect from me. Yet, you do the opposite: you don't respect others as you respect me, but you expect them to give you joy and behave ideally. When they don't meet your expectations, you are frustrated. You blame them, or curse them. In doing so, you lose your spiritual energy. Blessing them, on the opposite, restores the spiritual energy.

The world is full of diversities; arguments are inevitable. With clear-sightedness, or patience, work your way through with intelligence.

Honour everything in the Creation, including your own body. Have you ever considered your body with great honour? Have we ever looked at our own breath? "Oh, how beautiful it is; this breath comes in and out." It maintains life.

Give attention to every part of your body with great honor. All the feverishness will be transformed into love.

Look at the tree with honour. Feel grateful for the trees that are here. They purify the poison we are breathing out. Everything in the universe, the sun, the air, the moon, water, they all belong to you. Have you ever thought: "All these stars are mine? I have so many stars. These trees are mine; people are mine; everything in the universe belongs to me."

We have to develop a feeling of worshipping. Because we have stopped worshipping and respecting people, we have led our societies towards more violence. If all the people who walk around with weapons had more respect in themselves, more veneration, more care for the people around them, they would be very different.

It doesn't matter what people choose to worship. Whether it be trees, a cross, a person or such and such a symbol, it doesn't matter. It is this feeling of worshipping which is essential. Even if it is a pop star, it doesn't matter at all. This emotion must manifest authentically, from inside. It is important. Don't prevent people from idealizing, respecting and worshipping others.

In the East, according to the tradition, children worship their mother as a God, every day. Then the father is being worshipped, then the guru, then any guest in the house.

Children may quarrel with their parents during the day, but every morning, they have to reconcile, because they have to bow in front of them before starting a new day.

They may quarrel again, but at least, they start fresh on a new page every day.

Life has many different colours. We must accept life with all its colours and flavours. Today, we must educate people to worship more, to revere more, to appreciate better. Don't be paranoid about veneration; rather be paranoid about violence, arrogance, insults, foul language, anger, frustration, and not about veneration, gratitude, love and appreciation.

Love becomes devotion through dedication.
The blossoming of devotion is fulfillment in life.
When love blossoms, it becomes devotion.

♦

18. LIFE IS IMPERISHABLE

The final principle of spiritual life is knowing that life is imperishable. This is totally contradictory to the principle of knowing that life is impermanent, that everything is perishable. Now we say that life is imperishable; nothing can happen to it. Truth is always contradictory.

Gurudev Sri Sri Ravi Shankar also says,

Nothing belongs to you; neither your body, nor your thoughts, nor your emotions, nor your feelings. None of these are yours. They come up from themselves, stay for a while and go away from themselves. Remember that your nature, which is joy, peace and fulfillment remains the same forever.

You are not restricted to your present body, to the name you are wearing, to this present form, to your relationships with your environment. You may not know your past, the antiquity of your existence, but you know you have come a long way, and this is a start...

You have gone through many experiences, and nevertheless, you came out of them identical to yourself, shining, innocent, pure, unstained. In this respect you are the ancient love. Does this mean anything to you? Whether it does or not, what's the difference? If it means something, it's good, if it doesn't, it's also good. It is wonderful.

Truth cannot be understood through proof. Truth is beyond proof and refutation.

Truth is not linear, it is multidimensional. Truth is spherical. In a sphere, every point is connected to the others. In a line, every point is only connected to two others, the one before and the one after. In a sphere, a point is connected from all sides, 360° around.

Truth is existence. It is what exists; it is being in agreement with oneself inside. What we believe is truth comes from the event.

What exists is truth; what doesn't change is truth.

What changes is illusion.

6

MEDITATING IS BEING

THE ATTACKS OF THE *MEETING ROOM* CONTINUE, albeit rather hopeless at this hour. Gurudev sends everyone back to the meditation hall downstairs where he will make his way later, once the recording of the interview is over.

The agreed interviews with the international press are becoming more common. The name of Gurudev Sri Sri Ravi Shankar in the credits of big secular masses, throughout all continents, can't escape the media, intrigued by this unusual speaker. In the debating chamber of the United Nations, no problem, but at closing the World Economic Summit Conference in Davos, there is enough to surprise people – although several religious or spiritual leaders have taken up the invitation. The Master doesn't ignore modern means in order to spread some useful wisdom in the world. Any constructive exchange is welcome. He thus replies to the journalists' questions, without any preconception, whether they are open-minded to spirituality or not. Relevance does not always come from the expert, the big signature, or the influential media.

Any sort of questions can be put to Gurudev Sri Sri Ravi Shankar; he will not be offended by any. But when he is asked, "Do you still get snakes on the roads in India?" how could he not consider his time wasted? Or, when asked without too much thought, "Why is breathing important?" –"*Is that a question*?" he replied, so astounded as to still be telling it, "*Breathing is not important, it is just inevitable! Without breath, you simply die! What is the point of breathing? Are you aware of what you are saying? What is the point of loving? You can't use breath; it's that which uses you. It's the same for love. You always think about profit, about immediate pleasure. All the time you are calculating: "What am I going to get?"*"

The review is not glorious: the level of competence is often a disaster, the faking of the remarks soul-less, the result overwhelming and the impunity entire.

The Master judges neither the delivery nor the manner. He says simply, *"It's good to speak more and more about spirituality. The world needs it... People often take spirituality too seriously, and conversely turn games into war. So, the whole charm of existence is lost. Spirituality is not boring. It's the flavour of life. Don't make a serious topic of discussion out of it or it will become just another compartment. Spirituality should be like everyday chat: relaxed and personal. But soon that will change..."*

You won't hear Gurudev Sri Sri Ravi Shankar denouncing the perversion of today's means of communication: the continuous flow of murder on the entertainment and news screens, the hegemony of depressing news, the virtual exclusivity of the dark side...

He notes the distortion of reality, disastrous for people's spirits right from the first perfusion of the morning news. He says, "*That's not a reflection of real life.*" And without other remarks, he takes up his responsibilities by creating the Gurudev Sri Sri Ravi Shankar Centre of Media Studies. This school of journalism created by him in 2000 in Bangalore, a dynamic city in Southern India, was established to train observers clear initially with themselves, people who don't try to mould the world from their own image, to reinforce their own personal views through their reports. A certain number of professional people, journalists and directors of big worldwide media organisations, determined to break away from the bad press their job has, are disregarding their membership of competing media organisations and are forming the school council of administration. The new generation of news reporters, already out there, is making its difference.

Goofy saintliness is not the taste of the Angel Sri Sri, who on the contrary appreciates lively speakers, why not incisive ones – the exercise is but more perilous for the interviewer. And since there is nothing to assail, no-one to beat, the investigation at the end of the foil becomes the natural game of the interview without complacency which he enjoys: "What do you think of the New Age?

– *The age is always new.*

– New Age gave birth to the industry of salvation. Are you a trader of salvation?

– *The market signifies the needs of the people, and the needs of the people are happiness, peace and beauty. The industry of salvation? Business and spirituality evolve in opposite directions. In business you give less and take more. In spirituality you give more and take less.*

– What does it mean to have a guru?

– *In the West, having a guru is badly thought of. They think that you are giving up on your freedom. But in the East, we are convinced that a guru offers freedom. People are quite proud of the fact, they say, "I am a disciple of such and such."... A guru demands nothing of his disciples, but on the contrary helps them to expand their vision, gives them another dimension. In fact, not only do you retain your free will, but you gain in freedom, you free yourself from your cultural, emotional and religious atavisms, you lose your inhibitions. In India you know that by giving your ego up to a guru, you are in touch with God. That's why the guru-disciple system has always played an important part in our society: if you want to learn classical Indian dance, your teacher is not only a dance master, but also a guru. It's the same for music, wrestling... Isn't it?*

– What is your mission? What does the modern day world need most?

– *Human values; to bring back human values.*

– What are your plans for the future?

– *Nothing specific. We are always ready to do all that the moment, the circumstances require of us.*

– What does Indian spiritual knowledge have which other spiritual traditions don't?

– Each place has its own speciality. Switzerland has cheese, Germany has marzipan.[1] *India has spirituality.*

– Nowadays we are seeing everywhere signs of a renewal of spirituality and meditation. Is it special to the present time?

– When values rise, the time is special. Human values make a time special. Celebrations make a time special. What is special in celebration? It's celebration which makes everything special.

– So, are you optimistic about the growth of values?

– Spread the values, consolidate them and the time automatically becomes better. We can transform our time by enhancing our values.

– Is it then the attraction of spiritual alternatives which keeps gurus going?

– It's Man's quest for happiness. Through truth, you get to the destination. Truth is the last moment, the final.

– What is your message for the readers and for India?

– A truly religious person will be a layperson by nature. 'Layperson' means the one who thinks that all human beings are his. Every religion is concerned with its own sect and not with humanity as a whole. All our religious leaders compartmentalize humanity and take responsibility to a limited level. Spirituality is taking responsibility for all the peoples of the world. We need to create this awareness. All maulvis, bishops, pandas, priests and mahants must be in agreement. Only then will human values be sustained.

– But a man's faith can be murderous...

– The problem starts when someone wants to impose his idea about God. My idea about God and his idea about God could coexist. The basic principle of the Art of Living is to accept people as they are. Life is multidimensional. If you forget that...

– What happens?

– You see people, like Muslim fundamentalists, who have read no other Scriptures than their own. If they had studied the Upanishads, they couldn't commit certain acts. God was there before the Koran.

1 A confection made with almonds.

And we ought to take our responsibility. We haven't carried our knowledge of Yoga, of Vedanta, and of the Upanishads to the rest of the world. Just remember, there can't be just one way of living in this world. You can't make the whole world materialistic, as the communists tried to do – without managing to do so. And you can't make the whole world spiritual either. There is a place for each one in this world.

– How many people have benefited from your teaching?

– I don't pay attention to the result.

– At the age of 17, you had already passed the highest qualifications in physics, chemistry and mathematics. Is the scientific person inside you sceptical about the spiritual you?

– I don't label myself as a spiritual or scientific person.

– What's the difference between you and a politician?

– I don't know. I can talk about myself, but how could I do so about others? Don't compare yourself with anyone else in this world. Not even with me. You are a unique individual.

– What's the difference between you and me?

– Do you think there is one? So what's the difference between a flower and a flower bud? That's the difference.

– Are you never depressed or angry? For example, if there is a problem within your organisation?

– [Laughter] We have kept our organisation small, just enough to spread the knowledge. The organisation is the frame which supports the picture. It must be appropriate. If the frame eats into the photo little by little, then it no longer serves its purpose. At the same time, the photo cannot be hung without a frame.

– Often, when you talk about meditating and singing, people consider you a sect.

– What is a sect? They don't know. If it's a feeling of belonging to the whole world, then it's better to be part of a sect. There are two sects: one for the depressed and one for the happy. Sects are groups which exclude others, who think that they alone are good, and that others are bad. In the Art of Living foundation we include

all religions: they are part of a truth. Don't worry. Just be happy. Share this joy. Make plans of service.

– Have you made a conscious decision to target young people? You attract them in great numbers.

– We don't try to influence anyone, to attract specifically the young or anyone. I am just what I am. If you feel inspired by me, well fine! If you don't, then you do inspire me! That's the way we think and how all those who come to us think; they also become popular. Smile or make me smile. Inspire or be inspired.

– Some people say that nowadays *gurus* are commercialising spirituality.

– People are free to have their own opinions. I don't care about being or not on the front cover of magazines. I'm here to serve...

– Do you see yourself as a man or as a god?

– As a child."

He concludes, "*Jai Guru Dev*".

♦

The Master invites the visitors who wish to attend the before lunch meditation. The journalists generally accept his offer, less out of curiosity than a desire to have a bit of a rest. The hint of aggressive smugness at the beginning has vanished in the course of the meeting. They acknowledge this, the exceptional stature of the Sage commands respect, and his kindness touches. But it's after going themselves through the experience of meditation guided by Yoga Shiromani that they will appreciate more the interest of the practice and its inexpressible part. And when they have had before their eyes the saint in *samadhi*, they will take the measure of what they were trying to grasp. From then on, the articles on Gurudev Sri Sri Ravi Shankar will move away from the compulsion to denigrate which is in vogue. And the Master enjoys seeing that the apprehension about spirituality has moved back another step.

♦

Close to the platform, a few chairs are set out for the visitors, out of consideration for the stiffness of their bodies, or according to their position. Personalities from public life frequently come to attend a part of the programme. Spending a few hours in the presence of Gurudev Sri Sri Ravi Shankar will not be without effect. Something new will come out of it, something will move...

More often than not, the *ashram* is open to representatives of all spiritual and religious affinities. Gurudev honours their traditions: he will even be seen following their service – be they Christians or Sikhs – as a simple follower... He is keen that his disciples recognize his teaching under many forms.

At the present, the resident-guests are nine *swamis*, some Buddhist monks arrived from India, in their orange robes, with their bare arms and woollen bonnets to compromise with the Germanic winter. They are spiritual leaders and leading protagonists of the university life of their countries, each one being in charge of several hundreds of faculties.

Next to the *swamis*, a man in his seventies carrying himself proudly commands attention through his slightly austere countenance that a generous look dissolves. This is Acharya Ratnanda, known affectionately as 'Pitaji'. He awaits the arrival of his young Master, with this unusual and unique particularity: he is his father. On the ground, among the musicians, sits a beautiful round young lady in her dazzling sari: Bhanu, the sister of Gurudev, is there too.

Both these people bring their contribution to the knowledge. Pitaji's wisdom and erudition are considerable. He too is a doctor in Vedic science, an excellent practitioner in Ayurvedic therapy, an enthusiast in astrology which he has studied for half a century, like a Galilean researcher. He is a born orator who has mastered to perfection the art of story-telling. And thus he regularly treats the assembly of his son's disciples with stories drawn from the Puranas where suspense mingles with humour. The same lessons of life which he related to his children when they were small.

As for Bhanu, she teaches *sahaj samadhi* meditation and sings the *bhajans* in her nightingale voice.

The moment when the Master enters, Pitaji and Bhanu stand up along with the rest of the assembly of unobtrusive and glowing staunch believers. They wait, with their hands clasped together, for Gurudev to arrive where they are, and bow heads as he passes just as they have done for about forty years. No demonstration of their family links. Gurudev greets Pitaji with a hardly perceptible nod of the head. Once in position, he beckons his father to kindly join him at his side on the platform and invites the monks to sit down on the seats provided for them around him. None of them would think they could consider occupying the place before being invited to.

The Master praises his prestigious guests, underlines that they themselves have thousands of disciples in India, and reminds of their lofty responsibilities – particularly those of this learned monk, at the head of one thousand five hundred universities... Enough to put our complaints of overwork... and our intellectual feasts into perspective...

In response, the monks offer what they possess of high value: their *bhajans* from the north creating a wonderful mood with their deep and profound sonorities. In the returning displays of consideration, the recognition of the *guru*'s 'superior' dimension by these great mystics can be perceived. He does his level best to erase any distinction through his overwhelming kindness and humility.

Before starting the meditation session, when it is important to have no distractions at all, the Master casts a careful eye over the comfort of each person. He has a window banging too close to the head of one shut, has another one opened to avoid draught, spreads a few of the rows apart, brings the less well off further forward... For the rest, everyone is left to themselves.

Shoulders are covered in shawls, backs kept straight, chins tucked in. From the still floor rises the 'Om', sung three times, before awaiting instructions from the Master.

♦

Meditation is the focal point of spiritual life: "*Without meditation there is not the same depth, the same sensibility, the same perception... Life becomes more shallow*", says Gurudev Sri Sri Ravi Shankar.

In the Western World, you generally understand 'meditating' as absorbing yourself in thought, maturing a thought... Here it is the complete opposite.

"What is meditation? The mind in the present moment is meditation, the mind free of agitation is meditation, the mind which becomes non-mind is meditation. The mind which knows neither hesitation nor expectation is meditation, the mind which has returned home, to its source, is meditation."

The Master explains:

"All joy which you experience in life comes from deep within you. When you are capable of letting go everything you cling to, finding calm and remaining centred in this space, this act is called meditation. Meditation is the art of doing nothing, nothing at all. The rest is deeper than the deepest sleep you will ever experience. Many times deeper, because in sleep, there is always a place where desires linger on. In meditation you transcend all of these. This brings such calm to your brain! It's like putting your entire body into repair, like giving your mind-body complex an overhaul.

It's very important to be in one's internal peace. There is no need to wander off into the forest and to cut yourself off, no. Wherever you may be, it is possible to be in contact with the centre.

The most beautiful place in the universe lies within you.

When is rest possible? When you have finished any other activity; when you stop moving about, working, speaking, listening, watching, smelling, tasting... When all these activities cease, and that includes the thinking process, then you are at rest. You stop all voluntary activities and you repose. Only involuntary activities continue to happen: breathing takes place, your heart beats, your stomach digests food, your blood circulates; only involuntary activity remains within you, and all voluntary action comes to a halt. It is sleep, it is rest – however it is not complete rest.

When the mind dies down, meditation becomes spontaneous and you experience total rest. You sometimes go to bed in a nervous or agitated state, or in a state of desire. The mind projects, projects, projects... These plans hang around your mind. These ambitions linger. Superficially, it seems that they disappear one moment, but in fact they become more and more deeply immersed. That is why, when sleep is not very deep, you are full of ambitions and desires. Very ambitious people cannot experience deep sleep, because their mind does not become hollow and empty. It is not free. True liberty is to be free from the past and the future.

When you are not happy in the present moment, then you desire a brighter future. Clinging to the desire within your mind means you are not satisfied with the present moment. This creates tension within the mind. Each desire causes fever. Meditation is then far from being able to evolve. You can sit with your eyes closed, but if the desire doesn't stop appearing, then you are fooling yourself by believing you are meditating. You are day-dreaming.

What does it mean to be centred? It is to be satisfied with the present moment, to turn your gaze higher, to stay in this state of peace. If you are not centred, then your mind goes round in circles, there's no possible peace.

Each desire or ambition is like a speck of sand in the eye: it irritates. You can neither close your eyes nor keep them open. It's uncomfortable either way. Being detached from passions is like getting rid of the speck of dust or sand from your eye, so as to be able to open and shut it as you please. With detachment, you can take on the world with complete freedom and relax. You feel relieved. Total freedom occurs. It's liberation. You are neither concerned about the presence of things nor by their absence. Otherwise, without detachment, possessing things disturbs you and not possessing them disturbs you too. You have a partner, that's a concern. You don't have a partner, that's also a concern! You have money, that's a concern, you are frightened and you are always wondering what to do with this money. "Should I invest or not?" If you invest, that creates another worry: will it increase or decrease? How is the financial market performing?

If you don't have any money, that too causes you annoyance. Meditation is to leave anger and the events of the past behind, and to drop all your plans for the future. It is to accept the present moment as it is, to live fully each instant in depth.

Whatever your plans may be, whatever you may do, your final destiny is the tomb. Whether you live life as a good or bad man, whether you laugh or cry, whether you are a sinner or a saint, you will end up in a tomb. Whether you be rich or poor, intelligent or dull, stupid or scatterbrain, you will all end up in the tomb! What are all these little things which come to your mind and prevent you from finding peace, joy and love?

Whether you are loved or hated, you will end up in a tomb. Whether you love someone or hate them, you will both end up in a tomb. People have made war. Whether they won or lost, they both ended up in the tomb. What's the importance of this? The difference is a few years. Those who survived also suffered; those who disappeared quickly departed more in peace. The patient will die and the doctor too.

There are a couple of things which God laughs at: the first one is when a doctor says to his patient, "Don't worry, I'm here to save you." The second one is when two people say, "This is my land," and fight over this small piece of ground. Then God mocks them. He says, "You'll both end up in the tomb and you say, "This piece of land is mine!" Ha, ha, ha, let me laugh!"

Detachment can bring so much joy into your life. Don't think that detachment is apathy. There is a difference. A state of apathy is incompletion. Detachment is full of enthusiasm and joy; it brings complete joy into your life. It allows you to rest properly. When you rest properly, when you go deep in your meditation, you come out of it full of energy. You are capable of acting better.

Don't think that to move in the direction of detachment means to renounce everything and to run off into a monastery or a cloister. In monasteries, people also daydream of Paradise. [...]

Clinging to the idea that you are 'the doer' can hold you back. Clinging to plans can prevent you from falling deep into meditation.

This simple knowledge is sufficient. Let go, sit down and observe how much a few days of this practice can change the quality of your life.

The Self is like an unlimited ocean, the divinity lies entirely there. You are so profound, you can't conceive how profound!

Meditation is being.

Meditation is seeing God in yourself."

"When I sit down and meditate, old memories come back and bother me.

– *That does not matter, don't lose courage! Let them come! Say, "Come and sit down with me! Old memories going back five, ten, twenty years... sit next to me!" The more you'll want to flee from them, the more they will annoy you. Tell yourself simply: what a wonderful Maya game!*

– During meditation I struggle to keep my spine erect, so I can't completely abandon myself...

– *When you sit down to meditate, sit with your spine erect. When meditation comes, allow this something which modifies your posture to release itself. Your head can sink, your spine can relax, you can fall asleep, etc. Don't bother about keeping a straight back. [...]*

Let go... Abandon the bliss or the joy of your meditation. Don't even detain peace. When you try to hold onto peace, you just get disturbance. If you detain joy, you just get misery. If you don't worry about joy, you will never be affected by misery. If you don't worry about peace, nothing will disturb you. Accept and receive everything as part of life. When you don't cling to pleasure, you become free, and when you don't cling to freedom, you gain love.

Abandonment is an illusion which allows you to fight against the other illusions.

Effort is the key to the relative world.

Absence of effort is that of the absolute."

♦

"Om Shanti, Shanti, Shanti..." The song of Gurudev further deepens the rest while it brings back the mind to an awareness of

the surroundings. And at these words, "*Gently..., gradually..., at your own rhythm..., you can open your eyes*", the people gathered come out of their delectable retreat.

"*Are you well?*" Gurudev asks.

The majority just raise a thumb. Others, brought out of their torpor more quickly, add the word, "*Fine!*" Some, on the other hand, feel that they haven't been able to relax. Too many thoughts or emotions have come and upset their pre-fixed idea about what good meditation should be... Someone feels full of anger and tells the Master:

"I find it tough staying in this position, my legs ache, my back kills... I don't like meditating.

– *When do you feel better, when meditating or not meditating?*

– "I don't know... Probably when I'm not meditating...

– *"Then don't meditate. Simple!"*

♦

Today is Wednesday; the day for preparing the weekly wisdom sheet. The Master solicits everyone's help to finalise it. The outlines of the text have already been laid out in a sub-committee, but Gurudev submits it – intentionally in its raw form – to the audience: a chance to make an active contribution to the knowledge, instead of merely being fed.

Of course, the Master has his precise idea about the teaching which he wishes to spread throughout the world. His words are immediately re-transcribed. He says,

"I'm asked, "What is your message?" I have no message. To deliver a message you need to be a distance away. A message needs distance. A message is about the past or the future. A message is impersonal and lifeless. Knowledge cannot be a message. A wise man will not deliver you a message, but will only arouse you.

God will not deliver you a message. In order for God to give you a message, he would have to be far away from you. God is nearer to you than your own breath. How could he address a message to you?

Wise men have no need either of a message, or to forward one to you. Whosoever needs a message will not take advantage of it. And whoever can put it to good use won't need one.

– What is the difference between knowledge and a message?

– *You can read the ingredients – read a message – but when you taste food the information becomes knowledge. You can read over and over again what living in the present moment is, but it only becomes knowledge when you experience it.*

Put that too in the wisdom sheet..."

Pitaji listens to his son like a disciple who never stops learning from his Master. I was discovering this unique rapport between a father and a sage, his child, whom he considers with almost intimidated devotion. Nothing possessive, not even proud in his attitude, but rather a placid submission to the divine will which made of him the father of his own master.

He doesn't say 'my son', but 'Guruji'. Most often, when he talks about him, it is to quote him. As a bonus – the adornment of his own reflections. The day when Pitaji accepted to confide in me his more intimate vision, he had never done this in public before. He relied on my discrimination to assess whether it should be published. "All depends on how you describe Guruji, he told me. You can either frighten people, or bring them to love him." For his part he would deliver his pure truth without censuring himself.

"Most respected Pitaji, you were born in the midst of a very pious family...

– *My great grand-father did a hundred yagyas*[1] *during his life. My grand-father built many temples. My father was an associate of Mahatma Gandhi, they were very close... Guruji was born on the same day as Adi Shankara and was baptised on the birthday of the very great saint Ramanuja. These circumstances coincided for the first time in centuries. They symbolize what will be his enlightened monism associated with a unified dualism...*

1 Exceptional Vedic rites

– So what has your son taught you that this heritage hadn't, you who already had a learned knowledge of the Holy Scriptures and a very profound faith?

– *The most important thing that I have learnt from my son is to realise that love is God. Experiencing love makes a big difference.*

– Let's suppose that I'd never met Guruji, how would you talk to me about him?

– *Every period in history has produced great souls whose words and actions have gone far beyond our concepts of normality. Modern times have also produced great masters, who, by their actions and their ability to act, have undertaken to lift us from an abnormally low level to the highest degrees of the fundamental values about life and love. The Devine responds to dismay and despair by bestowing his blessings via benevolent messiahs. These extraordinary beings move among mere mortals with love, compassion and grace, their eyes towards God and their hands laid on mankind.*

His Holiness Sri Sri Savi Shankarji is one of these messiahs of modern times, simple in his attitude, sincere in his action, innocent like a child and mature in his wisdom.

For me he is a messiah who teaches quite clearly that love is supreme. Lots of people think this way too.

– "What do you do about this conviction of yours? Talk about it or keep it quiet?

– *Guruji himself says nothing. He makes no claims regarding this subject. He says simply that he is a messenger of love. A rose has a beautiful smell; there is no need for it to be advertised.*

– But you, you don't hesitate...

– *I have the right to say these things. I am his father and his first disciple.*

– What sort of education do you offer to someone like Guruji?

– *Even messiahs must go through the processes and laws of life. He had to go to school, to university. He knew already what he was learning, that's the beauty of it... He absorbed everything very quickly because interior awareness was there.*

– In what circumstances do you exercise with your son your role as a father?

– At the very moment he was born, according to his horoscope, I knew that I was to be his disciple one day. You can be both a father and an admirer at the same time. Admiration leads to acceptance which leads to obedience. I know that Guruji belongs to Mankind. I was lucky to be his father. But I know I can't totally proclaim it. The sun protects you, but you can't say it belongs to you. I used to say of Guruji that he was both 'my son and my sun'.[1]

– Have you ever feared or are you still fearing for him that the world does not understand him? Or on the contrary, do you feel that his existence and the very concrete work that he does on this planet make him a man of his time, and that it is going in the direction of how things are currently evolving?

– Even Christ wasn't understood. He was crucified. But he did say, "Forgive them for they know not what they are doing." Guruji says exactly the same. He is building a real empire of love. The present period can count three great men of wisdom like him... But great emotions must be experienced, not explained."

♦

On his way out of the meditation hall, Gurudev went straight to the kitchen. He checks out the provisions, checks on the freshness of the products, double-checks that nothing has run out, points out any wastage, and oversees any hygiene issues... Strict cleanliness must be kept throughout. It is... almost. The Master has noticed a few crumbs left out on a table. He has no need to pass comment. He has been understood.

And here he is, standing in a corner of the dining hall, ladle in hand. This particular lunch, it is he who serves the rice he himself cooked that morning. With his head covered by his white veil, he feeds everyone, present for each person, 100% in all he does...

1 The Christian name 'Ravi' also means 'sun'

He who has no real need to be there, he who could live being served like a king, give alms of his public appearances, exercise all his powers, have statues built in his honour and even cathedrals, makes himself available to all with the simplicity of a supreme being. He is not a master who serves, implying that he can also be humble; he *is* the service. For everyone here, Christians, Jews, Muslims, Buddhists, he is the prime model.

7
RELAXED SPIRITUALITY

WOMEN HAVE DRESSED UP FOR THE OCCASION and so have the men. Everyone has dressed up a little more than usual for the special New Year *satsang*. Traditional party dresses from the various countries: Gurudev does not encourage Indian fancy dressing, except when it is necessary. On the contrary, he appreciates 'the global image' show of the various cultures and folklore represented at the *ashram*. The buboes of some of the African women bring a spicy touch to the colourful range of ceremonial silk shawls and modest seersuckers as well. Backs are covered with a flower field of embroidered shawls. Hair has been tied up, and perfumes are discreet.

Tonight everyone enters the meditation hall as a ball room... The only difference is that shoes have to be left at the entrance. It can then be noticed that feet have not been included in the appearance package: sports shoes have conveyed dressed up bodies from their bedrooms to the main hall...

As soon as one is in, they'd better forget the amount of time spent ironing their evening dress: up to two thousand people are sitting on the floor, knees to knees. Many have come to spend the last hours of the year in the presence of Gurudev Sri Sri Ravi Shankar, and will return home during the night.

The late comers have difficulty in finding a place to sit. With experience, one sees the smallest open space among the assembly and squeezes in without considering whether the spot is free or not.

As usual, it has been a real battle to find some space in one of the front rows, the ones that are the closest to the stage. Some made a fruitless effort at attempting to reserve some personal space by installing all kinds of cushions, comfortable mats and varieties of personal belongings indicating the area of their territory and dissuading anyone from sitting there. Their belongings will end up being spread out across the room. It is a time when peaceful hearts may undergo some internal frictions... Most of the time Gurudev's precept works quite well: "*So what...?*" Irritations disappear before any real friction has time to burst out. There is no time for friction; motives are seen for what they are: pathetic. The presence of the Master is enough for the discordance to be dissolved and for the sealing of a new reconciliation in typical *ashram* mode: the automatic jubilatory hug. One hugs a lot here.

Being concerned about seeing or being seen by the Master does not make any sense since there is absolutely no space in the room where anyone could not possibly be considered by the Master. And above all, no little game would be clever enough to catch Gurudev's attention against his will. He does not allow anything to be dictated to him, not even an earth quake, as it was proved in May 2002 in the United States, during a *satsang* in San José for his birthday. The earth had been trembling for a few seconds. The entire building was shaking, but the Master's facial expression did not change at all. He just carried on with his talk. Thanks to his calmness, panic was avoided. People started spontaneously to clap.

Someone asked: "Guruji, didn't you feel the earth quake?" He answered, laughing: "*No, I have enjoyed the rocking movement.*"

So, imagine catching his attention by way of clothing efforts! He appreciates the sense of celebration that is related to the special care given to the clothing appearance, but the best way to become transparent to him is to try to look one's best and wanting him to admire you.

It has happened that he complimented me for an outfit that I was not wearing for the first time though. At the beginning I used to say, "But you have seen this dress before!" And I noticed that the day he noticed my dress was the day I had totally forgotten what I was wearing...

He says, "*When you are trying to use your charm on someone, you produce the opposite. You should rest in peace with a smile.*"

Singing starts: '*Om Namah Shivaya... Om Namo Bhagavate... Ganesha Sharanam... Satyam Shivam Sundaram... Shivoham Shivoham... Kali Durge... Radhe Govind... Jay Jay Jay Guruji Ki Jay...*'

Each *mantra* is repeated, repeated, repeated endlessly, and no one knows how long it will be sung along with by the gathering... However, as a sign of a profound unity that the singing creates among all the spirits, and without the need of any prior indication, the thousand voices stop singing all together on the very same music note!

One of the devotees installs the *asana* on the couch. The Master never sits on a chair that is not covered with this special ritual shawl. This is done shortly before his arrival, so it will not be long before he is there...

Up there, in the *meeting room*, Gurudev is finishing some interviews or having private and relaxed breaks... He does not wear a watch. In general, he asks around for the time. "*Oooh, it is late! Eight-thirty already*!" And he claps his hands so that everyone leaves the room: "*Quick, quick... Go down to* satsang... *Come on go down*!" No one moves, but he does not get upset. He goes into the bathroom, comes back roughly combing through his long hair with a plastic gadget comb with extravagant teeth... On top of his *dhoti* he wears a Kashmir shawl embroidered with golden threads, but a devotee from Abu-Dhabi has just offered him the complete set of an Arabian sheikh – white keffieh and dress, and a black cord to put around his head. He puts it on top of his own clothes and starts playing desert rhythms on a drum in front of a small assembly, who is delighted not to have listened to him and left. Playfully, he brings the keffieh to the bottom of his face, like a veiled woman. He says that in the beginning, Mahomet had encouraged this practice to protect women from violence and brutal temptations; meant to protect them and bring them more safety, the use of the veil has then been misinterpreted, and used for wrong purposes. The Muslim also gives him a copy of the Koran as a present. Gurudev reads it through and puts it respectfully aside.

Another day, a Jewish prayer shawl was given to him by an Israeli devotee. He adopted it for a part of the evening, and took it off: the sacred aspect was honoured and at the same time was relieved of its seriousness. The dressing up does not matter. Gurudev does not give excessive importance to things.

So the Hindu sage will celebrate the Christian calendar New Year dressed as a Bedouin sheikh.

He moves forward slowly into the lane drawn by the crowd, and stops very often to greet some of the newcomers: "*Oooh...! When did you arrive? Where do you come from*?"

Once he is sitting on his couch, he starts meditating, and very soon casts off... Disappeared, in *samadhi*... Inaccessible to the loud fiesta going on around him. His closed eyes are smiling. Christ face... Divine presence.

"*Although you exist with a body in the state of samadhi, you are not there at all. In other words, you can say that living as if you did not exist at all is the state of* Samadhi."

People are dancing some kind of jerk dance to exuberant *bhajans*... Then tiredness comes and musicians start playing more quiet chants. Between two melodies, one increases the silent pause to indicate to the Master that the assembly is ready to listen to him. But tonight Gurudev seems to be in an eternal state of *samadhi*... Inexpressible beauty of the Holy Spirit. Some cry...

Finally his big black eyes open, sparkling as a water mirage under the sun. One is tenderly hypnotised by their purity. From where have they come back? What have they seen? Each one is surrounded by their beneficial life-waves.

Someone asks: "Guruji, when you look at us, what do you see? Do you see our auras? Do you see our future? Do you see our *karmas*?"

He answers, "*Just* bambinis..."

He leaves space for laughter and asks, "*So what do you want to talk about tonight*?"

Some of the classic themes are called out to him, but the Master carries on almost immediately:

"For each of you, your body has the capacity of the five senses. You can see without your eyes; eyesight is part of consciousness that is why you can see in a dream, without your eyes.

You can feel without the skin. This is why people deprived of one limb can feel a itching there.

You can smell without the nose and taste without the tongue.

The five senses and the capacity to think are all present in the consciousness. So, each cell of the body has the potential capacity to perform all the functions of the senses.

When somebody tells you something, you are all ears; you listen with all the cells of your body. In India we say, 'to look with a thousand eyes' – 'To be all eyes' in English. All the cells are made of the same tissue; all DNA has the capability of all the body functions.

Consciousness is inherent to each cell. Every stimulus of the senses conveys the knowledge which is the nature of consciousness. Eyesight passes on a knowledge: blue, red, green. Knowing is the nature of consciousness.

Somebody says, "Some people who have lost one of their senses see the other senses develop."

Gurudev replies, *"It is not necessary to lose one sense to develop the others. You can sharpen them all through deep silence."*

A disciple named Mickaël carries on, "And if you have no sense at all?

Gurudev, *"Then you become like Mickaël!"*

Laughter.

New Year's exercise: think that each one of your cells has the potential to see and hear. They all have eyes and ears. Sit down comfortably, close your eyes, know that you are all eyes and ears...

"God is not an object of sight; you can never see God. God is not an object of hearing, God is not an object of smell and taste. God cannot be perceived through your senses, or through your mind.

You can experience God, you can be God, but you can't 'see' God or perceive God as if it was a separate object.

God is in you, as you, in all his forms. Don't imagine you are going to see God one day as a separate object.

There is no separation between God and you. If you are here, it is because there is God, what is God is God, what is is. It is the Divine.

In your most intimate Self, in its purity, clarity, you are not different from God.

Don't try to see God inside you... It is not necessary to tell others you have found God inside... If others see God in you, then it is fine.

– When will God come?

– *Never! One who is always here doesn't have to come and go!*

– Can you give a definition of God? What is God? Can one live without God?

– *Can you live without love? God is love, space; Love is God. So you are made of God. Our world is entirely made of God. And that is what God is. God cannot be separate because everything is in God. Everything is God. There is nothing outside God. If you don't want to use the word God, you can say 'energy', or 'intelligence'. The very foundation of the creation is to be found in every existence.*

God is not the Creator; he is creativity itself. There is no God sitting in Paradise with a white beard. God is here and now. And how to reach Him? When you meditate, when you feel at ease, at home with everybody, you are in contact with the divine force. When you are at peace, you become aware of what reality is. God is omnipresent. If he is not everywhere, then he is not omnipresent. Even if you go to hell, God will follow you. It is said in the Upanishads: "Kham, kham, Brahma." What is God? Space is God, in which everything exists, and everything dissolves. God, in English, spells out 'G' as generator, 'O' as operator, and 'D' as destructor. God is this field in which everything happens.

Questions about God sound so silly...

– *How can I stay centred on God's love?*

– *By being grateful for everything you have. Your body belongs to the world. Your spirit belongs to the Divine. The Divine is your only security.*

God is not just here to fulfil your petty demands. There is a story about it. When God created man, man got into the habit of calling on Him for every little detail: he was asking for favours and complaining about everything! Man was praying for God to visit him. But if God came, he said, "Not now, come later! You came too soon!" If God did not come, he used to protest, "I have called You so often, and You come so late!" God was fed up. He wanted to go and hide somewhere, but it wasn't that easy. He knew man would go to the moon to find him! At that time, God met a wise man who whispered in God's ear, "Go and hide in man's heart; he never goes there. Ever since that day, God has been hiding in man's heart. Whoever ventures there won't be able to complain any more. Every complaint will disappear by itself. One person out of a thousand goes there. And when this person discovers God at the bottom of their heart, they no longer have any complaints.

– When we offer everything to the Divine, is it through our thoughts, or our feelings, or both? Is there a special way to do it more efficiently?

– Don't complicate things... Nothing belongs to you anyway! I say, "Offer" because you think you possess. You are holding on to things and you worry how to deal with them. So I say, "Offer" It is a relief for your head. It is like somebody travelling by train and carrying all his luggage on his shoulders. What would you tell him? "Put your luggage down and relax." You are on the train and the train carries the luggage anyway. Don't be eager to discover what the most efficient way is. It doesn't matter. You have a tendency to want to be perfect and this anxiety to be perfect makes you imperfect. Don't worry.

– Who has created the illusion of the separation from the Divine? Does the Divine love us all equally? Is there somebody in this room who is more important to the Divine than another?

– It is you. Although there is one sun only, this sun can enter a lot of houses. The fact that the sunlight has entered this house through the window doesn't mean it isn't also in the next house. This is the logic of the small mind. There is a natural desire in you to be special. Everybody wants to be somebody special and close. I tell you, you are already.

You are very special, very unique and very dear! It doesn't matter what you do, what you have done, where you are from. It doesn't matter.

God is in everybody, in dogs, cats, leaves, and ants... in all the Creation, in pigs too! Through the window, you cannot but see Him because the window is so transparent! This love and this silence, you cannot but feel them. You cannot pass by the power of existence. All is one.

– But why did God create the world to start with?

– [In a severe tone of voice] *Who told you God had created the world? Is there evidence for you? Who said God had created the world? God has not created the world, God has* become *the world!*

– What is the difference between religion and spirituality?

– Religion and spirituality are two different things. Spirituality is the essence, the substance of religion. This distinction has to be clear in our mind. I often give the example of the banana. Spirituality is the banana, and religion is the skin. Don't hang on to the skin and throw away the real stuff! People have thrown away the banana and hang on to the skin!

Religion is a set of outer rituals and habits; it is a way of life. Spirituality is the quest for the source of life; it is going back to the source, knowing deep within us that we are part of the Divine.

Symbols are in religion, and their meaning is the essence of spirituality.

On this path, everybody has to travel alone; nobody can walk it for you. You cannot walk in place of somebody and say, "Yes, I travelled on the path." Nobody can eat or drink for you. "Relax, I came to drink tea for you!" It is not possible. This quest represents the real need of the soul, of any growing soul.

– What is the value of religion?

– Every religion, every prophet who came on this earth has brought a lot. It is immeasurable; one cannot assess it. Every major tradition has brought its contribution to wisdom. The message of love and service in Christianity is incomparable. The message of meditation and the theory of observation in Buddhism is incomparable.

The knowledge of the universe, of the Self and of life in the Vedic tradition is incomparable. The theory of karma in the Jaïn tradition is incomparable.

It is not necessary to consider that one tradition is better than another. Read the sacred Scriptures of each tradition and see them from a new angle. They all lead you to the basic human values of love, compassion and joy. You won't find a religion that will not defend truth, peace, service and caring for life.

Different teachings have appeared according to different people, different periods. In every religion, there are three aspects: first, the values; second, the practices; and third, the symbols. These values are common to all religions. The teaching may seem contradictory but it isn't. The values are the same. On the other hand, practices and symbols are different – and that gives them their own charm. There is diversity. God loves variety! It is a good thing that different approaches should exist – but all teachings are yours. You are the child of this Creation, of the Divine. Everything the Divine provides belongs to you. Knowledge and wisdom are neither mine nor yours, nor anybody else's; they belong to everybody. And when you are ready to realise it, you will discover masters everywhere. A tree, a bird, every human being you meet will teach you something.

So if you limit yourself, "Oh, I am a Christian, I only speak of Jesus." or, " I am a Hindu, I only speak about this philosophy" or, "I am a Buddhist, I have nothing to do with anything else," then you miss many things. You own them all.

When we identify with something limited, the capacity to love becomes limited. The capacity to know becomes limited.

A Hindu says Hinduism is great, because he is a Hindu, not for what Hinduism is. A Christian says the Bible is great, because he is a Christian. Muslims say the Koran is the greatest book, because they are Muslims. If a Hindu says, "The Bible is magnificent", it is a more authentic than the same statement coming from a Christian. If a Japanese says, "America is fantastic" it has more value than an American's declaration. We think things are good simply because we belong to them. We are stuck with this limitation. Why not wake up and see that everything that has existed in this world for eons belongs to us? Humanity's whole wealth belongs to us, whether it is in the Gita, the Koran, the Bible, among the Sikhs, or in Jainism. All this wealth is mine.

A mature person will claim the whole world's wealth. To be mature is to fix no limit to the world's wealth and not to divide it. "Everything belongs to me and I belong to all:" this is enlightenment.

For an enlightened being, everybody is a form of God; everybody is an expression of Divinity. When an enlightened being speaks, they don't take this position, "You are all ignorant, I am very enlightened, I am going to reveal something to you." No. They know nature. It is the Divine who offers this wonderful knowledge, which is only expressed in a different form. An exchange is happening. In fact, everything in life just happens!

There are some very good people today who have realised the futility of dogmatic religious practices and who try to adopt other methods. But they make a small mistake; they say, "We are making a synthesis of the East and the West. We are linking Eastern spirituality to Western spirituality. We are bringing them closer." An enlightened person will never say the word 'synthesise'. There is nothing to synthesise; everything is One already. If you see duality, you are mistaken. It is as if you draw a line with a stick in the ocean and then say: "I synthesise the left side and the right side of water!" You initially created a difference, then say you were synthesising. There is nothing to synthesise between Christianity and Hinduism, or any other religion. It's no use!

The search for unity is the true spiritual path. Unfortunately, this so-called spiritual path has divided human beings and torn society apart.

When we celebrate Christmas at the ashram, we celebrate it in the intimacy of our hearts, in the deepest silence of our being. This celebration of the Being, being in truth, being in the Father's principle is true and authentic... We discover Christ, who is eternal, in the depth of our being as our Self.

We don't use a cross, but we nevertheless celebrate Christ. The cross has become the symbol of a 'Christian', and the fight starts with the feeling of attachment to the cross, not to Christ, not to the Christlike consciousness. If you tell somebody, "You can be a Christian without the cross", they think it is almost impossible. You can be a Christian celebrating Christianity in your own way, without necessarily performing the same rituals as the others.

We have left the real substance and are stuck on the periphery, on the rituals. But here, we are approaching this place where truth reigns –enlivening the consciousness Christ gave rise to through his enlightenment.

It is a Big Mind that became Christ, and before Christ, this same Big Mind manifested as Buddha, and before Buddha, this same mind manifested as Lord Krishna, and before Krishna, this same Mind manifested in another form; a Big Mind reflecting in all its purity. Like you, with different names and forms throughout the ages, and it goes on. Today, this awakens in you as your own mind, deep in your heart, in your deepest consciousness.

Christ does not belong to Christians, Christ belongs to humanity. Krishna does not belong to the Hindus; he belongs to humanity.

People would like to bring religions closer! What ignorance! There is no need for a synthesis.

Walk in Christ's steps. He said, "Be in peace and know thyself!" Have you ever been in peace? Have you ever contemplated this Kingdom of God which is concealed so deeply in our heart?

Please note: there exists the Unique, and nothing else. In the Bible, it is said that Christ is the only Son of God. It's a slight translation mistake; they should have rather translated that Christ is the son of the Only Father. The Father is one. The source is one. And Christ has come again and again! He has already come before! He has also been born as Christ.

Be in this supreme Mind. This supreme Mind is Jesus. This supreme Mind is the guide. Jesus has said, "I am the way". What did he mean? He meant he was reflecting this Supreme Mind totally. He also said, "Whatever you do, it can only happen through me in you, me, the supreme Mind.

– So, do you believe in Jesus?

– Of course! Jesus is all love, and so are Buddha, Krishna, Mohammed... and so are you!

Jesus and love are synonymous. If you say love, you need not say 'Jesus'. If you say Jesus, that means love. Such a complete expression of love you find in Jesus. [...] Love goes with courage, and look at the courage of Jesus. He completely overthrows the common concepts of people: 'the strong will inherit the earth'. He turns it around: 'the meek shall inherit the earth, the meek shall inherit Heaven.' For Love makes you meek. However strong you are, when you are in love, you are the weakest. Yet love is the strongest force in this universe, and it makes you meek, it makes you weak.

Even a macho man will cry when he is in love. A macho man will be like a mouse behind somebody he loves very much. Love makes you weak, but brings you the Kingdom of Heaven.

Jesus says, "Love each other as much as I love you!" It was impossible for anyone not to recognise the love Jesus was, but since love makes you weak, it is also scary. Among thousands, just a few followed him. Many heard, but just a few came, that's why he said, "Very few shall pass through the narrow path." "The gate is wide; very few shall pass through the narrow path." Even after showing all those miracles, only a few, a handful of people, twelve, thirteen people really could recognise and follow Jesus. They were not high intellectuals. They were simple, innocent people. When Jesus said, "The Kingdom of Heaven is within you", they would not understand; they asked, "Which side of God will you be sitting, right or left?" Once you go inside, there is no right or left! There is no front or back! They were not very intellectual people; they were more innocent, simple people. He had to tell parables in many ways and repeat them, to help them understand a little more. That much patience and compassion can only come out of love. [...]

And Jesus had made all his efforts for one to cross the mind and get into the soul, the spirit, the source of life, the Self. Break through the limited relating yourself with something or somebody or identities and recognise your Divinity within you, recognise that you are much more than just a human. You are part of the Divine, and you inherit the Kingdom! And it is right here, right within you. [...]

The mind cannot understand Jesus; only heart can feel the presence of Jesus.

And those who crucified Jesus are not bad people, they were ignorant; they were stuck in their heads. They were not born out of spirit but they had read all the scriptures and books. They thought he was being blasphemous and had done something criminal.

Jesus himself has said in one place, "All those who came before me are robbers and thieves." What did he mean by that? They are robbing your mind of the present moment! You cannot love the people who are right in front of you, you cannot experience love with those who are around you, but you are dreaming of someone in the future, or glorifying someone in the past. Divine is in the present. Divine is the conjunction of presence and present. Here and now. So your mind has been stolen away by the past or the future. I am here to bring it here now. I am the only way. If you can't see Divinity in me when I am right in front of you, do you think you can see Divinity in the past or in the future? Forget about it. I am the gate. Look at me. See what I manifest; that is what you are! I have come home; I am standing at the doorstep to bring you home. Take a step, come on in. You are not going anywhere else! You are going where you are. Jesus leads you to your own Being, your own Self; your own Divinity that is deep within you.

Unfortunately people think a chariot is going to come and that they will all be sitting in the chariot and it will go with their body up somewhere in the clouds. In this century, where science has advanced so much, people are still caught in an unscientific mind. That is amazing! That shows time has not changed much. Maybe a little bit here and there. [...]

Jesus has said, "I have come to put one against each other; I have come to set fire, not to make peace". He had to say this because he had seen the depth of slumber of people. When you say something nice, peaceful, everybody will go to sleep. When there is something sensational, people wake up and listen. The newspapers are filled with such stories. This is human mind!

– How do we understand the concept that Jesus suffered for our sins?

– Jesus has never said, "I am suffering for your sins." That was a way that people used to awaken people, "Look, Doomsday is coming! Come on, wake up!" See, when Jesus was on this planet, those were the darkest days, the darkest period on the continent. People were slaves; they were not highly educated, nor aware. It was necessary in those days to say, "Come on, wake up! There's going to be a disaster! Be good, be compassionate, pray, do something for the sake of the spirit!"

Fear wakes one up from slumber. Otherwise, one is doing the same thing, being dull and not opening to knowledge. Teachers in those days knew this psychology of the human mind, so they used these tactics to awaken people who were so thick-skinned! Fear need not be a tool for someone who is sensitive. But just a pinch of fear works on someone who is very thick-skinned. Today, you don't need to induce fear to tell people to pray, you go through love, you can go through gratitude, gratefulness, helplessness. The wise had many ways to lead one towards the truth; so that was one of the ways.

– What is your feeling about conversion?

– We need to be converted from adulthood back to childhood. This is the conversion we need, from hatred to love, from being somebody to being nobody. This total conversion is what we really need. We need to be connected to God, to the Divine within us. A simple belief system is not enough. It is really the experience, the authentic experience that can change our life, which can change the world. We become one with the Divine, deep within us. It is so simple! It is not necessary to worship an idol if you don't want to, but feel free to do it if you fancy that, in any form. What is a cult? Simply loving the Divine. It is just a way to express one's gratitude. So, it isn't meaningful to idolise, neither is it necessary to prevent oneself from doing it. The opportunity to feel grateful is one of the most precious moments in life.

Two thirds of the people practice a religion, but this leads to many wars. If there were no religions, there would be no wars. In all these cults, there is no joy.

– What about the rituals?

– It is good to have rituals, but keep it to a minimum! Rituals are not really necessary, but there is nothing wrong to have them.

– We have a '*Jesus hall*' and a '*Buddha Hall*' in the German *ashram*; why don't we have an '*Allah Hall*', or a '*Mohammed Hall*'?

– We can have an 'Allah Hall'; *we have an* 'Allah kutir' *in the Bangalore* ashram. *It is very fine. We can have an* 'Allah Hall', *or a* 'Mohammed Hall' *here. Give any name, it doesn't matter.*

– What is the meaning of atheism? Often, atheists are very strict and firm about their position.

– There is nothing great in being an atheist. Somebody very stupid can become an atheist. It doesn't require much to disprove God – you can easily do it. But to prove the existence of the Cosmic Intelligence, you need to be intelligent. Only an intelligent person can have faith in God – not only believe – but have faith, which is deeper and comes from the depth of your heart. When you know you have faith; when you don't know, then you can only believe. Do you see the difference?

By reading books and listening to what people say here and there, you can acquire a conviction. But faith is created within you. Faith is an event, a stage of maturity of your knowledge. When knowledge ripens, it becomes faith. [...]

A pure atheist cannot exist. An atheist is someone who refuses to believe in what is neither concrete nor tangible. Yet, life is not always concrete nor tangible, neither is the universe.

Whether in the realm of affairs, sciences or arts, one often has to make suppositions, build up hypotheses, and resort to imagination and intuition. All these fields are by nature ethereal and non-tangible. As soon as an atheist accepts, even hesitatingly, a field that remains unexplainable, he ceases to be an atheist. No sensible person can evade the mystery of life, and consequently cannot honestly call themselves atheists! The so-called atheists are maybe only denying some concepts about God. [...]

An atheist is one who says, "I don't believe in God." But in saying so, does he believe in what he says? At least, he believes in the one who says it. Does he know who he is? No. It isn't possible to be an honest atheist. The one who says, "I don't believe in anything", does believe it. Okay. But does he know who he is? [...]

If you are an atheist, at least you believe in your existence. And yoga doesn't exclude an atheist. There is no blasphemer in Hindu philosophy. If you criticise somebody, you must have a complete knowledge of his thought system. The very structure of Indian philosophy is such that you can never be a fanatic.

– Was Buddha an atheist?

– In a way no, because he was professing the vacuity, which is very difficult to accept for an atheist. And on the other hand yes, because he was professing no concept about God. But he used to say, "Go inside yourself, and you will see. First come to the path, and you will discover it all." Buddha has never said anything about God.

Buddha never let himself be trapped in a philosophical discussion. He stated several questions he would not answer, and about which he would keep silent, "Does God exist?" "When has this universe started?" "What will happen to the soul after enlightenment, where will it go?" These questions were inappropriate; he would not say a word about them.

– An atheist believes only in what he says, but Buddha said that all we see is not real.

– If only all atheists today could be Buddhas. A true believer is one who acknowledges his ignorance. He knows that there is a lot that he doesn't know. He sees the potentiality in things. Have faith, believe, because there is a lot that we don't know, that we cannot know about this existence. There is a Power, an Intelligence behind this Creation, and there is evidence of this Intelligence. Acknowledging this supreme power is enough to gain depth.

One who keeps his mind open is like a pot. He is hollow, he is light, open. Alive is the quality of a believer. Here, ignorance makes you alive. An atheist believes he knows it all; he is dull like a stone.

– When an atheist comes to you, how do you teach him?

– Atheism is to believe neither in values, nor in abstraction. When an atheist comes to the guru, what happens? You start to experience your own form, and you discover that you are in fact without a form,

hollow and empty. And this abstract no-form becomes more and more concrete in you! The guru makes the abstract more real, and what you believed to be substantial clearly appears more like imaginings. Sensitivity and subtlety start to dawn. The perception of love, not as an emotion, but as the substratum of existence becomes more evident. The formless spirit shines through every form in Creation, and the mystery of life increases the breaking up of atheism. Then the journey starts. It has four stages.

First stage – *Seeing the form in the formless. Seeing God in all the forms. Often one feels more at ease seeing God in the formless than in the form. One feels a distance, a duality, a fear of being rejected and other limitations. In life, all our interactions are with forms, so the awake part of our life remains separate from the Divine. All those who accept God to be formless use symbols, and they maybe love the symbols more than life itself! If God happened to tell a Christian to drop the cross, and a Muslim to relinquish the crescent, they might not do it. To start, loving the formless is only possible through forms.*

Second stage – *Closeness. Feeling totally close to the form you have chosen, and seeking to reach the formless. This leads to a sense of intimacy with the whole Creation. At this stage, one has overcome the fear of being rejected, and so on... but it is restricted in time and space.*

Third stage – *Feeling the presence of the Divine, through whom you transcend the limitations of time and space.*

Fourth stage – You are well established in the Divine, then, you realise you are one with Him. There is a total merging, a fusion with the beloved, and duality disappears. This is that, and that is this.

– Does a believer also go through these four stages?

– Indeed, the atheist and the believer go through them. People used to think that saying "I am God" was blasphemy. I am telling you that saying "I am not God" is blasphemy! When you say "I am not God", you deny God his omnipresence. You are made of love. If you say "I am not God", you doubt that God is love. If you are love and you say "I am not God", you are saying that God is not love, and this is blasphemy.

"I am" is your consciousness. When you say, "I am not God, you deny that God is conscious, alert and awake. You exist. When you say, "I am not God", you refuse God a part of existence, and this is blasphemy.

In the same way, you deny the Scriptures that say, "God made man in his own image." If you say, "I am not God", you deny God.

– Can you please tell us about enlightenment?

– Enlightenment is going from being somebody to being nobody. This is the first step. We think we are somebody – "I hate this, I love that." First, get rid of strong feelings of aversion or attraction; become like a child. The second step towards enlightenment is to move from being nobody to being everybody. To go from the stage when you are nobody to the stage when you are everybody, this is enlightenment.

One can't even speak about 'an enlightened person'; one can say 'enlightenment'. When the person's personality disappears, dissolves, this is enlightenment.

– Please describe enlightenment.

– Enlightenment is like a joke! It is like a fish looking for the ocean! Once upon a time... there was a meeting of fish discussing who had seen the ocean. None of them realised they knew the ocean. One fish said, "I think my great grandfather had seen the ocean!" A second fish said, "Yes, yes, I've heard about it too!" A third one said that yes, certainly, his great grandfather has seen the ocean. So they built an enormous temple and erected a statue in homage to the remarkable great grandfather. They wrote these words, 'He had seen the ocean, he had been in contact with the ocean!'"

Enlightenment is the real core of our being. Go into the heart of your Self, and live your life from there. We all came into this world endowed with innocence. But gradually, in becoming more intellectual, we lost our innocence. We were born with silence and as we grew up, we lost our silence and filled ourselves with words. We lived in our hearts, and as time passed, we moved to our heads. Now the reverse trip is enlightenment. It is a journey from head to heart, from words to silence. It is getting our innocence back, in spite of our intelligence. Although very simple, it is a great achievement.

– Is enlightenment really possible for the average man?

– *Yes, a big yes! Indeed, enlightenment is easier for an ordinary person than for somebody who thinks he is very special. See, when somebody thinks he is special, his ego becomes complicated. He thinks, "I am a great teacher", or "I am a great writer". This is ego.*

Enlightenment is dropping the ego. Your real nature is enlightenment. It is already in you as a seed. When you let go of all tensions and become natural, then it is in your hands! We simply need to let go of the old patterns in our minds. Then you see something beautiful dawning and blossoming in you.

When you think enlightenment is not within your reach, it means all the good qualities of enlightenment cannot manifest in you. When you think the highest state is impossible for you, you gradually eliminate the next possibility, then the next, until you lose what is called self-esteem. Then you think you are incapable of anything.

These potentialities of enlightenment cannot be revealed or awakened if you don't desire them. You cannot force someone to learn meditation if he doesn't want to; he must want to learn it.

– When two enlightened beings meet, what do they tell each other?

– *Oh, very simple things. "What is your favourite brand of chewing gum?"*

Enlightened people may seem to express very different things, but they mean the same. Ignorant people may seem to say the same thing, but what they mean is very different.

– Can a Christian or a Westerner be enlightened?

– *One who believes he is a Christian, or a Hindu, or a Muslim, or who believes he is somebody cannot attain enlightenment. As long as one adopts such an attitude, one is far away from enlightenment. A human being can be enlightened; a Christian, a Hindu, a Muslim, no. Can you see the difference? If you know you are only a human being, and if you know you are only Being, you are enlightened already.*

– How do you know you have reached enlightenment?

– It is as if you asked, "Do I have a headache?" You know you have a headache; it is the same for enlightenment, you will know it, you won't ask me.

People tend to think one only denies truth: the more you assert a thing, the less true it appears. One day a man asked me: "Are you enlightened?" I said, "No." Then he insisted, "You're joking, come on, tell me the truth..." But if I had said "yes", he would have assaulted me with endless questions and suspicions... Much better so, at least, I stay in peace!

– If God is omnipresent, how come there is hatred and suffering in the world?

– Like in the cinema, whether it is a tragedy or a comedy, whether the end is happy or not, in the absolute, there are no opposites. All opposites belong to the relative world. It is not the total image. Good and evil, true and false, everything is relative. Nothing is ever completely good, or completely bad. Everything is simply there.

– But where does all this evil that I feel in myself – not only in others – come from?

*– This is evil... [*Guruji ties a knot with a corner of his shawl*]. This is good... [*He unties the knot*] Evil is nothing else than a knot. It is not a substance. It is not our nature. It is only stress and tension. If a good person is constantly put under pressure, prevented to sleep and deliberately stressed in different ways, unless this person is quite enlightened, they will become violent.*

Evil and malevolent things are only lack of love, lack of knowledge, lack of happiness. It is like gloom, darkness... What is darkness? Is it a substance? No. It is only absence of light. Is stress a substance? No...

There isn't a single bad person on this planet. This is why Jesus said, "Love thy neighbour as thyself!" Love everybody like yourself. Even when he was crucified, he said, "Forgive them, they are ignorant!" He did not curse them, saying, "They are bad people." They were ignorant and lacking knowledge.

– You told us to see ourselves as the most important person in the eyes of God, to see abundance and to be grateful for it. I have been thinking about my childhood and my mother who left me when I was only five and I did not feel any gratefulness. I was thinking, "If I am so important in God's eyes, wouldn't I have grown up in better family conditions? I also remember a friend whose legs are paralysed. He says he doesn't want to surrender to God, because he thinks God did not really take care of him... How can we, he and I, feel grateful or feel God's love that you are talking about?

– If you simply look at what you don't have, you can never be grateful, and everybody can think the same. You say you haven't had a family, somebody else will say they should have had a better health, or more wealth, or a more gratifying position. Somebody else will be sensitive to the fact that they were not born in the White House, or they will say, "If I was born in Buckingham Palace, I would be part of the Royal Family. Do you know how the guards feel when they are standing in front of Buckingham Palace and see the queen, the prince and the princess go about? All they can do is just stand there and serve them.

Don't concentrate on the lack. Look at those in wheelchairs, or look at the blind, deaf and mute! At least be happy for what you have! You could be living in Ethiopia, under a scorching sun! People in Ethiopia realise your life is much more comfortable! There is no end to it. If you want to be grateful, you can be, at any time. It is like considering something half full, or half empty; it depends on the way you look at it.

– Guruji, why am I given non-stop trials? As soon as I have tackled one, as bravely as I can, here comes another one. Why are the hardest things to overcome always placed in front of me? Continuously!

– You see, the problem is you encounter pitfalls that make you stumble, huge difficulties, one after the other. And the question is, why always you? Am I wrong? Now, do you know what? Every time you encounter difficulties, you try to 'immortalise' the situation, or to generalise it. Suppose in a group of eighty people, ten of them catch a cold. Do you know what you would say? "Oh, everybody got sick!" Isn't it so? Every time a difficulty happens, we generalise and dramatise it. Whatever the problem, you say, "Oh, I am always

like that! If you get angry several times, you say, "Oh, I am always angry. Oh, I always have trouble." But it isn't really the case. If people have not been cooperative four times, the fifth time, you will say, "Oh, nobody is cooperative with me." What does it mean? Does really nobody want to cooperate with you? Has the whole world suddenly become bad? It isn't so. But the mind does it all the time. Doesn't it? It always generalise, it 'eternalises'. But it isn't so.

Look at your life, see how many wonderful moments you have experienced. You have been overjoyed, and you also have had to face difficulties. All this has made your life more interesting, because you have been able to overcome these difficulties and you still have the capacity to overcome them. This is why you have to face some challenges.

Always remember this: nature will never confront you with a problem you cannot solve. If you are facing a problem, it means you have the capacity to solve it. You already have the answer; this is why the question appears in front of you.

The first thing to do is to stop 'immortalising' problems. This is already a big thing in itself, that you don't welcome them all the time! Let's not attract them. Never say, "I am bad, I am useless." When you keep saying, "I always have this problem... I'm always sick..." it becomes a sankalpa, like a wish in you. You are sowing these seeds in your mind. Some people say, "I can never succeed." So the seed is sown. "I can't do this, I know." It's again another seed you're sowing in you.

Or you consider yourself as unlucky. "I am very unlucky, I have never been lucky in my life." If you say ten times that you have never been lucky in your life, then you get a lot of weeds in you which will take over everything. We should never say, "I have never been lucky." Oh, you have been so lucky!

So we should pull out all these weeds from our mind; through trust. What do you think of it? Hmm?

Surrender means what? Letting go of all these things. If you let go of all judgments about yourself, that is called surrender. Do you get it? All judgments about yourself, you can drop them, this is surrender.

If you understand this, you will gain a lot of self-confidence. Confidence will grow. Every doubt about yourself will disappear. This knowledge is very precious.

You should always remember this. Unless you go from grumbling to gratitude, in your life, unless you start considering yourself as lucky, the seeds of misfortune will remain there. "I am not lucky with money, I am not lucky with relationships, I am not lucky in my work." Pull all this completely out of your head.

– How to pull out the seeds that are already there?

– Let go. Surrender. Say, "I surrender to the Divine, to the Master. My life is very lucky now, I have found a way." This is the beginning. "I am very lucky." Start with this, "I am very lucky." You are thus sowing the seed of one who is lucky. "I am lucky!"

– Guruji, in your work, do you have to bear people's suffering?

– When you love something, then nothing is hard to bear. If you love your work, it doesn't matter. What gives you the most joy is the hardest.

Suffering is created by our own mind. Pain is inevitable; suffering is optional. A smile that cannot be removed by any event is a real smile. Suffering is remembering the events, chewing them again and again. In the slums, people have the strength, the courage and the dedication to move on despite their problems. To have compassion is natural; to have pity is degrading life.

In the world, there is suffering, and there is a cause for this suffering. You can't be unhappy without a reason. You can be happy with or without a reason, but you can't be unhappy without a reason.

Buddha said, "The first truth is... suffering exists, the world is suffering." When this truth is crystallised in your mind and in your experience, then only are you able to see what is beyond this world, this something, this spirit, which is joy.

There are only two ways to learn in life. The first one is to observe the world around you and to learn, through others' suffering, through their petty occupations, that it is a waste. The second way is to experiment by yourself and discover that life is painful. There is no third possibility.

The more sensitive you are, the less you need to experience all the suffering yourself: you can observe those who experience it and become wise. If it isn't possible, never mind, you will experience it yourself! You will come out of it complete and wiser. For sure! Life is immortal. The only question is to learn the lesson, sooner or later. Suffering exists, one cannot deny it, and there is a cause for this suffering; that is the second truth.

The third truth is, "It is possible to put an end to suffering." If suffering was your nature, you could not eliminate it, but it isn't the case; it is possible to come out of suffering.

The fourth truth is, "There is a way, a road, a path to come out of suffering." The path indicated by Buddha was an eightfold one. The path of right practice, right meditation, right serenity, right vision, right Samadhi, right silence.

Buddha was born at a very interesting time in India's history. Unlike Jesus, Buddha was born at a time when India was prosperous and had attained peaks in philosophical thinking. People were highly educated and prosperous. In a very intellectual society, people think they know without knowing. They think they know it all, but they haven't gone through experience.

It was the case in India. The highest philosophy was already available, within hand's reach: yoga, Vedanta, darshans, meditation. People thought they knew everything about these subjects, but they were stuck in their heads.

Buddha called this path, "Come and see, come and experience." He could not discuss and get the upper hand with these people who thought they knew it all. A discussion is a discussion, you can extend it forever, it is limitless. So Buddha said, "See, I suggest you try four very simple exercises: observe the body, observe the sensation, observe the movement of the mind, observe your own nature. Observation. Come, I have a very simple technique to offer you, come and sit! Put aside any other concept. You can have your own concepts, whatever you want, but come and see; sit down and observe." Intelligent people always like this kind of talk, they like to do something practical, so many people came to him. [...] People should be open, innovating, ready to listen and not have a closed mind – it is the sign of an advanced society. So Buddha spoke and taught.

Ten thousand people came and sat in peace, observed, meditated and were freed in attaining enlightenment. Ten thousand people, it had never been seen before in History.

– Can everybody in this life succeed in transforming all their possibilities, all their sufferings into happiness?

– *Yes, it is possible, very possible.*

– In a week?

– *In one instant even, it's possible! You're never given a problem that you can't solve. Every problem you encounter allows you to achieve your capacities, to discover how much more you can pull out from yourself, to what extent you can create more talents, skills and joy. Problems stimulate our mind and intelligence. When do we really need our intelligence? When a problem arises. Without any problems, we would be like cows. Cows don't have any problems. They chew grass, drink water, and sleep. In the same way, if your life is too quiet, without any challenges, all you will do is eat and drink, and become more and more lethargic. The Divine has given you a brain so that you are alert, and every problem is there to make the brain work.*

Instead of that, we do the reverse: we don't use our brain and we lose ourselves in complications, or we use it to create problems rather than solving them! When we have a problem, instead of looking for a solution, we make a mountain of it, or we imagine the worst. Don't give back to God an unused brain!

Now and then, touches of inconvenience happen. Do you know why? To make you aware of the pleasant moments. Suppose you've never any unpleasant moments in your life, you would never have had any pleasant ones either. You wouldn't have known what enjoyment is. Your life would have been heavy and dull! You would have become like a stone! So, to keep you awake, nature gives you a little pinch now and then, here and there. It adds spice to your life. Accept it.

God does the same to you; now and then he gives you a pinch. Then you start crying, but look back and tell me honestly, every time you have had difficulties, haven't you been pulled through? Every time you have had problems, you have found a helping hand. Someone pulls you through.

I don't mean you should spring now into the ocean to see if somebody is going to save you. No, what I mean is, you don't have to be afraid in life. There is always a relief. Everything that happens to us is there to make our life less dull and tastier. That is why God – creation, eternity – is called mad, crazy. You see, there is no purpose in life. Otherwise, why should people go on being born and go through all these experiences as they are going to die one day? Is this life? Were you born only to pay your bills? If you were only born to pay your electricity, phone bills and rent, life would not be worth living.

Sharing your misfortunes doesn't make them less. But if you don't share your joy, it will decrease. Only share your problems with the Divine, not with your friends, which would only increase the problem. Share your joy with everybody.

– Guruji, many people pray, but for me, it remains somewhat rather enigmatic... What is prayer?

– Prayer is not a practice; it is a happening. When you feel helpless in the depth of your heart, this is prayer. When you are successful and aware of it, a feeling of doership rises in you.

I don't mean to say we should all be unhappy in order to pray. But when this feeling of helplessness overcomes you, prayer can really be authentic. This authentic prayer can bring a power in us capable of transforming life.

When you succeed in doing something, you are very happy and proud of it. But you don't need to be happy about your success. If you have made a success of something through your own effort, it means you had the capacity to do it. What pride is there in achieving something you are capable of! Such a success doesn't really mean anything.

Everything that is worth having in life comes from prayer. And prayer can only happen when you know something is beyond your means and you cannot achieve it.

Who can pray? Only those who feel helpless. If you think you can do something, you can achieve something, no need to pray. But when you become conscious of your incapacity, when you become conscious of the futility of your efforts, when you become conscious that you are insignificant, that your existence is insignificant in the world, then you can pray. It is just a matter of perception. If you continue thinking you are a very important person, very influential, or that you achieve great things, prayer cannot happen in you.

For thousands of years, many people have come on this earth, and have disappeared without trace. Among the thousands and thousands of galaxies, the billions of stars, the whole universe, you are nothing. You are not even a particle, on this scale. How can one be so blind not to see this reality? See yourself on the scale of the whole universe. An intelligent man can conceive this; he will feel very acutely that he is nobody, that he is nothing.

Every person is facing this reality. There are times when you feel great because you have achieved something. You say, "Yes, I did this!" At other times, all your efforts fail and you don't get the results you were hoping for. So, you have two options: either to brood, feel upset, depressed, unhappy, or use the circumstances to pray. Become conscious of your insignificance and transform the situation into a prayer. Every moment of helplessness is a golden opportunity to pray.

You can think you are doing things in your life. What do you do? You can think you have planned your life. What have you planned? It reminds me of the story of a lizard. Do you know it? No? A lizard had come to visit another lizard, to ask him out for a walk. But the other lizard said, "Oh, but how could I move from here? I am supporting the roof; if I move, the roof will collapse!" We are no better! The lizard may seem very stupid; so are we. We think that we are holding everything, that we insure the cohesion of things.

What have you achieved in your life? Where are you today? You can be a doctor, or an engineer, a teacher, whatever. What have you done to become what you are today? Very honestly and sincerely investigate the events of your life. You have become an engineer or a doctor, or whatever else, when different parameters all fell into place to make you what you are.

Now examine if you have succeeded every time you have put in effort. Many times you have given 100% of your energy and yet, you have failed, haven't you? And how many times, putting no effort, have you not failed, but just gone through the situation?

There must be a limit to ego.

The thirst for the Presence is called prayer. It becomes a plea. Whether or not there is a God to whom you are praying, your simple 'state of praying' is enough. The first step consists in 'feeling' the Presence. The second is to realise that you 'are' the Presence. You have become one with this Presence; you are not distant from it, 'you are the Presence'.

You sing the bhajan *'Om Bhagawan...' What is this 'Bhagawan'? It is the presence, the Lord. What is the meaning of 'Lord'? Lord 'is' the Presence.*

The real meaning of your life is prayer. Your very Being becomes prayer. Your walk becomes prayer, your work becomes prayer. Everything you look at with gratitude in your heart becomes prayer. Look at a tree and feel grateful. Try to feel some gratefulness. Stand in front of the ocean, and admire the immensity, the depth and the huge and impressive waves rising up. You feel then a very deep emotion in your heart; this is prayer. You are praying, "Oh, I am totally fulfilled to be in this world, at this place."

Silence is the most beautiful form of prayer. Prayer could not come up through words. Prayer is everywhere and everything is prayer. Your breath is prayer and when you are simply sitting fully conscious, aware, your whole life is prayer and your seated body is in prayer.

When you see people grumbling, with bloodshot eyes, go into prayer and feel happy inwardly. When you see someone shouting, screaming, and punching themselves, let a prayer come up in you, "Oh, how beautiful. What a beautiful action, what a great action; this is wonderful." Are there questions?

– Is prayer asking for something?

– When you have something to ask for, prayer is a request. When you have received, your prayer is to be thankful.

But prayer is not claiming something from God: "God, heal this, heal my leg, heal my eyes, heal my stomach, heal my tummy!" You are violating all the laws of nature, and then you go and ask God for healing; as if God was your servant, you ask, demand, order. And then you say, "If you do this for me, then I shall play this part, or do this thing!" You are blackmailing the Supreme Existence, the Supreme Intelligence. This is impossible! It is all a game of your mind. Have a look at it.

Praying is not demanding. Prayer is not asking for something. No. Prayer is gratitude. Prayer is being in the totality; it is to be conscious of the love God showers on us at every moment, of the enormous waves of love which eternity blows in you. If you are intelligent, you cannot be asleep.

– Does God come first, or does prayer come first?

– *"Let me know God, and then, I will pray? And whom should I pray to? Without knowing to whom I am praying, how can I pray? No, no, no, this is not it. You pray first. Wherever you pray, God is there. You don't have to go to the churches, the temples, the mosques; wherever you pray, there is God. The atheists say, "Let me know God, and then I shall pray." It is like saying, "First I will learn how to swim, then I will go in the water." No! Prayer comes first. You pray! Praying is being grateful for everything you have been granted. With eyes, ears, a nose, you have been granted the whole world; feel gratitude for all that! Feel some gratitude for everything you have now. This is prayer."*

– Why should I pray?

– *This is not a question at all. "Why should one pray?" No! If you have prayed, you know how futile the question is. It is like asking why should one live? Why should one want peace? Why should I want to be happy? Why should I want to give love and be loved? Prayer is the blossoming of your life. The nature of an evolved human being is prayer. Prayer is a sign of evolution. If you aren't grateful, you might as well be an animal. Even animals are grateful. Everything in Creation is grateful. There is something fundamentally wrong in you if you are not full of gratitude. If you don't recognize the presence of infinity around you, then you are not normal, you are not established in your true nature.*

Nature has induced pain in your life in very many ways, and gives rise to a quality of prayer through it. When we find excuses and discreetly sneak away – we are very good at sneaking away! – We miss every opportunity to pray and we try to remain in our little shell.

To know to whom to pray is not at all a priority. It doesn't matter to whom you pray. Whether it is to Rama, Krishna, Jesus, Mohammed, Allah, it doesn't matter! Prayer depends on the one who is praying. Prayer depends on you and you alone. If you are there, it is enough. You are more than enough for a prayer to happen.

Devotion is a very intimate feeling. It is very personal. You cannot simulate prayer, you cannot copy prayer! Prayer happens spontaneously! You cannot just implore something and keep on chanting and reciting it. This is not prayer. Prayer is very original. If it isn't original, it isn't prayer.

Prayer is very personal and intimate. It is not repeating something. You don't have to repeat a thousand times, or a hundred times: "Ram, Ram, Ram, Ram, Jesus, Jesus, Jesus, Jesus." No! When you call from the depth of your heart, this is prayer. Each devotee, each saint has been singing his own words. There have been many songs before Mira, before Kabir, but they have not sung the same old songs. They have connected themselves very personally to God. There are no rules. All rules atrophy prayer.

There are no rules in love. When you love somebody, you have no obligation to sit on this side, or on that side, to love in this or that manner. Nobody goes to school or to college nor reads any books to learn how to love. You don't have to become a student to love. Love, devotion are your own nature.

Nobody else can pray for you. Your prayer is your own prayer. But you can be helped.

– And in this case, if needed, can words help?

– Prayer is not possible though words. Certainly not. Words can never reach that source where prayer dawns. You can use words to bring up a feeling. It is in the depth of feeling that prayer starts. So don't worry about words or terms. Prayer doesn't come from

outside to go towards something far away from you. Prayer is starting to become conscious of the Presence, to feel the presence in the depth of your feelings.

– What is the best time to pray?

– You can pray at any time, there is no fixed hour when you should get up and pray. And it is not necessary to pray in a particular way. I know a man who got up when everybody was sleeping at home and started to sing and chant in a higher and higher pitch at three in the morning! He disturbed the whole household. His wife and children were very upset about it. You shouldn't pray like that, so early in the morning or very late at night. At every moment, you can pray. Praying is not a mechanical action. It should dawn from within you. It is a spontaneous happening which takes place when your life matures. The more mature you are, the more devotion you have.

Praying is not a serious thing. You don't need to be sad to pray. Prayer is joy! Prayer is rejoicing, it's a game! If you have once tasted the joy, the ecstasy of praying, you will never forget it. A devotee jumps at every opportunity to pray, seizes every chance to dance, every opportunity to let God appear. This is evolution, isn't it?

– What to do when prayer becomes mechanical?

– You stop as soon as you feel it. But don't analyse yourself so! Sit down, prayer just happens, like in meditation. This feeling to be at home is a delicate, tender sensation... It is a great force, to be used properly. There is a strength beyond emotion in silence. If you base your life on emotion, you will be ruined. If medical students follow their emotions, there won't be a single doctor! Your life is based on commitments towards yourself more than on emotions. Most people are slaves of their emotions. "I feel like this, like that". Never mind, I want to do something good, to bring good things to people.

– I lost all enthusiasm and confidence; how to deal with the feeling of uselessness which derives from it?

– You cannot force enthusiasm and confidence to come back. The more you try to gain your confidence back again, the more your condition becomes disastrous... When you feel useless, use this time to be in prayer, in deep meditation. This is what happens when you

feel very gentle, very humble, very subtle, deep, soaking in a state of diffuse love. Feel that. Use this time to be in prayer. Tell yourself, "I am nothing, not good for anything. Take care of me; I am here for You. I am part of You."

Use this opportunity to be in prayer, and you will see that soon you will regain your confidence and enthusiasm beyond what the craziest imagination could let you hope for, because you have become part of the Divine. The Divine is all confidence, all enthusiasm.

The real prayer is when you are happy, when you sing and dance! This is real meditation. Meditation is a fountain of joy and ecstasy. People glorify suffering. The Divine prefers your happiness by far.

Real laughter is a real prayer.

There are two things that hamper you: the fear not to have what you want, and the fear to lose what you have. This is stupid, absurd, everything will be given.

♦

For this New Year's Eve party, an international singing contest is organized at the *ashram!* Gurudev Sri Sri Ravi Shankar asks the participants to come on stage and present a song or a typical dance from their country. We have now got the habit to introduce the Master to the most joyful or sacred songs of the national repertoires. As he doesn't really fancy the sad or nostalgic tunes, he remembers first of all the Latin-American or Italian music rhythms. To hear them sung, he strikes up the song first, *"O sole mio..." Or, "Eh, bonita...!"* Everybody is mimicking the *Passionata...* Gurudev, easy to please listener, laughs, and makes every effort to remember the words, in order to be able to sing them when he pleases. This leaves us with enjoyable scenes to imagine for the future... He can also have fun in improvising a jazzy *bhajan...*

Every country has its turn, with its 'hit-song'. We realise many songs already belong to the international cultural heritage. The song recital becomes an opportunity to learn other songs, so that the regular 'course goers' can sing in many languages, included in Chinese. From the French, Gurudev Sri Sri Ravi Shankar likes to hear a Christian hymn, "Ecoute, écoute, les pas du Seigneur vers toi..." ("Listen; listen to the steps of the Lord coming towards you..."). As everybody is not a fan of this song, the French will sing tonight, "Y'a d'la joie!" by Charles Trenet. Personally, I try to escape it in sneaking nearer to the Israelis... We sing more and more Hebrew songs during *satsangs*. Even when they are not that joyful, Gurudev is not insensitive to them. In the end, he sings along, *"Shalom...Shalom..."* As if he was saying, with long suspension dots, "Peace...Peace... Ah, goodness!"

The show allowed us to approach midnight with the pleasant feeling of having had an escape outside the ashram doors. Now we feel again the privilege of being inside these ashram doors to welcome the New Year in the atmosphere so heavy with meaning created by the Master.

He says,

"This year is fortunate because you are living at this time. You are not living for yourself, but for the world. When you are living for the sake of the world, the world is fortunate! Whatever the world needs or wants, you are there for that. So this year is fortunate that you should be on the earth at this point of time... Usually, people make a wish for the New Year. This year, make no wish! Let the New Year celebrate you! If it wants to bring you nicer things, let it! Usually you are lost in celebration. When you let time celebrate you, you are a witness amidst celebration. You keep smiling as ever. A poor man celebrates the New Year once a year; a rich man celebrates every day. But the richest man celebrates every moment! How rich are you? Do you celebrate once a year? once a month? every day? If you celebrate every moment, you are the Lord of this creation. Review the past year. This will be your homework. What have you done? What have you achieved? Have you been useful? Sit down on New Year's Day for one hour, and think of each week, a minute per week, and see the progress of the year in less than an hour. With a flower, offer the whole year to the Divine.

The message for the New Year is, "Simply be!" which doesn't mean be lazy... No! Be very busy... And just be!"

Whereas outside, the celebration in towns and houses is at its climax, the feverishness here has come down; the passage to the New Year happens in silence and quietness. The voice of the Master leads the community in meditation, eyes closed, through the mythical frontier of time. Counting the last minutes...

"New possibilities are opening up to this new age... Welcome these new possibilities... Four and a half minutes to go... Four minutes... Just two minutes... One minute only! Thirty seconds... Chant Om!"...

The tremendous vibration of the thousand voices seems to bless the entire earth, and greets the next three hundred and sixty-five coming "today".

Tonight and tomorrow, remind yourself of all the people to whom you must be grateful for something. Think of what has been given to you by them.

And Gurudev adds, *"Before going to sleep, cover yourself with a blanket of grace. Wake up tomorrow with a smile..."*

Amateur fireworks are organized outside, in the snow. Everybody gathers to watch them. But Gurudev goes up to the first floor to see it... I followed him with a few others. Elbow against elbow at the windowsill, we overhang the group of disciples, with their heads raised now towards him, now towards the plumes of sparks banging in the black night. So near the forest, the powder is thundering with a power amplified by the resonance chamber of the trees, so much so that it releases a mini avalanche between the trunks. Everything seems to me very beautiful. Utter happiness! Gurudev is resting his shoulder against mine, as he often does with the clarity of his innocence. I look at him; his face is serious, displeased. He worries, "*Oh... We are going to wake the birds up*!" To make his intentions known to the firework operators, he goes away towards his apartment, and says again, "*We are disturbing the birds*!" Nobody other than him had thought about that. Even in an atmosphere of celebration, when everybody seems caught up in fun, the Master keeps an attention and a sensitivity to everything around him. To be celebrating and feeling in the same time; he constantly gives us something to learn!

On January 1st, Gurudev Sri Sri Ravi Shankar will say, *"The general theory of evolution presents human development as linear. The idea is that man, in the beginning, was a barbarian and uncivilized being, and that with time, he gradually became more civilized and better off. Let's not rush to conclusions. If you go back to the first human civilizations, you will discover that there existed then very intelligent people. At no time has nature deprived man of civilization, culture and refinement. Of course, at certain times, life has been more civilized than at others.*

Time was once perceived as a wheel or a circle, rather than linear. A circle means you always come back to the same point; from the Dark Age, you come back to a golden age. With time, the knowledge of one civilization gets lost, then is rediscovered later. What we today call the 'New Age' is nothing new; it is all very old.

The transition from old age to the present New Age is a passage from prestige to self-esteem. Look at the past centuries, or even the last decades; the values were different. People liked to show off, or were very concerned by what people would think about them. With the beginning of the New Age, we see these values change. In the old days, people believed in a God somewhere in Heaven. With the New Age, the idea that God is in you, that you are the Divine is becoming dominant.

People in the New Age speak of angels and consciousness; they emphasize values, love, meditation. A few decades ago, if someone had spoken about love, people would have thought it was phoney, unscientific! The former age was more head oriented. The New Age is more oriented towards the heart. But people are still seeking something more substantial. A large part of the so-called knowledge of the New Age is not structured; it is as we could put it, a little bit hare-brained.

During the former period, the accent was on things such as pesticides and antibiotics. With the New Age, the accent is now back on natural and organic farming. To be close to nature and use natural remedies based on herbs is an ancestral knowledge. A few decades ago, yoga was considered very bizarre and not at all a proper thing to do. To sit down and crouch on the floor was not a common thing. Today yoga is very much in fashion. Wherever you go, you see people practicing yoga to keep fit, and scientists have studied its benefits. What was once considered as primitive has become very meaningful, and what we thought was very advanced technology has proved to be very destructive. This is why I say time is not linear, it is a wheel, a circle and it reverses back to itself.

People consider old times as barbarian, but look at the toys children use today, are they more refined? more civilized? Look at movies and television, do they show any sign of refinement? We are coming back to a new age, because time has arrived at its darkest point. You cannot fall further down! This era has gone to the end of barbarism, it cannot fall further down. When you are at the bottom of the wheel, you can only go back up! This is why people are becoming more conscious of values. Parents are more concerned with their children and their value systems; they are wondering how to nurture the human values in everybody. This is exactly what the ancient rishis, wise men and saints did thousands and thousands of years ago. You can trace them in Ayurveda, yoga and many other texts relating to the same principles, in a deeper and more methodical way than what we today call 'New Age thinking'.

I think we are lucky to live in this period, because we are leaving behind barbarism for an era more oriented towards confidence, love, compassion, service and solicitude for others. Not only are we more thoughtful and caring for others, but we have also started to take care of the planet, which had not been the case until recently. Environment has become a favourite topic in the last years. A few decades ago, nobody cared about environment. The word itself was unfamiliar whereas it is today very popular. The main topic of discussion was business; love was secondary. Today, love is in first place. We can speak about love without feeling shy or ashamed. Emotions can today be expressed, while one was not allowed to express them a century ago. This is particularly true for men. In the past, a man could not express his emotions, it was considered bad. Today, expressing one's emotions is accepted, and even encouraged.

The best attitude is to combine the old and the new, to adapt them to modern life, and to current situations. When people started to invent planes, for instance, it took them decades before arriving at the right model. There were many obstacles to overcome before a plane could take off, because no blueprint existed from the past.

What the knowledge from ancient times offers us is a blueprint from which we can base our own research. The path towards the inner awakening is an individual quest. Everybody must walk their own path and ancient knowledge can guide us. This knowledge will be like lanterns lighting our way from time to time."

♦

Seeing the sadness in the eyes is enough to let you know that the time of departure is near. The master has no consideration for this sentimentality, "*Get busy*!" he says. "*You have so much to do*!" Somebody asks him, "I feel very happy and stable here, during the course. How do I keep this balance when I am back at home?

– Only plants need to be watered and nurtured. Trees are stronger and don't need to be watered.

– Guruji, me too. When I am at the *ashram*, when I meet the people here, I feel very good. But at work, emotions change. I can't be the same in my office. Why is it so?

– I think I should go and see you at work! [Laughter] You have received the knowledge; see how you can apply it outside.

– Guruji, when I live in the *ashram*, I don't feel like going back home; so my family doesn't allow me to come to the *ashram*. What should I do?

– Make your house an ashram. *What do you find in the ashram? Peace, love, joy, knowledge... Create a similar atmosphere at home. When you have guests at home, you usually discuss mundane things like money, clothes, jewels, etc... Talk rather about knowledge. Create such an atmosphere that your uests will go home full, joyful.*

– But Guruji, we don't have your *darshan*[1] at home!"

– I am everywhere. When you are joyful, have a look in the mirror, you will find me."

1 Literally, 'vision'; the Master's power, looking at the disciple, to pass awakening.

Before heading to the airport, the Master guides a last meditation. But by the time he arrives at his car, he finds it already surrounded with disciples. Instead of scolding them, Gurudev uses a trick. He pretends that he is going for a walk and starts walking down the road. Clusters of people immediately cling to him, happy to enjoy his presence a little longer. The road winds down and down... People are starting to wonder how long it will take to walk back up... Gurudev, in his sandals, bounds down the slope, almost running, without throwing a glance behind him and without caring about his disciples in the middle of the road, where a car might come, he who is usually so protective. Besides, strangely enough, no car does go past. But where is he going? Far behind, a car moves near and insists on passing, until it reaches the Master, who gets in the car, waves good-bye and disappears around the bend...

On the plane, in a comfortable seat, Gurudev Sri Sri Ravi Shankar is finally alone. He rests and meditates. Nobody here really knows who he is...

Meanwhile, in India, people are getting busy to welcome him... And to smother him with more love!

8

THE *GURU*'S INDIA

THE VOLUNTEERS HAVE SLEPT VERY LITTLE. They only had a week to oraganise the Divya Satsang where Gurudev Sri Sri Ravi Shankar will come right after landing. But the tour de force has been successful. The huge waste ground assigned to the public event is now ready to welcome the venerated *guru*.

In town, banners over the main roads, and series of notices on the walls have announced the event in the middle of advertisings for the most motley. Once in a while, the beautiful face of the Hindu saint emerges from a slightly suggestive picture of a film... Never mind. At the crossroads, giant portraits of the Master, resembling as much as the cardboard allows it, overhang the assembled automobiles and *rickshaws*. Furnace, dust, uproar, strong smells and all colours, the dense crowd of poor people smiles, be that as it may, at its fantastic hell.

Immoderation is the yardstick of India. So, the reception organised in honour of the one that everybody here calls 'Guruji' is a big one: a gigantic platform designed to welcome the great number of musicians, dancers and V.I.P. guests, a lotus-shaped throne perched at the top of stairs, several metres above the ground; an elephant band in ceremonial dress which puts the knowledge, living and strong, under the safe guard of Ganesh, the Master's favourite god.

No debauchery of expensive things. At most the decorum has reached the art of celebrating with very little: these green birds flying in the shape of arches of triumph are only cable-knitted bamboo leaves; the sumptuous scenery is only dressed with paper and flowers – hangings, panels and carpets are made of roses, carnations and jasmines... India doesn't skimp over this luxury offered in abundance by nature... The bare ground has become a *made in India* 24 karat gold love case.

Three hundred thousand persons walk into the open air enclosure and take their places on a simple newspaper sheet put down right on the ground, in a quietness that already tells a lot about the respect they have for the *guru*. There is no medical unit planned and practically no police forces other than the volunteers themselves for this meeting that puts together religious communities often at daggers drawn in this region. A lot of Muslims and a lot of Hindus, mostly. But there will be no incidents. The police don't even think of it, as Guruji is here.

Celebrities come to relate about the victories won over themselves, thanks to their meeting with Gurudev Sri Sri Ravi Shankar. They follow one another in front of the mike to pass the message with simplicity. It is Rhéa Dutt, one of the most famous film stars of India, an Art of Living teacher between two shoots, who, after signing autographs, sees to the conference introduction.

Christian nuns, sitting on the platform in the first row, also bring their support to the work that 'Guruji has come to do on our planet'. One of them is also a teacher for the Foundation.

♦

India has listened to its Masters for a short time; since misery started to lose ground. "How to pray when you are ravenously hungry?" said Ramakrishna. Since the time when Wise men decided to leave their far retreat, only approachable by a few spiritual seekers, to get involved directly with uneducated populations. After a materialistic experience detour, increasing numbers of privileged persons realise the irreplaceable richness of their forgotten tradition and want to make something other of themselves and their country than mere Western clones. Since the corruption of the world of politics and the deficiency of the system discouraged the population to hope by this way the improvement of its condition...

The main effort of education of the masses depends today on spiritual masters. Who else to remove children from the working market, to jam the women's prostitution machine, to bring care where no doctors go, to clean up villages and houses, to purify waters, organise the picking up of the garbage, bring solar energy? Who else especially to bring back confidence to the resigned populations, crushed under the weight of 'enough is enough'?

To the urgent aid, – less financial than benevolent, because money is lacking, Gurudev Sri Sri Ravi Shankar's humanitarian organisation adds the essential complement of not replacing misery by charity: the learning of human values and harmony in diversity.

Today, you can count the villages revived this way in tens of thousands. And this is still quite little! The job is gigantic, but through hundreds and hundreds of trained volunteers, its evolution has gained ground..

Moreover, India is modernising at great speed: new technologies are spreading almost everywhere, next to utmost poverty. Still there remains, despite everything, something deeply homogeneous, due to an unshakeable, an invincible and unspeakable faith among the people born on this earth.

"If India had been another country, with this poverty and this violence that we have, it would have been torn into pieces. Only in India can you find this strength that holds us altogether... That is all due to the marvellous streams of spirituality that flow in the baratha desam",[1] says Gurudev Sri Sri Ravi Shankar.

The Master devotes most of his time to India. He especially likes these poor people whose brightness of smile and look is never tarnished by any of their misfortunes, the deprived nation whose first impulse remains rather to give than take. Gifted with the most precious divine qualities in today's world, and the most promising if they can find a way to express themselves in the best manner.

Destitution is a reality, but *"unhappiness and sorrow, it is all imagination, says Gurudev. Fear comes from duality, superimposition. I... me... my. Duality is the source of sorrows."*

1 All of the numerous administrative regions and subdivisions in India.

He says that a study about happiness directed recently in different countries ranks India fifth, America forty-third and Germany forty-fourth... He also points out that there are no psychiatric hospitals in India...

♦

Gurudev Sri Sri Ravi Shankar car has just stopped over there, at the end of the carpet unfurled for him. He gets out, with flower necklaces and armfuls of flowers, and he starts the long walk to the stage, preceded by the fight of television and still cameras. The crowd has jumped to see him closer and tries to force the security cordon that doubles the barrier protection. People stretch out their hands to him, call him... A huge clamour of joy comes up from everywhere... He signals to sit down, to stay quiet... On a giant screen, the images of his progression along the main aisle are broadcast... We people celebrate him as a god back home; without hysteria. Guruji has got rid of the flowers as he nimbly steps up onto the platform, but garlands and crowns are arriving again from everywhere... He plays at avoiding them, true to form. Someone puts on his head a kind of symbolic mitre, quite striking for western eyes, which he keeps for the moment.

At the end of a dance show presented by children, the Master says,

"The sound displayed... is music.
The movement displayed... is dance.
The spirit displayed... is meditation.
And the life displayed... is celebration."

He informs that some of the young dancers have broken their foot bracelets and asks them to watch the splinters scattered on the stage. Then he leaves his seat and goes down to pick up himself the little pieces of glass. He carefully paces the platform, still speaking to the crowd... There is so much grace and care in his gesture... A few volunteers run to help him, but he has already seen to it.

During journeys that I will afterwards have the good fortune to take with him, I will see him sometimes intervene to avoid an accident or a drama that he only could sense. One day in Kerala, as he was being assaulted by the devotees and swallowed by the number of those who were pressing round him to receive the '*darshan*', a breach was made in the compact shield of people behind whom he had completely disappeared: I could see his face that indicated to me the flame of a little oil lamp down by my feet, ready to set fire to my dress, that nobody next to me had been able to bring to my attention. How many times will I see him thus avoiding for me the consequences of careless mistakes? And how many opportunities to note that he always watches over each of us?

Charismatic and informal, Gurudev Sri Sri Ravi Shankar walks on the stage, holding the mike... He speaks as often as possible in the language of the area, mostly in Hindi, the most widespread, or in *Kannada*. Many Indians don't understand English, and the Master doesn't know all the spoken languages in India[1] – even though he generally understands them enough to denounce the translating mistakes...

For the ones who worry about the generalisation of English and the *risk of losing the national languages*, he answers,

"For two hundred years, the British have governed our country, but they couldn't destroy even one of its languages. Have faith that none of the languages will be destroyed. Our Hindu culture is from such a special essence that it cannot be destroyed. A tarred road can be damaged, but not a dirt track. It's been there for millions of years."

In *satsangs* in India, Gurudev Sri Sri Ravi Shankar comments occasionally on some habits dating back from the English colonisation – like wearing a tie for young schoolchildren. He explains the origin, showing the absurdity and the hindrance that it mentally represents for the children... He encourages us to renounce it. He also explains the meaning of Indian customs.

One asks, "Depending on the religions, some burn the corpses after death, others bury them. What is more proper?

– *See the origin of the customs: Islam, Judaism were born in the desert. The desert is dry sand, trees are rare. It is practically impossible to burn corpses there. In such circumstances, it was better*

1 Fifteen principal languages and hundreds of dialects

to bury them. The sand would decompose the bodies. Five to ten thousand years ago, India was much greener than it is now. There was a huge amount of woods. So, the best method was to burn the corpses reducing them into ashes. We didn't have that much land: the whole ground would have been a cemetery. Cremation doesn't damage the environment. Nature goes back to nature. Nowadays, electrical cremation is what's best. It is an environment-friendly method. Today, we end up to a unique culture.

– Why is there a class difference between the higher and the lower castes?

– In our course, there is only one class, the one of love. No differences of castes. Where there are slums, where there is no spiritual consciousness, do a satsang, *give* prasad,[1] *do* seva. *Politics divides people, Vedanta establishes the contact, connects each one to the knowledge. With hate, there is no peace and neither is there any progress. Surrender to Vedanta. Vedanta teaches us that everything is just One! So many saints have worked for the elimination of caste differences... Do you know about the book entitled 'Heritage of Dalits?'*

– You say that God is amusement. So, why the expression, 'fear of God?'

– Not in this country. Here, God is always in leela, *which means in Sanskrit at the same time life and game, as in 'Krishnaleela'. Singing, dancing and acting are part of our spirituality, but we seem to have lost the meaning of entertainment. The fear of God is a Christian concept. We only have devotion, no apprehension.*

– Why are Saints most of the time men?

– Because it is from men that saintliness demands the most! But don't think that only men are saints... Male saints have only become more famous. So, many mothers and wives have saintly lives in the houses and the villages..."

The celebration of knowledge in great ceremony in public *satsangs* in India appeals to Gurudev Sri Sri Ravi Shankar. It's very revealing of the space that people give to spirituality in their lives.

1 Blessed food.

But the dimension of the welcome that is reserved for him doesn't change his attitude one iota. In these almost papal surroundings, Gurudev moves at ease, natural and happy.

At some point, he turns towards his seat perched between sky and earth and, as if he was discovering a little bit of excessive solemnity, he says, "*Oh, how big this armchair is! Bah, it's not important... And what a beautiful decoration! So many flowers! Nice! Flowers or no flowers, everything is fine. Your smiling faces are like flowers that I really appreciate very much.*" He takes boxes of candies and asks a devotee to go and offer them to the security people. "*They have been hungry for quite a long while.*" he says.

In India, he is more paternalistic, more of a teacher. He may occasionally scold a bit, appear a little firmer on the directions to take. More critical too than he allows himself to be in foreign countries. To manifest authority and love, strength and even, eventually, anger, is in this country what is expected from *gurus*. A nation of a billion human beings on which weigh centuries old natural disasters, economic handicaps, and war threats, needs spiritual guides who are full of compassion, but ones who have 'some spirit'...

"You say, 'India is a sleeping lion'. When will he awake?

– *He's waiting for you [laughter]. We need to waken up our people. We are not aware enough of our own richness and of our own qualities. We don't even know, for most of us, how many Upanishads are at our disposal. Western people, on the other hand, have understood their value and appreciate it. Do we have to wait for their appreciation to become aware of it and wake up? For example, the printing rights of the Yoga Vasistha belong to a New York agency...*

– Could India, with all its treasures of knowledge, become the worldwide number one?

– *Of course! The Indian culture says that the world is all ours. 'Vasudhaiva Kutumbakam' means that the earth is a family. Number one worldwide? Yes, you can, we can! All the potential is there... We have brilliant minds, a deep wisdom... We have all the resources, but we stay stuck in tiny small things!*

– India is spiritually rich, but economically poor. What can we do? What's the solution against economic and cultural terrorism?

– Think global, buy local. Adopt the good things in each culture, but never forget your own culture – food, dressing, dance, etc.

– Can we resist globalisation?

– Operate it skillfully.

– Give us spiritual principles to revive the industry...

– See your weak points and improve them. In India, weak points are a lack of unity, imperfect marketing strategies, bad quality negotiations, lack of self-confidence, a slave mentality, low self-esteem. During a conference in the States, I met a fragile woman who worked in a small traditional handkerchief business. She was supposed to say in seventeen points why the handkerchief that she had made was the best in the whole world. After all, it only was a handkerchief... But the way she was introducing it made all the difference! She was confident, and so proud to explain why her handkerchief business – by its size, its colour, its seams, its corners... – had, in seventeen points, the qualities that made it the most beautiful handkerchief in the world! When you are so proud, how could you not succeed? In our country, the so-called journalists and the so-called communists, and the so-called intellectuals have systematically sabotaged the confidence that we had in our own heritage. It has been systematically belittled!

– How to welcome a disagreeable remark?

– Don't welcome it. Otherwise, what happens? You lose your sleep. Don't do anything that disturbs your comfort. If you can respect yourself, then you won't be upset. An elephant is not scared by the barking of a dog. If you are distressed, who can say they have succeeded?

– How to eradicate political corruption?

– Who elects the politicians apart from us? So, before electing someone, we must examine what kind of candidate they are, what their career path is like...

– Must we vote?

– You must vote. When there is an election in India, if I'm lucky enough to be there, I never miss the chance to vote. It's my duty. You must enlarge your vision. But don't let politics do your head in... They are only people talking about one another. Why pay attention to that? Don't let politics divert you from the path. However, if you're afraid of politics, you won't be able to succeed in the spiritual field. You have to get over the barrier of politics. It's a test of your strength, of your commitment and of how much you are centred. You can't avoid politics, but you can let yourself be consumed by it or not, it all depends on you. There was politics between the twelve apostles and with Buddha. And Krishna was up to the neck into politics. And you say that you don't want politics? The more you will reject it, the more it will invade your mind. When you can recognise politics in any meeting or satsang group, it is a blessing for you to go back to the centre, deep into yourself. You can do that without blaming the group, running away from it, or 'sneaking off'. This can develop your ability to act and to become detached.

To get involved in politics presents many advantages. It underlines the diversity of people. It confronts you with different points of view, approaches and tendencies. It increases your ability to communicate and act. It makes you centred again and detached. It gives you a shake and makes you equal to the knowledge. It makes you more tolerant and ready to take things as they come. It makes you aware that life is only a game. Get over the threshold of politics and come to the Divine. The strong will get through smiling, and the weak will moan.

Why has only the Mahatma Gandhi got independence when so many people as intelligent as him didn't succeed? This is all due to the satsangs he was giving mornings and evenings. He was making people sing bhajans: it was a major strength for our independence. So, companions, give as many satsangs as possible...

– How can India speak of non-violence when they are in possession of nuclear arms?

– Who will speak of non-violence other than someone who feels strong? Only the 'strong' one is qualified to talk about non-violence. The weak one will not talk about it. Have everything you need to

defend yourself and your country, and then speak about non-violence. So, we have the nuclear arms and we feel strong: this way we can speak about non-violence...

– When will peace arrive?

– *Now. Peace is in the present. Peace is always with us. Somewhere in the world, right now, it's morning, isn't it?*

If you are peaceful, you can transform the non-peace around you into peace.

Violence brings noise about, whereas non-violence is born from silence. Violent people make a lot of noise; they shout their violence out. On the other hand, non-violent people are discreet. But the time has come for the non-violent to be heard, so that violence declines. The message of non-violence has to become high and clear, so that it can be perceived very early in life.

– When you see terrorism and injustice everywhere, do you advise people to be quiet and serene?

– *Being quiet doesn't mean staying passive! When you are calm, you are able to make intelligent decisions and interfere at the right moment. Be calm and dynamic.*

– When does violence end?

– *Violence ends where love starts.*

– Can we be right making war?

– *The worst act of reason is war. Every war has a reason, and reason justifies the war. That's how people that get into a war reason. But reason has its limits, and when the reason changes, the justification falls apart. All the reasons invoked for all these wars appear legitimate to some narrow minds and for a limited time. From there, war becomes unavoidable on this planet.*

Human beings are the only ones to make war. No other species in the Creation gets involved into war or mass destruction, because they have no reason to do it; animals have their preys and let things be. But the human kind, from time immemorial, has been into wars, because man lives from reason. Man finds a reason for each one of its acts and justifies it and as the reasons change, the justifications collapse. Man must transcend reason, only then will he be able to realise Divinity. Then he will not get involved anymore in wars. It's only when people become reasonable, get over hate and give access to a higher consciousness that it will be possible to stop war.

– Why are there wars?

– *Wars have always taken place on one side or another of the planet, in the whole human history. Like alternating current, war and peace alternate in the world. It is surprising to see how completely devastated countries during the Second World War have developed into economical giants, and this very quickly. Today, Germany, at one time vanquished, supplies food aid and assistance to Russia that has itself been completely wiped out. The same thing happened in Japan, which has accomplished a fantastic leap forward.*

We think that only peace can be profitable to man, but it's not true. War has also its utility! War is useful! It's not desirable but it is not against the laws of nature.

As long as each human being has not reached a higher level of consciousness (the change will happen only on this condition), there will still be wars on this planet. It cannot be otherwise. War is only a tendency of the human being brought to its paroxysm. Watch yourself: people around you bother you all the time, or you cannot stand yourself any more, isn't it? Inside you too, war rages. [...]

As long as violence has not been eradicated from people's minds, war will be unavoidable. But when war has become unavoidable, there is no use saying: "No, I am for peace, I keep quiet." We must get completely involved, keeping in mind that they are the two facets of life. When there is an outside pressure, you gather.

Let's suppose that you're arguing. It is very easy to reconcile by provoking an outside constraint, a danger or a threat coming from somebody else. You will reconcile for sure! It's very obvious in history. Christianity at its beginning has developed in reaction to an outside threat. Facing danger and pressure, a handful of people have united, dedicated and reinforced in the intensity of their fervour.

Whatever country it is, whatever community, even the smallest one, the most disparate, as soon as a mutual outside threat gets more precise, everybody gets together. It's the same thing in a war context; it exalts cooperation and harmony. As in peace.

Something can apparently seem fabulous, but by scraping a little, we discover a flaw, a much less pleasant germ. On the other hand, something very unpleasant on the surface can reveal to be deeply very beautiful.

After Buddha, India had lost the courage to fight. After Mahâbhârata war, a gigantic world war happened. People were so fed up that they didn't want to hear about wars anymore. Buddha arrived and peace settled. They abandoned completely the army and every idea about the protection of the country. Buddha was a king, an emperor, and he had become a 'renouncer'; he had renounced everything. Buddha's example of peace and a renunciation frame of mind was prevailing in the country. It was then very easy for a little group of Arab invaders to conquer this huge territory of seven or eight million souls. And they dominated it for a very long time, not only a year or two! Because everybody was peaceful, in peace! "So what do you want? Go! You want to take the wealth? Okay, go! You want to reign? No problem, sit there! Here's the throne... You can do everything you want!" They gave up; they did not have a spine anymore! The country lost all its forces, all its power, all its beauty, everything! And it has sunk more and more into poverty! There is no comparison between the India of the past and what has remained. In the name of peace, in the name of kindliness, in the name of values, everything has deteriorated. You see?

It is clear that discernment and wisdom are absolutely essential. Wisdom consists in understanding that what cannot be avoided now is a matter for the law, the divine Law. Keep your mind really hollow and empty.

Jesus, he too had said "I came to bring fire. I didn't come to bring peace, but the broadsword". When the broadsword imposes itself, peace is essential. When peace is there, war is still essential.

Some of you think: "What! Guruji advocates war!" No, no! Try to understand what I'm saying: don't tense up against what's happening. The infinite Being is infinite love and if He allows some things to happen, it is because they have their meaning.

You too, you act according to your nature! But I'm certainly not in favour of war!

♦

Today in India, the conflict with Pakistan and the problems related to Islam haunt the minds. In front of the obscurantism of an ideology which drives people to crime, Gurudev Sri Sri Ravi Shankar most of the time just takes up in public, word by word, the sentiments of the fanatics. For example, he says, "*They think that if we kill a Jew, we go to paradise.*" And he bursts into laughter...

The Jews have problems with the Arabs... Christians have problems with the Arabs... Buddhists have problems with the Arabs... There must be a problem somewhere... In the same way as a person can be stuck, a nation can also be stuck..."

The crowds standing in front of him, agitated by hostile feelings towards Pakistan and threatening current affairs, seem to be expecting signs of complicity with the Indian cause from the guru. To rejoin a camp or decide between the responsibilities is not exactly Gurudev Sri Sri Ravi Shankar's way of intervention, and neither is preachifying.

"*It's pitiful,* he says. *The Pakistanis have fallen into their own trap... They have the same root as ours. Their ancestors were used to singing 'Om Nama Shivaya'. But now, they have cut themselves from their roots. They have only lost the knowledge of where they come from. Their history is not only five hundred years old. It's not all their history... That's why there are so many problems. But don't think that all Pakistanis are bad. They are very beautiful persons, a very beautiful people. Only, they follow a delinquent ideology. There is only one world, one divinity and many paths. But we all are 'Om',*[1] *we are all human beings; no difference... Respect all the traditions.*

– How do you define religious fanaticism?

– *Fundamentalism is what doesn't include everything, what separates, divides, judges. It's basically ignorance. In each religion,*

1 'Om' is the original sound, the universal sound that is found in 'Amen', 'Amin', 'Shalom', etc.

there is space for progress, to adapt to the changing times. The religions which don't do it stagnate or regress. It's this refusal to adapt to the modern times, in Islam for example, that recently triggered tragic events. If each religion feels superior to the others and is ready to use force, either psychological or physical, to convert the 'pagans', such events will probably happen again. But all that must not prevent us from seeing the best in each religion be it Islam, Judaism, Buddhism, Hinduism, Christianity or Jainism.

The very structure of the Indian philosophy is such that it can in no way drive anyone to become a fanatic.

– What are the factors that bring people to terrorism? What is its cause?

– Frustration and the rage to reach a goal... Confused emotions... The lack of perspicacity and an impulsive action... The belief in a non- verifiable concept of paradise and merit... A childish concept of God who would favour some and would be wrathful against others, a concept that undermines at the base the omniscience and omnipotence of the Divine...

Terrorism is a purely destructive act, which inflicts sufferings to oneself as well as to others. Perpetrating such an act, the terrorist ridicules human values to achieve their goal.

Terrorism gives rise to an irrational fear in the world, amplifies poverty, suffering and entails the loss of human lives with no apparent advantage. Instead of suggesting solutions, the terrorist looks for destruction as a response. If you only criticise without proposing a solution, just know that the criticism is stemming from the same seed as terrorism.

– What's the difference between the fight for liberty and terrorism?

– If you live under a regime of freedom and you advocate destruction, you are a terrorist. But if you try to obtain your freedom, then you are a combatant for freedom.

– What's the remedy against terrorism?

– To instil a broader vision of life, put life over races, religions and nationality; to teach human values to people: kindness, compassion,

cooperation and moral elevation; to teach methods to eliminate stress and strain; to cultivate the belief that you can attain your noble purposes by pacific and non-violent ways; to arouse a spiritual elevation that can eradicate destructive tendencies...

– How to overcome the after-effects of terrorism?

– *By faith and prayer. In the face of the disaster, anger is unavoidable. To make sure not to react, you must show wisdom and not let yourself be taken over by emotional rage. A mistake cannot be corrected by another mistake. Do your best to dispense a multicultural and multi-denominational education and let spiritual education reach all parts of the globe. For the world will not be a safe place as long as pockets of ignorance – even small – still subsist."*

It's on this calamitous ground, that usually bewilders the leaders in charge of bringing solutions, that Gurudev Sri Sri Ravi Shankar exercises, in the most convincing way, all his influential wise man's know-how. It's him who, negotiating with the Muslim authorities has succeeded in calming down the bloody riots that shook India last spring. He is claimed to be the government's official mediator – which is, of course, not the case – but he is still often induced to calm down the conflicts...

Muslims respectfully discuss with the Hindu wise man. They listen to him. Negotiators know they are safe in every way with him. There is no antagonism, no rivalry, no proselytism, no possible condemnation between them... Moreover, this fair interlocutor has a most rare proven talent: he succeeds in making of yesterday's enemies tomorrow's friends.

Being able to gather those who don't resemble one another and make them feel even better – what he calls 'to recreate harmony in diversity'– Gurudev Sri Sri Ravi Shankar makes of it a demonstration in Kosovo, in Bosnia and in Croatia for example, in Afghanistan, in Kashmir, in South Africa and in all the places where hate poisons the communities. Since 2001, he has delivered his anti-discrimination arm to Pakistan! Proof, if necessary, that there are no crippling conditions.

Gurudev Sri Sri Ravi Shankar, who knows all the mechanisms of the mind and the machinery of violence as a musician knows his scales, is perfectly well understood by the warmongers, to whom his science shows 'coldly' that they are striving towards aims with methods that deprive them of every chance of victory.

One day, an armed group of thirty-five men had suddenly appeared in an *ashram* in Rishikesh, where the *guru* was staying. In this area, gangs are trying to take Westerners hostage, a more profitable bargaining chip than the local population. (For this reason, Gurudev had exactly asked the Europeans and Americans not to come with him). The Master explained to them the qualities of a terrorist: absence of fear, a form of courage, devotion to a cause, enthusiasm, zeal, a sense of sacrifice... "*There is also love: even if they only love their ideal, they love something. Nobody gives their lives for mathematics or geography.*" The qualities, after all, of a military officer. Virtues, unfortunately polluted, "*that create hate and misery for the others*". Gurudev Sri Sri Ravi Shankar says, "*We should learn from the things to never do: put ideas and concepts higher than life; to have a narrow perspective of life and not to honour its diversity...*" Twenty-five among the hostage takers said 'Okay to follow right away an Art of Living course! It's one of the Muslim teachers who conducted it. There was a small problem: the fighters never thought of getting rid of their arms! The teacher only told them that it was necessary not to wear leather on the body for the yoga breathing processes, because it held up the circulation of energy... All of them unbuckled their belts and laid down their equipment in a corner of the room. When the 'bandits' took them back four days later, they were not the same. A revolution they were not expecting had happened in themselves. Not by a miracle, but simply because the teaching of Gurudev Sri Sri Ravi Shankar, that highlights the real value of people, had twenty-five more times confirmed its soundness...

At the time when the disarmed group was having its civilisation course, in the active sense of it, the Danish TV, that has already produced a film about Gurudev Sri Sri Ravi Shankar, called 'Great Wise Man of our Time', was preparing a second broadcast about him. They had no trouble interviewing them as they had so much to say. One of them came this close to telling off the Master for not having intervened earlier in his life! Another one was saying: "I now realise that we were animals". These events are not at all exceptional any more. Gurudev Sri Sri Ravi Shankar has even managed to put together war groups, sworn enemies, involved in the resounding massacres of the Bihar, around Buddha's birthplace. A woman of the group had committed sixty murders and two men more than two hundred and fifty...

The conflict management programme met with the usual success. Followed by unhoped-for consequences: the fighters, once back in their territories sent contingents of two hundred people to make them live, in their turn, the experience that had so deeply influenced them. It was then seriously considered to start working in villages.

I remember a similar British documentary crowned by the Albert-London prize, that was broadcast on French TV on the programme 'Envoyé Spécial'. A gang of extremist criminals, fearing neither God nor man, incarcerated for life, ready to kill for a simple bet, without any reason, were there saying unbelievable things. They had agreed to take part in a course, very close, in the spirit and method, to the one that Gurudev Sri Sri Ravi Shankar has set up in jails. They had agreed to participate, laughing, with the firm intention of making a mess of it all. But the course, driven by a remarkable woman to whom the brutes had promised the worst, had made them see inside themselves an unknown truth that turned them upside down. Their metamorphosis was astonishing: the barbarians of the week before were so touched to have discovered this humanity in them that some were crying, with words that they would never have thought they could pronounce... What they were saying about mates that they would have easily bumped off for a bad look was beautiful. It was on 'France 2'. Nobody talked about it anymore: the matter was closed.

For more than ten years, Gurudev Sri Sri Ravi Shankar has run a programme especially devised for prisoners. By teaching them how to handle their stress and their urges, he prevents crime and favours social rehabilitation. The total absence of repeat offence has convinced the American government to subsidise the programme in their prisons. Tens of thousands of delinquents have benefited from it today, with results that every year bring the American authorities to renew the contract. In the every other country where the project is organised, its promises are kept.

It is this same basic course, adapted to criminals, that a certain Mohammed Afroze, close to Osama Bin Laden, convicted of planning a deadly attack on London and now incarcerated in Bombay, took in March 2002. What comes next looks like a cock-and-bull tale: this key character of Al-Qaeda has been so transformed that he now wants to become an Art of Living teacher for criminals around him in jail. He says he feels he has lived until then without understanding anything. He wishes he will be able one day to spread the knowledge all over the world.

Today, without abandoning his Koran or his ritual prayers, Mohammed Afroze joins every morning the yoga and meditation session with the sixty prisoners who, like him, follow an advanced teaching in prison... Up very early, far before the others, to reconcile everything, and again another yoga session in the evening.

Two big Indian newspapers, The *Times of India* and the *Times News Network*, have done their investigation. They tell the story in details, under the headings, 'The Art of Living has quietened down Afroze; meanwhile standing trial, he is looking for peace' and, 'really incredible! An Al Qaeda terrorist refuses his release on bail to follow an Art of Living advanced course in prison! The journalist describes the atmosphere of the yoga session behind bars, the stupefaction of the director of the prison who can't believe the change of attitude of Mohammed Afroze and the quality of the relations among the prisoners. The *Times* reports the declarations. "The course has brought me a tremendous amount of peace; I have no more anger and I don't bear anybody a grudge anymore. When I get out of prison, I want to teach this course to my family and to the members of my community."

His enthusiasm still doesn't go so far as to claim that his Al Qaeda 'ex-colleagues' will not hinder his plans... But who knows in whose favour the scales will end up tipping? How far will Mohammed Afroze's example in the prison of Byculla be followed? In Bombay? Or that of this Pakistani from Karachi who would have applauded with pleasure the use of an atomic bomb not long ago: He writes, "Respected Guruji, let God grant you ever-growing success and let your message spread in every nook and cranny of the sick world".

From violence, we know what to expect. From scepticism also: "*Go and sleep with your pillow on your head, there's nothing better against confusion...*" the Master says, paraphrasing a Chinese saying. The unknown is in the mobilisation and the dynamism of the heart: "*The ones who wish for a peaceful world are not strong enough advocates of action*", Gurudev Sri Sri Ravi Shankar remarks.

9

THE SERVANT OF SERVANTS

GURUDEV SRI SRI RAVI SHANKAR began to observe a long silence in the Himalayas, near the source of the Ganges.

Before sunrise, he bathes in the Ganges, whose pure waters seem strangely gentle, in spite of the cold. The river is still only a stretch of smooth water here. Far from the riverbank, the meditating figure seated on a rock can hardly be distinguished in the morning mist. Gurudev is in Samadhi, with his wet clothes clinging to his body. Nobody asks him any questions, or runs after him, nor touches him here.

Just a little further down, it is necessary to cling onto a rope bridge swinging above the water to cross over the hardly recognisable river. It has become a real mountain torrent here. Same dramatic contrast as with the crowds Gurudev left after his recent tour of India. Between twenty and fifty thousand people filed past him every night to receive his *darshan*. It could last until morning, thousands and thousands of heads waiting for his blessing, hands touching his feet, bodies lying down, stretched out in front of him, and arms daring to hug him... Even though Gurudev lifted each of them up, let them know that, in spite of their tradition, it was not necessary to bow so low, just slightly was sufficient, the fit of frenzied devotion, a bit cannibalistic, was overwhelming. It was, "you and me, no difference" taken literally... The Master came out of it exhausted.

It is now Sankalpa. An intention: to become aware of the two million years passed since the creation of the earth, since his coming in current space and time, in relationship with the universe.

Prayers, *"for the benefit of all the inhabitants of the planet, for the health, happiness, prosperity, for knowledge and enlightenment; to reduce to a minimum conscious or unconscious negative karma;*

to negate the effect of any unkind or ignorant action; to clarify the intellect, and calm the spirit of all the devotees, particularly; to impart common sense to those engaged in violence, and to bring peace to the world."

Glory of the saint with his aura of light and bliss. It seems that each one of his cells is a sparkling diamond. This is the incarnation of the ultimate consciousness.

He will come out of his silence in front of a big group of devotees. The first word pronounced in these circumstances will always have a special tone. With infinite tenderness, Gurudev Sri Sri Ravi Shankar blesses humanity: "*Jai Guru Dev... Om Nama Shivaya*!"

As if the privilege of being present were not enough, some want to kiss his feet. "Don't touch him! Don't touch him!" shout others, horrified. A protective human chain is formed around him to prevent this sacrilege.

A little later, the Master reappears, refreshed, seeming younger.

He says, *"Love doesn't age. It is like the Ganges: the river doesn't change, but the water is always fresh and renewed; the river doesn't grow old. Equally, love remains forever fresh."*

Dynamic and lively, he starts off again to travel this terrible world. He is going to cover about fifty cities in three weeks. In Ahmedabad, two thousand people meet him privately during the day... From Calcutta, he flies off to Japan and back... Then on for a new tour to Johannesburg, Los Angeles, Sydney, Hong-Kong or Mauritius... Everything is possible... He visits the planet just like we go on a weekend trip... He has to give a television interview after thirty-two hours of flight, but he is fine. Nothing can upset his equilibrium.

♦

Gurudev is on his way to Bangalore and the atmosphere in the *ashram* has already changed. The energy is always lower when he is away. The small band of young masters, with black hair and white *kurtas*, who look like his younger brothers, are longing to see him. For them, he is away too often and goes too far. They tell him on the phone: "Come back soon; it's too cold for you over there. When you come back, we shall lock you up and never let you go away again!" The Master appreciates this sign of real intimacy, where all different moods are expressed with love.

Just knowing that he is approaching the *ashram* is enough to restore harmony. Last night's *satsang* sounded like a terrible cacophony. Tonight's is punchy again.

The Master arrives.

It is two o'clock in the morning; only a few of us are still waiting for him. Is it worth it? Nobody knows. No plan is ever written in stone with Gurudev. He may very well decide to go and visit somebody in town, his sister Bhanu for instance, and maybe stay there...

It is raining; one more reason not to miss being here if he comes. A few of us fall asleep on the floor. Others are talking – always about the knowledge. Sharing personal experiences is more inspiring than chatting about this or that. Talking about the Master is a passion. It revives the feeling of carefree happiness. Confidence in him is total. No matter what is required, one knows it will be taken care of in the best possible way. It is as sure as one plus one makes One.

At the airport, under the permanently exhibited portraits of Gurudev Sri Sri Ravi Shankar and Sai Baba – another famous guru in Karnataka – the expression on the faces is an unmistakable sign that Guruji's plane has just landed. The authorities, the customs' officers and the staff are getting ready to welcome him. A crowd and sprays of flowers follow... and here comes the white figure in front of which the policemen bow.

Gurudev gets in the small car that has come to fetch him – any car will do; they all have four wheels... He doesn't have a limousine.

The *ashram* gate finally opens up in front of a car's headlights. Yes, it is the Master, sitting on the left of the driver. The little group comes running to meet him. He smiles at each one. He exclaims, "*Oh, you're here!*" pretending to have only just discovered my presence. Then he adds in French, "*Comment ça va*?" I hold his hand against my cheek: I am very well; I fall in love every day... with the same person!" He laughs.

Although it is late, Gurudev doesn't leave straight away. He lets those who have been waiting for him until so late sit down around him. He takes care of everybody, asks how they are doing, and hands out fruit...

An Englishwoman is here to take the Teacher Training Course. The Master asks her, "*Have you been singing here*?" she answers half-heartedly, "Yes, a little bit". Surprised, he says, "*A little bit? Tomorrow, you will sing*." The young woman is a soft-rock singer in the Sister India group, nominated for the BBC Awards. Without needing all these precisions, Gurudev knows that she will sing all over India in the future. And this is what is happening since then... Her music is ideal for the introduction to spirituality conferences in colleges.

♦

A story is told that, when demons were devastating and destroying the earth, thousands of years ago, the Divine Mother replied with fervent prayers and came to kill the demons. A new life was thus offered to a suffering world... today, the Hindus celebrate her victory during the nine nights of Navaratri. On the fourth day – after killing Mahishasur, where the city of Mysore is now situated – the Divine Mother came to the place where the Gods and the wise men had assembled to express their gratitude to her. The legend says that she then blessed all the people who had meditated on this land, which became sacred from then on.

Centuries later, when Gurudev Sri Sri Ravi Shankar announced that he had found the location for his future *ashram* – nothing more than a stony hill, without vegetation or charm – the devotees were wondering what he was up to! We now know that the rocks on which the Master had the Sumeru Mantap built – a coliseum of which he was both the architect and decorator – is the place of the mythical meeting. Buddha himself is said to have stayed on this hill overlooking the area, exactly where Gurudev Sri Sri Ravi Shankar has just built a temple, in accordance with his own plan

– a vast amphitheatre for meditation – the Vishalakshi Mantap – dedicated to Amma.

The light, the panorama, the vegetation, the indigo lake in the palm garden, the flowers and the fruit, the colours and the fragrances, the smiles and the melodies, the comfortable kutirs,[1] the delicious ayurvedic food, the attention to detail in everyday life, all the positive effects of the presence of the Master, the days and the nights spent here give a fairly accurate idea of what one could envisage as 'paradise on earth'.

However, an absence has been felt since November 9th: Amma's. Every year, the Master increases the celebration of her memory. One evening, he said, "*I have a wonderful woman in my life." And after a while, he added: "It is my mother...her photo is there, in front of me... My mother was my first, most gentle and precious contact, with this planet... I never told her that I loved her and she never told me that she loved me either... But we loved each other... and we still do.*"

Amma's portrait has pride of place beside him, decorated with jasmine garlands. Candlelight shines upon it, every day. Gurudev shows everyone another photograph of himself, as a child, in his mother's arms: "*She loved me more than herself. We shall dedicate this* satsang *to her...*"

Amma behaved like a mother towards her son up to the end. She scolded him as if he were a ten-year-old boy. She took care of him, ensured that he ate well, rested enough, and did not get cold, which made him laugh a lot. In fact, she was the only one who remembered that the *guru*, no matter how divine, also had a physical body.

"*His mother is particularly privileged,*" Pitaji told me one day I was asking him about it. "*The older her son got, the prouder she became. She was very proud to be his mother; she was the personal witness of everything that happened to him.*"

She would refuse access to the *kutir* for no good reason. When Gurudev was resting, she would be adamant. So much so that, one day, when she was called away, the young doorman devotee,

1 Round bungalows

sorry but inflexible, refused to let her back in. That the boy had dared to refuse her entrance for the good of the Master impressed her. She set him up as an example.

But ever since Amma is no longer there, no one has succeeded in maintaining peace and quiet around the *kutir*. Gurudev even asks sometimes to be locked in from outside, so that people standing in front of the padlocked door would think he has gone away! After many a struggle, three successive blocks have been set up... This did not distance the Master, but demanded the necessary respect for his increasingly busy timetable.

♦

Gurudev Sri Sri Ravi Shankar is working today in an emergency. How to break the cycles of violence? How to bring back human values? How to make people responsible for themselves and for society as a whole? How to infuse in them again a taste for life and for action? How to teach them to depend only on themselves? How to bring them to appreciate diversity – and not only to tolerate it?

Gurudev Sri Sri Ravi Shankar does not need to gather commissions, nor to create committees, nor to publish white papers to find solutions. He knows what the solutions are. He knows very well what can work, and what cannot, what is better to do or to avoid, which is a minimum, on the part of a wise man. So he has created programs of action adapted for specific issues that today's society is unable to solve.

The tools exist, only the volunteers need to be found. The Master does not count on the politicians to roll up their sleeves. He seeks it, but doesn't expect it. In any case, without the selfless help of the volunteers, who set a contagious example that inspires others in turn, the task would be impossible. Hence the importance of kindling a fiery zeal to serve in as many people as possible.

More than ever, Gurudev Sri Sri Ravi Shankar is leading his humanitarian organizations briskly. The time wasted is only a benefit to misery. And the time saved is counted. The *guru* is not immortal, at least in his present appearance. He puts pressure on his disciples to become more selfless and move in the exact direction of devotion. He says, "*The utmost in devotion is to bow in front of oneself. 'I' and 'you' dissolve, and one can see what IS.*" His closest devotees are those who can do without him. If his life is going to be short, he must leave solid, autonomous and active spirits behind him, who will contribute to the spreading of knowledge, generation after generation, and not inconsolable spineless individuals.

This is what occupies him, exclusively. One way or another, he works hard at it. His Buddhist friend, His Holiness the Dalai Lama, who comes to visit him at the *ashram*, does the same with his own personality, history and means.

The Tibetan spiritual leader's travels are very different from those of the Hindu *guru*: they are those of a state dignitary, with a ritual and a very strict protocol, even during these casual circumstances. The night before, some monks from his close circle had preceded him at the *ashram* to announce his arrival. They had chanted their *bhajans*, of a more austere beauty.

In the morning, a procession of about fifteen pearl grey cars, strictly identical, went into the *ashram*. The considerably important person was in one of them, but, security measures, nobody could guess which one. The ceremonial preliminaries, with the sound of the horns of the Buddhist pope, were in fact provided by the guest himself, with all traditional rigour. Right after that, the two wise men kissed each other without ceremony, were laughing with the joy of meeting again, and holding hands in the *ashram* alleys. The Dalai Lama has difficulties walking; the *Guru* supports him.

To see them together, to stay in their presence and meditate with them is a precious gift for whoever can appreciate it. But the interest of the meeting lies somewhere else.

Apart from the moments the two saints reserve for each other – we can imagine how they play together and what pleasure they take in sharing their common visions – Gurudev Sri Sri Ravi Shankar and the Dalai Lama are glad to be seen together, equally honoured, to send a strong message to the Buddhist and Hindu twin communities, pestered by ridiculous dissensions.

A huge public *satsang* will take place in Bangalore in the evening, during which the two spiritual leaders will speak with one voice only. Only the clothing will be different. His Holiness the Dalai Lama sums it up thus: "The only difference between us is the beard!" And the town will resonate with his huge child-like laughter.

♦

In the *ashram* gardens, the burgundy and white uniforms scattered in the greenery or hanging on the swings tell it is playtime for the school children. Indeed, here the usual release of wild shouting of children let out of the classroom cannot be heard, because the *ashram* children have no excessive stress to release after class. They play with the liveliness of their age, they may shout and sometimes quarrel, but there is no over excitement or fighting.

Violence is no threat; it is simply not a thing that attracts the children here. Gross behaviour, aggression, make them laugh more than get angry; violence has gone right out of favour and cannot set in here.

"*Humour is the only lever that can change disrespect into respect*" says the Master. As long as it's not directed against somebody, to laugh about everything, and first of all about what happens to oneself makes the personality of the children blossom, and develops non-violence in them.

"*In any group of children of some importance, there will always be one to hurt or insult the other. You can't expect a whole class to behave like saints all the time. But when they can welcome the one who has insulted them with a smile, they free themselves of ready-made reactions.*

Today, aggression seems to have become a way of life", notices Gurudev Sri Sri Ravi Shankar. "*Pride is associated with aggression instead of compassion. This has to be changed.*" This incentive concerning aggression leads young people to have, in crime, feelings of superiority rather than shame.

"*When I was at school, whoever would have only spoken of weapons would have felt ashamed. All the children would have said, "Oh, he said weapons!" Today this aversion for weapons has disappeared. In the same way, formerly, if somebody had shouted in class or lost their temper, everybody would look at him. Such a fuss was so abnormal that the person would feel sheepish; it was automatic. These values have disappeared. The students who speak out loud in the classroom are those who tend to get the most attention.*

Society has sowed seeds of violence in children. Wherever they look, toys and games are violent. They lost the sense of the meaning of life. This violence gets into their system. Children don't perceive the refined qualities they have in themselves. Television has made them tough: people are fighting, tearing each other to pieces... Nothing evokes unity or union. Only violence stays in the conscious or unconscious mind of the child. Of course there can be shocks or accidents, but too many influences of this type create in the mind a faint unconscious tension. When children reach the age of ten or fifteen, you can perceive it on their faces. They don't look any more like bubbles of joy and bliss; they seem crammed with interior cramps.

We have to do something. It is essential that we create an atmosphere favourable to their growth. The teaching of non-violence is dramatically absent. School can be an ideal place to introduce these values. It is most important: children spend so much time there. The teachers should tell them inspiring stories about non-violence and teach them that compassion is a sign of dignity. This could really initiate a change."

It is evident that today's youth hasn't received a proper education. For Gurudev Sri Sri Ravi Shankar, the increasingly precocious violent behaviour of teenagers comes from the fact that they have no tool available for them to channel their negative emotions. They have no idea how to get rid of their mental tensions. Neither at school, nor at home have they been taught to express themselves correctly.

The Master attributes part of this aggression to an impaired self-esteem, and to the incapacity to criticise, or bear others' criticism. But above all, "*The absence of a feeling of belongingness in the children, and their incapacity to understand others are the key causes of their desire to inflict pain on them.*"

Physical activity and control of emotions through the breath are classic and proven methods of tempering teenagers' aggression. Gurudev Sri Sri Ravi Shankar also stresses the impact of bad eating habits, which are not adequately taken into account. He emphasises the need to reduce the consumption of sweet or salted snacks and fizzy drinks that increase restlessness. He draws attention to the importance of entertainment and of the example given by adults: "*We have to show the young how they can be broad-minded, kind and cooperative, through our example. They observe everything you do and get inspired from it. If the basic education in human values is failing, Human Rights cannot flourish.*"

Gurudev Sri Sri Ravi Shankar maintains that children are born with these values: "*They have compassion, cooperation, benevolence, the smile, the laughter, the lightness, the desire to help, the feeling of belongingness, the desire to take care of each other... Recognising life is inborn in them... All these qualities are present, they just need to be nourished and brought to expression.*"

Children come to the world in a state of yoga. The Master underlines how, in the cradle and even in the womb, all their physical positions are inborn yoga postures. Like the position of the fingers, which is called '*mudras*', the thumb inside the other fingers that are closed around it or the thumb held up for sucking, the index finger and the thumb together... Every gesture has a deep and precise meaning. The same is true for the body: "Look *at a child's poses, for instance the way he places his limbs on the floor when he is playing; he is the best yoga teacher.*

All children were born with this natural conscious state of joy. Simplicity and naturalness are the qualities of an enlightened person as well as of a child. But with time, a child loses its innocence."

– From childhood to adult state, by what have we been transformed?

– I am wondering... Let me know if you have the answer! As they grow up, children have not learnt to value the basic notions of life.

The first thing we want in life is love... and the last is also love. In the beginning, like a small child, we were in a state of love; after breaking the dictates of ego thanks to the knowledge, we are again in a state of love. Only, between the two, there is a lot of confusion and problems...

– If children are in an enlightened state, why do they tend to be selfish, quick-tempered, etc.?

– *They just follow mum and dad! They want to keep you company... Teachers should know that the human physiology is very similar to the atomic structure. In an atom, the centre, the proton, is positive. The electrons, or negative charge, are on the outside. All the negativity you see in a child is really only at the periphery. Negativity is not the real nature of the child. With care and love, which does not exclude being firm, you can kindle positive human values in them. The teacher has to kindle them. During their childhood we have to favour the sense of service and friendship...*"

To state ideals as regards education has been done many times. But what does a wise man do, concretely, to combine theory and practice? Only a few concrete examples can be given here.

Gurudev Sri Sri Ravi Shankar makes this observation: "*When we observe a group of thirty to forty, or of two to three hundred children at school, each one is friends with only three or four, maximum ten children. And they will stay together during the five or six years of their schooling. Ask your children how many friends they have, they will list them to you on the fingers of one hand. If you cannot be friends with two hundred children in your school, how then can you be friends with the whole world when you come out of school?*

Basically, we can only be friends with two to five people we meet; check for yourself in your own life. We don't even know how to live with the people around us. Have you noticed it?

Do you know why we go into conflict with people? It is because we are not open."

So the Master asks the schoolchildren to make a new friend each day; to go and meet somebody new to discover... The widened contacts of the children with one another do not allow the sectarian gang mentality to have a say in the matter any longer...

In the classrooms, the children must also sit at a different place everyday, next to a new classmate. Very young children do it spontaneously, but usually, the teachers attribute the same seat to them, in order to teach them discipline and also to make things easier for themselves... Then children get attached to 'their' seat, and even fight to keep it! Their seat ends up becoming their property. "*This is very bad*!" explains the Master. He encourages the teachers to place the child with the best results next to the weakest of the class. In his schools, the good students look after the less talented. The former become more responsible, and greatly strengthen their knowledge, and the latter lose the humiliating feeling of mediocrity and make considerable progress, without special care.

It is a widespread attitude with the *ashram* students to encourage the weaker, whether in games or in studying. "*Let us suppose you are weak in a particular field, and everybody came to help you, how would you feel? You would no longer feel your weakness. Although you are not strong, you will feel strength. It is important that children learn how to support each other.*

This process elevates both the helper and the one needing help. They are used as a support for each other, not only through a lesson, but also through their behaviour.

This generation needs to cultivate much more these supporting values; we are responsible for it. Today's children will be the society of tomorrow. Teaching human values is not only a wish – it is for us an obligation."

So, no students are left behind in Gurudev Sri Sri Ravi Shankar's schools. Not a single outcast! His educational methods don't need a very large budget, but are not thrifty either. There is no shortage of anything for the children.

The teaching covers both modern and traditional subjects. There is a 100% pass rate in the national exams.

The Master says, *"The secret of successful studies is to have fun with life, to feel light, fresh and happy. Then you only have to skim through the pages once to understand them."*

The mind is clear only if it is not chained up. So the wise man recommends the children not be good, not to fit the school mold, in their own way: "*To be mischievous is fine! You have been told so much not to be rascals, but I tell you to be one*!

Our youth needs to have a deeper knowledge of its roots, of its heritage, and at the same time, to broaden their vision of life. When I say broader vision and deeper roots, I mean to be responsible with ease, calmness and equanimity.

– According to you, what are the most important qualities the young should tend to develop?

– *The young are always looking for success. They need to change their parameters of success. What you do think success is? The parameters of success are changing. A few years ago, maybe twenty years ago, wearing a lot of jewels was the symbol of success. It is no longer so today. To me, the sign of success is an undying smile, confidence in life, and a feeling of belongingness with everybody; this is what our youth should focus on.*

– How to free the young from the negative effects of drugs and alcohol?

– *We get into these bad habits assuming they will bring us the happiness we are looking for. There is only one way out of it, it is to see that a spiritual dimension alone can bring you unlimited joy, and that it is not a stern path, but on the contrary, a path full of fun!*

– Why should secular educational institutions in India speak about spirituality?

– *Because it is a basic human need! Religion and spirituality alone can bring emotional comfort. Who knows what will happen if this is denied, as in Russia...*

– What is the problem with the education given by our teachers?

– *The lack of belongingness between teacher and student.*

– *I* have difficulties with my students. I cannot obtain silence in my classroom. Should I make the children meditate?

– *Of course not! They just could not! No, no... You just need to speak louder than them. Shout louder. All of a sudden, they will be quiet. Then play with them. How old are they?*

– Between six and ten.

– *No, don't make them meditate!* Guruji repeats, surprised by the question. *Impossible. It is so evident!*

– What is your message for the youth?

– *Don't look for labour dignity. Be active and involved. To be active gives you an opportunity to be creative."*

Gurudev Sri Sri Ravi Shankar educates thousands of children in Bangalore. Boys and girls diverted from the professional work they were intended to do. As a compensation for the wages their families are deprived of, the Master gives a bit of money to the families and replaces their tin-covered hovels with permanent small houses, simple, basic, but clean and healthy. The global support for a child amounts to one euro a day...The courses given throughout the world finance this.

The full education given in the ashrams explains why the Indian elites, so much valued in the West, often come from these schools. Gurudev Sri Sri Ravi Shankar's former pupils are today grown-ups. They haven't chosen an international career; they went back to their villages to take care of them themselves.

It is not an insult to say that in the West we are at a loss to find a solution to violence at school. The teaching staff admits that they are out of their depth, and aggression among the young keeps growing. Gurudev Sri Sri Ravi Shankar thinks one should supplement children's education with outside programmes. Everywhere, it has become necessary to support teachers, to "i*nstil in parents and children a greater respect for teachers*." If the teachers themselves lay down new rules, it may well not work. So Gurudev Sri Sri Ravi Shankar has set up a programme that is meant for India as well as for the rest of the world, called ART Excel – All Round Training for Excellence.

Some American states understood its value very early on. In particular those states where one child in four goes to school with a weapon. Since the tragedy of Littleton, Colorado, where college students shot their classmates with no apparent motive, people are starting to realise they are not a leading power in every field.

Gurudev Sri Sri Ravi Shankar's very subtle teaching skills get a good score too, but in a totally different way... Gratitude is expressed by covering him in honours – the 'Gurudev Sri Sri Ravi Shankar's Day' has been declared as a day dedicated to Human Values by the city of Washington. The cities of New York and San Francisco, the states of New Jersey and Florida have granted various awards to the wise man for his 'active part taken in improving our children's lives'. He is the only non-western member to sit on the Divinity School Counsel at Yale University. These are appreciable tributes that are a sign of a growing consciousness, even if they aren't always backed up with concrete actions.

♦

Gurudev Sri Sri Ravi Shankar says, "*When you live for others, others will live for you. If you live only for yourself, then you must carry all the weight on your shoulders.*" This is the secret of the lightness in the Master's house. Anybody can come and stay; the door is open. But it is no market place where the adventurers of spiritual tourism can come and go. Nobody stays here longer than necessary. Gurudev Sri Sri Ravi Shankar does not want to make a factory of lazybones out of his paradise.

They are preparing a stage at the *ashram*, for the official prize-giving ceremony for all the tilers, plumbers, electricians, painters, masons, welders, mechanics, electronics engineers, who have just finished their training here. They are going to receive a document which sanctions their training, which is recognised by the Indian Government as 'the best programme in rural development.' It is a long way from the days which they spent sitting outside, idle, only a few months ago, until they recently realised that through work, they will be able to get things moving again around them!

Here they are, ready to go back to their villages with a job under their belt and the capacity to train young apprentices in their rural area, still kept out of the main trends of the national life. Needless to say they go back with ironclad confidence and strength.

In the *ashram* workshops, about forty new apprentices are already taking over from them to receive free training in turn from volunteer professionals who offer their personal time to come and teach. The full amount of the benefits from the sold production is put back into the apprentice community. If they had been told, "Come, we are going to train you for a job", they would not have come. The motivation was not there. But the key word to convince them to accept was to say, "Guruji is going to take care of you!" On average, four out of ten men in these communist villages know the value of this promise.

When asked what has been the main change in them with this experience, these former Marxists – as most of them have been – answer, "The sense of service". They say that they find again through the Master the values that had made them dream about a brotherly and fair society, a long time ago, only without the same failings. "In communism, there are many words... Here, we work following our own feeling. There is no ideology. In every act of life, these are glaring differences. The *guru* can make communism a reality. And when things go wrong for one's self, the answer will be individual and not only collective. We believe in action, in *karma*, and in knowledge; no longer in beautiful speeches. We cannot change the world, but we can spread this state of being, this consciousness that the world belongs to us."

An awakened minority is enough to stimulate action around them. The purpose being to allow all the villagers – for whom daily life is a struggle – to lead a more exciting life.

The direction given by Gurudev's humanitarian work is self-development. Teaching people how to be responsible for themselves, and to help each other beyond all divisions: what could be a better solution?

Such a program might seem a utopia outside India. But Indian mentality makes it very realistic, on the contrary: if you are able to be of service, you are grateful for it.

Somebody asks the Master, "Will a time come when everybody will be happy?" He answers, "*When everybody is happy, whom will you serve? Harshly afflicted people do you a favour by giving you a chance to be useful to them. Be grateful for it*!" Very many people perceive these words as evidence. The *ashram* is the place where thousands of volunteers come throughout the year to graduate as seva warriors... An easily attained figure, as each course trains one thousand people here. Particularly the programme called 'Youth Training Program'. It is about training the young to answer the basic needs of destitute villages in terms of housing, hygiene, health, human values and harmony in diversity.

♦

Nayak will go back to his village now, but will do his seva in another village. The Master advises that they start work in a new environment so that they don't fall back into old family or neighbourhood patterns.

Nayak is a Muslim. He has learnt how to behave with his friends of the same religion, in order to underscore the stupidity of clear-cut opinions in the realm of religion or spirituality, without creating conflict through tactlessness. He has also learnt how to smooth out the differences with the other sensitivities.

Nayak tells me he feels ready. He knows there is a lot of good work to be done. He is certain to achieve it. The programme has boosted his self-confidence. He has already convinced some of his Muslim friends to do this YLTP course and they did it together and loved it. For two weeks, they have experienced great brotherhood between young people of various origins. They weren't used to that. It is even the first time they found themselves mixing with others so closely. The group came out of it wonderfully united – one thousand young men – now knowing, deep in themselves, that it is possible, easy, and joyful.

Nayak has just finished his studies and is looking for a job. Whether he finds it quickly or not, he is going to start his *seva* – supervising the homework of all the village children he is now in charge of, after school and free of charge. Poor children cannot, of course, afford private evening classes. Besides, nothing is organized for them by the national school system. So Nayak will look after their academic progress to bring them up to standard. This kind of help is very popular with the illiterate families.

After four to six weeks of practice, Nayak may be invited to do the second part of the programme. If he seems to have the requirements for the mission that lies ahead of him – after some further training – he will be placed in charge of ten villages. He will have to supervise *seva*, attend to general hygiene, to the schooling of all children, girls included, and to arrange a medical examination for all the inhabitants... Fifteen thousand villages are already involved with this self-development program.

♦

On the road, right in the centre of Bangalore, a horrible, stinking, narrow strip of land leads to one of the many slums of the city. In the alleys and the slums, the level of poverty is extreme. Men, women and children live there without having ever received medical checks. Three hundred people are in urgent need.

Gurudev Sri Sri Ravi Shankar does not favour systematic hospitalisation, even when it is possible. The sick people, cut from their links, just sink there. The outpatient care formula is more convenient. The doctors have to assess the necessity for hospitalisation on the spot. Generally 5% of the examined population absolutely needs it.

Doctor Raddha is a surgeon; her sister, doctor Ragini is a dentist. But they serve as general practitioners in the slums – they have to give three to five hundred consultations a day.

There is a long line waiting; the people are surprised that the pains and aches, that had been forgotten by getting used to them, are going to be miraculously taken care of. There is anguish in the eyes and solemnity to be the object of so much attention. The camp is set up and running smoothly. It is written on the sign: '*Free medical camps*' followed with Gurudev Sri Sri Ravi Shankar's name. The news spreads by word of mouth – it means that Guruji is there for them. They touch his face on the portrait that has just been hung on the wall, and put their hand to their eye – if only they could open up! Everybody is carefully holding a small piece of paper on which a figure is written his or her age. Yes, there will be medicine for everybody, and with the necessary explanations. Don't worry...

By force of circumstance, things go very fast. People have hardly sat down in front of the doctor when they have to give their place to the next person. But in this so short time, I can see that Ragini and Radha give maximum attention to each person. They are focused on the technical interrogation, full of compassion to calm down the anxiety, and manage everything. Diagnosis is made without hesitation. The symptoms are clear. Typical malnutrition problems, intestinal worms, infected wounds, cuts in the mouth, cataracts, and blindness due to the intense light in India... Then, there are the pains that have a story you want to talk about. A woman shows her arm damaged with a burn that is also on all of her child's body – the furious husband has burnt them with a flame because the dowry hasn't been paid yet. She does not remember how long ago. Aggression happens everyday. Another woman, for the same reason, has her hair pulled out – a few sparse long locks of hair are still hanging.

A mother who is a child herself shows her baby to Ragini; its lips and extremities are blue. She knows it suffers from a heart disease. She speaks English; she wants to show me her house. The grandfather is sleeping in a kind of hole, the grandmother in another one. There is no word other than disagreeable to describe the kitchen, and the 'bathroom' corner. Above is her place, with the child's; a little bit less appalling. The intrusive loud presence of television is overwhelming. It doesn't bother her. She would like more explanations from the doctor, so we go back together. She is well aware of the seriousness of her baby's state of health. But she is smiling. "How is life for you?" She answers in English, "Fine."

Ragini confirms that the child must be sent to hospital. A cloud passes over her eyes, but she doesn't let herself be overwhelmed with grief.

Gurudev has asked me to come here and sing *bhajans*. I had not foreseen I would be alone... But I sing, with a casual air... People are smiling, they like it. I encourage them to sing along and they do, especially the children... It is pure joy. The Master was right. The medical atmosphere has become lighter. To play with the children and exchange *bhajans* with songs learnt at school; everything finally happened very naturally. There are many who want to feel the touch of my hands and who want to cuddle in my arms. Some parents try to maintain a distance that they pretend to accept for two seconds and then come back. Where's the problem? *No problem*. The slum has become a place of a festive frenzy. They also start laughing in the waiting line. Radha is disturbed in her work and frowns, but straight away smiles to me. Gurudev is doing a good job. Good! Never mind if I get lice.

A week later, I hear something new happened here – people have cleansed the slum of all its dirt, outside and inside. In the coming days, some volunteers of the Foundation are going to bring them some basic notions for a well-balanced life. Those who understand what it is all about and who show some interest will receive a basic training. And with the enthusiasm shown by the newly trained, the slum will start to come out of the abyss.

The ball is in their court now. The doctor's next visit won't be for another six months.

Other appalling places are waiting for this providential minimum. Ragini and Raddha don't stop, torn between their private consultations and the slums or the villages. I will go with them for some time, with two volunteers who have started to clear away the grounds. We will do the trip together, the car filled with buckets full of medicine, of nutritional sachets, of sweets and fruit. One grape alone per person, which is received, each time, as an exceptional thing. We will be driving for two to three hours, with a large portrait of Gurudev on our lap. Hollow and empty... Good.

On our return, absolutely exhausted, we will bring back the piled empty boxes and buckets. Everything has been distributed, right up to the last pill, but there has been enough. Gurudev's portrait is supporting our back...

The only words we shall exchange will be figures: 450 + 300 + 350... A race after figures. During the year, the two women doctors have taken care of sixteen thousand people. They went back to thirty-five villages and twenty slums at least twice. The number of these 'Free medical camps' is flourishing.

The courses are going well everywhere. *Shambo*!

"Health is not absence of illness,
it is to be established in the self,
it is the dynamic expression of life."

♦

It is starting to become very hot in India. Summer is here. Usually, at the beginning of March, Gurudev sends me back to France, "*You're going to get sick, go back to France*!" This year, he doesn't recommend anything. He goes on opening *seva* doors.

I finally found an opportunity to go and visit Pitaji, at Vista India, his charitable organisation, in order to find out how to help him.

After he retired, Gurudev's father's wish was to serve in a place in India about which one could say it would be the final solution to misery. On this Indian land – poor almost everywhere – where were the most ignored peoples? He was told about Uragapura, named 'the snake village', trapped within mosquito infected swamps, inhabited by *Harijans*, untouchables, forgotten there like a sub-humanity, in a daily tragedy nobody cared about. The closest naturopath – thirty kilometres away – had had to treat over six thousand snakebites. And this number did not include the victims who did not make it that far. Everybody discouraged Pitaji to come and settle down in this hell. There was no drinking water – people drank the water used to wash the cattle and materials, no energy – they cooked food on bricks, no schools, no medical care – the women were brought to hospital on ox-drawn carts to deliver their babies, no chance for girls to escape prostitution – the work in the fields gave employment to only a few of them... Violence in the family was the only diversion. What's the use of investing energy in an impossible task?

For the last seven years now, Pitaji has been living under a hot tin roof, in a small room decorated with his son's and the great Master Maharishi's portraits, in the middle of this region that he has completely transformed.

First, they had to dig two wells, one hundred and thirty metres deep, in order to have water. Then they had to dry out the belt of marshland for basic constructions, plant some coconut trees to ensure a minimum income for the families, create a herbal garden to treat the population through Ayurveda, and create an oasis of flowers and greenery for the Art of Living.

Above all, he had to set up the means to remedy the people's extreme poverty, on a long-term basis. Pitaji banked on the women and on their qualities. To help them first it was necessary to increase the material support to all the family. The same trust could not be given to men, who often drank their salary. It is also meant to save these low caste women from a double banishment; even today in India, their living conditions are horrifying.

In surroundings where everything is conceived for their well-being, Pitaji brings up one hundred and fifty young girls from age fifteen to twenty-five. For two years, he brings them the education they haven't received yet and teaches them to be seamstresses. Every month, he deposits one hundred rupees[1] in a bank account so that they will have a small dowry essential to get married. At the end of their training, they have learned to be autonomous and not just financially. Pitaji provides them with a job in a factory, or gives them a sewing machine if they want to be self-employed.

Due to this incredible effort, almost one thousand girls in twenty-five villages around have been pulled through, so far.

1 Equivalent to approximately 1.5 euros or 2 US dollar,

The essential thing is to maintain this help. The means are missing to extend Vista India. Not enough places, not enough teachers – two hundred women are still waiting for their only chance to escape their terrible fate.

Pitaji is fighting to hold on. The old machines work, but electricity is whimsical and the generator often breaks down, so it is difficult to ensure regular productivity. The girls work well, but on materials that are not of the best quality, often stained. The clothes or bags carefully made in the workshops end up sold-off in the markets.

At the same time, in Bangalore, international ready-to-wear factories run at full capacity, thanks to the cheap local labour. The most famous brands, that are successful on the streets of the big capitals and that have relocated in India to produce at lower costs, make huge profits, and the waste of expensive materials does not even make a dent in their turnover. For the slightest flaw, thousands of pieces are just thrown away. Wouldn't there be a way to salvage some of these brand new scraps?

I went to see the largest French clothes manufacturer in Bangalore. I told him, "I came to rummage through your garbage cans." He said without me suggesting it to him, "Fine, one hundred kilos of a good quality material per month, is that Okay with you?" It wasn't enough, he agreed. He took action to come up with more realistic solutions: training women to be managers in Vista India and taking the apprentices for a trial period, even if it means sacrificing a few dozens of shirts in the beginning. But let them be careful; business is still business!

What will come of it? Maybe a lot, maybe nothing. The same acts can be useful or not, according to God's will... Not to be attached to the outcome saves one from becoming discouraged.

To be out in the field for seva has shown me the futility of self-satisfaction in commitment. Nevertheless, I enjoyed the contentment of these busy days.

Because, who is serving whom? At that time, when I returned from the slums I wore the filth as an ornament, but the story told by Vinod set the record straight.

Vinod Kumar has a large number of responsibilities. Active and disciplined, he supervises most of the programmes. Present in India on all *seva* fronts, he is a kind of Seva *generalissimo*.

In the beginning, Vinod was very proud, and even more than that, to be an accomplished *Sevak*. This gave him the privilege of travelling with the Master. Once they were staying in one of the biggest hotels in Taiwan and, towards 10 pm, Gurudev sent everybody away from his room, except for Vinod, whom he invited to sit on the couch. Vinod did not want to accept and sat down on the floor. But Guruji insisted and Vinod had to give in. Then the Master asked him what he wanted to eat. Even more embarrassed, Vinod said he would have dinner in a restaurant and come back to see if the Master needed him. "How can I tell you what I want to eat, it is not fitting!" Once again, Gurudev did not take his refusal into account, "*Order what you want – French fries, milkshake, veggie-burger, whatever you want*!" Vinod's protests were of no use – he finally said what he wanted. Gurudev called for room service and had the meal brought up. Soon, somebody knocked at the door, Vinod got up to open the door, but Gurudev ordered him to stay seated, opened the door himself, took the tray and brought it to Vinod who was so shattered that he just stood there. Gurudev pushed him onto the couch and he sat down on the carpet! Vinod was devastated and couldn't help getting up. He couldn't prevent Gurudev serving him the French fries and the veggie burger... After a while though, the devotee started to get used to the situation, and even to enjoy his meal. Finally, he felt quite comfortable. Suddenly Guruji stood up, and in a very different tone of voice, asked him, "*What do you think about yourself*?" Frozen and disconcerted, Vinod remained voiceless. Gurudev went on, "*Do you think you are serving me? The Divine is serving you! Every second, the Divine is serving you, day and night. He brings you seasons and cultures, the sun and the moon; he caters for all your needs; isn't that a service? God takes care of you, but you think you are serving the Divine*?" It was a big turning point for this exemplary servant's ego. Since then he no longer thinks of showing-off his record of service.

The Master says, *"Do seva as God wants it. He has no expectations and does not let you feel that he is doing it."*

♦

Thursday April 11th. The heat is becoming unbearable. My plane for Paris takes off at 1.15 pm. Since our detour through the clothing factory, the taxi driver can't find his way out. He claims to have understood the given instructions, but asks the way all the time. It is now 1 pm. The airport is still far away. We still try to reach it because it is India. It is 1.13 pm. The absurdity in going on driving doesn't even cross my mind. I sink back in my seat; we'll see! The car stops. What's happening? It is the airport! I leave my suitcases with the driver and rush into the hall, throw my attaché-case and other bags, heavy as lead, onto the security belt and run to check in. Too late! Everything is closed. The plane hasn't left yet. Isn't there a way, Sir? Not at this time, Madam. His attention is fixed at something behind me for a few seconds. He changes his mind. Hurry up! Where's your luggage? Outside! The taxi driver is not allowed to enter the airport. It is 1.16 pm. Two security agents take care of my suitcases. You have thirty-five kg of excess luggage, madam! That's right, Sir. He lets everything go. It is 1.17 pm. I must still collect my hand luggage. My attaché-case is open. The customs officer smiles warmly in front of the books and photos of Gurudev. So, that was it... The two agents still help me, carry my bags all the way to the plane, go on board and put them on the rack! Thank you, ever so kind of you! Don't mention it. I hold a banknote out to them – No! Please, no! They say, "Jai Guru Dev!" 1.19 pm – the plane is moving towards the take-off strip.

10

CELEBRATING SILENCE

EVER SINCE LAUNCHING THE PROJECT of writing this book, I was worried about not having enough interviews with Gurudev to write it. In India he would tell me how busy he was, and in Europe there were always other things in the way. When I told him about my fears he would chivvy me along: "*When are you going to stop being anxious*?" he said to me one day, shaking me by the shoulders... He would shy away from the usual newspaper interview yet, at the same time, he was reassuring: "*You'll have everything you need* – Yes, but it's interviews I need – *Yes, all right, we'll talk*." Each time I requested to remain in his presence in unusual circumstances for the needs of the book, he would accept. But when I decided on my own, he would say, "*Have you had something to eat? You should go along and get something*", or else, "*You are tired, go and have a rest*." And if I protested, he could tell me in quite an authoritarian way, "*Well, anyway I am*!"

The predefined project wasn't coming along. All I could see was how behind things were getting, and the material complications... How was it that Gurudev, who was so attentive, was putting me in such a difficult situation? I begged him to tell me straight out whether I was to complete this task or not. He answered yes, but sounded irritated. And nothing changed. So I eventually wrote to him: 'I'm giving up.' A few hours later, he asked me, "*Have you finished your book, then*?" And he announced publicly that it was being written. But I was still asking for the interviews that had been planned.

One afternoon, he had gone down to the kitchen to make some lemon rice. I was waiting for him to come back, standing by his door. As soon as he saw me, he said to me in French, "*D'accord [all right]*" and led me by the hand into his quarters. Like a real professional, I had my notepad and my tape-recorder at the ready. He was up to his eyes in urgent tasks, but it amused him to massage my neck muscles, to jostle me, and lead me off in a jerky dance... He said to me, "*So what it is you want? Quick, quick...*" The telephone rang again, and he took the call himself. Ten minutes of bursts of laughter, all the time glancing at the sheets of paper with my questions which were written out in my regular hand, and neatly laid out... Finally the Master was ready, he wouldn't take any more calls: "*Over to you now, quick, quick, come to the point*!"

From my very first question, he began doing gymnastic exercises. An answer in the stretching of his arms, and a roll of his neck... At my second question, he relaxed his back, stretched his leg muscles and jogged around the room... At my third question, he left me speechless, coming up behind me, shaking me around and jumping up and down! Gurudev's joyful contortions contrasted with the stiffness of my own exercise. How could I have thought that he would meekly submit himself to the exercise? Almost all my questions focussed on the shortcomings of the Western system. He didn't want to talk it down. And so, despite his display of flexibility, I was met with a firm refusal.

The aptness of the situation had delighted me. I gurgled with laughter and thanked him for the joke.

At the bottom of the notepad on which I described the incident there happened to be printed the following quotation: "*Be a bit crazy – you'll rise above the situation. Life isn't a serious matter. If living becomes a problem that needs solving, you will never be crazy, and you'll become an intellectual person; you'll become a doer. You need to know that life is a game; play it.*"

The answer always comes back, in one form or another.

Three months later, I presented Gurudev Sri Sri Ravi Shankar with another series of queries that were supposed to correspond to the big questions the public were asking: euthanasia, human cloning, abortion... The opinions of a wise person like him promised to be highly original. I also asked him for his definition of the principal social functions – what is teacher, a historian, a soldier, a businessman, a Head of State? What is a family, a society, a nation? Etc. I also wanted to hear what he had to say about the relationship between the sacred and the earth: the name of God linked to earthliness... The Master had had prior warning of the questions as I had given them to him in person. And he had been so kind since then that I was convinced that they had met with his approval.

I had an appointment. At long last, this was it... As soon as we start talking, Gurudev is off to rummage through his luggage in the other room and answers inaudibly, going back and forth between the two rooms. "*Follow me*." And he starts rustling bags of sweets in front of the microphone. He rejects my questions one after the other: "*Next*! Suivante!" From time to time, fighting against boredom, he consents to make a terse comment: "*Organ donations*? *Yes, that's all right... Next*!" Euthanasia? He can't see...

He says, "*These are unintelligent questions*," and I reply, "Is that not what you do all the time, answer silly questions?" To lighten the atmosphere, he hugs me and rubs my back as one would do with a child who has just fallen over, saying it's nothing, it'll soon stop hurting, it will be all right... "*Isn't it better to play*?" He takes me by the hand, and has me jumping and dancing with him. But this time, my heart is not in it. The gruelling experience has flattened me. I don't understand. Then he starts boxing with me, and we pretend to fight each other.

That evening, during satsang, he gives me the beginnings of an explanation. I'm still in such a state of shock that I jot down some notes so that I can think things over when my head is clearer: "*The intellect makes life more complicated, and weighs it down... We must embrace life as it comes. If you want to build a house, you take the slope of the land into account; you don't level it off... The same thing goes for cultures... If the land is on a slope, you farm in terraces...*

When you are not doing something right, I point it out to you so you stop doing it that way. If you love someone, you want them to point out your errors to you. You want the Master to maintain his authority over you. Can you describe saying "It doesn't matter, go on, do it that way", as love? No. This moment is there to improve you, not to accuse you... Not judging yourself, not feeling guilty, but being conscious of one's errors; that makes a lot of difference... If you complain, you spoil this moment... Do not search for justifications or explanations... When you try to justify your position, it becomes a source of stress, and each time you seek to defend it, it leaves you weaker... Everyone has the right to give or not to give. This is not something that can be bought... Don't worry. You will get what you are entitled to. By the same token, there is no way you will get what you are not entitled to. But what you are entitled to will come to you quite simply... Something that is a bit uncomfortable now but will be a comfort to you in the long run is a good thing."

The Master also says that what begins in chaos will end in bliss. That initial difficulties, though not a necessity, augur well for the future. That there is a Sanskrit proverb which says, "When you have something important to do for others, the road is very steep." And he goes on, "*But it is not obligatory. If the road is not, that is just as good. It's all right.*"

Once I had set aside the ridiculous idea that Gurudev Sri Sri Ravi Shankar might have been trying to scupper my efforts, I just had to trust him. Something Gurudev once said came back to me: "*You see, most of the questions you are asking me – I say most, not all – are ones you already know the answer to. You can buy books on all these issues in bookshops. Now, what you want is my 'opinion' on these questions. But my opinion doesn't count for anything! A teacher has opinions, has concepts about things, because he lives in the dimension of the intellect. But someone who has fully realised himself does not live in the intellect: he lives in another dimension. This is the dimension of silence. Do you understand? The dimension of the heart.*

What cannot be expressed in so many words can be contained in a single glance. And what cannot be conveyed in many glances can be expressed by a moment's silence. Isn't it? As long as we rely on words, our communication is very superficial. When we talk face to face with someone, we may both be trying to say the same thing, but we are still exchanging arguments. For someone overhearing our conversation, it will sound like a discussion. When we speak from the heart to someone else's heart, even if we say different things, there is still agreement. Words do not mean a lot. The feelings behind the words are much more important. Do you see?

For instance, when a mother gets angry with one of her children, she might say, "Clear off!", but that does not signify that she means what she is saying. When a lover says to his beloved, "I could eat you up," that doesn't mean that he is actually going to do it... The words lose their meaning, and it's the emotion which comes to the fore. Truth cannot be grasped through the intellect alone, because the intellect only corresponds to part of the brain. Nor can it be understood by emotion alone because, again, emotion only corresponds to part of our existence. The basis of both, intellect and emotion is silence. It is the true essence of our being. So, when you are very calm and silent, the emotion that wells up within you is truly serene, positive and pure.

Putting your trust in words is ignorance;

Transcending words is wisdom.

Words aren't powerful enough to express the Truth..."

♦

What I had hoped of Gurudev was the exact opposite of what he taught: that he would provide decisive answers, tell one how to behave, weigh up the different possible courses of action... His role is to wake the mind of the person who puts him or herself in his hands. The Master does not teach if he is not allowed to do so. Hence the fact that certain limits in development cannot be got past when the ego and the mind create a barrier. It is then up to each individual, 'in full knowledge of the facts', to determine themselves in their lives, in all good conscience.

A real Master will not answer all your questions then and there. He will rather proceed in such a way that the answers develop within you. In fact, he will put the answers away from you. He will keep you in wonder. A Master helps you go from the head to the heart.

"Each answer only pushes the question a little further along, and each question raises even more questions. A question and answer

session is endless. It can last indefinitely! When you answer a question, it raises ten other questions. Question and answer form a pair, a couple that has never heard about family planning!

Buddha said, "Go beyond your questions, do without an answer", for your being possesses an answer to all questions. Turn every question into wonderment; 'Oh!'..."

The question asked is a source of violence. You require feed-back. Wonder creates silence. The aim of knowledge is to lead to wonder – to this innocent state in which 'I do not know'. The Master himself is in wonder – it may sound like a joke – when he says, "*I don't know what I am talking about*." But the person in this state knows everything.

Spiritual exercises, such as *Sadhana*, serve to swing questions round in this direction.

"We formulate questions and answers that are perfectly pointless. We fill our minds with irrelevant information and overload our memory. Take pity on your brain, give your mind a break... and without your mobile phone!"

♦

All Gurudev's attitudes seek to make one stronger. The failures that he gives rise to, incite you to more creativity, more skills. And he is more or less demanding, proportionately to the disciple's ability to cope with difficulty. I understand it now. Granting me classical interviews, without critical intention, as, by the way, he does in an appropriate context, was an easy option which he spurned. What was at stake in going beyond was, to his way of thinking, more important than the interest of a book, even a potential best seller. Gurudev values nothing more than those things which encourage maturity, and hence the happiness of the disciple for whom he has taken responsibility. Not even the precious diffusion of knowledge, which would not be well served by mediocrity in effort. And this requires so much love...

Today, I know that he enabled me to write the book I wanted to write; to the best of my ability at the time.

When I look back at the reality of this 'wasted' time, I now appreciate how far the Master managed to bring me to fill in significant gaps. I see his Christ-like face lit by a light which at times outlines a crown in the middle of his forehead. I can see his gentle smile and cheeky gaze. He calls out to me: "*Got it*?"

A few years ago, I said to him, "Thank you for everything you give me, and also for what you refuse me, which is an even more handsome present."

And then, from time to time one's consciousness has a little snooze...

Some evenings, Gurudev Sri Sri Ravi Shankar asks his assembled disciples to sit facing the back of the room, and to turn their backs towards him. When faced with the prospect of taking their eyes off him, many people find they can't do it. They fudge the issue, and sit slightly sideways...

The Master says, *"Do not follow me. The fact is you cannot follow me, because I am behind you. I am behind to push you forward. You must leave everything behind and go forward. Everything – your experiences, your relationships – belongs to the past. Leave it all behind you. Leave the whole world of your memories behind you, including me. Go forward and be free. Stop searching. Then compassion will flow from you. You cannot follow me, because I am behind you and within you. For a long time, you followed like sheep; now it is time to be lions. Be alive!"*

Every day God gives, somewhere in the world, a *satsang* takes place in his presence. The baskets are always full, especially with the same questions. There is the freshness of discovery in Gurudev Sri Sri Ravi Shankar's answers. But sometimes he remains mute, giving his teaching in sign-language. At such times he mimes the way knowledge enters one ear and comes out by the other... The fact that there is no point..."*So what*?"

One evening, the Master even said that he didn't feel 'motivated', and added, with a weary sigh, "*Blessed is he who has forgotten everything*!" The joyful game of ping-pong was to recommence the next day:

"Guruji, you are so full of knowledge, it is like gold. Where do you get it from?

– *I have a mine within me.*

– What is the secret of your smile?

– *It is just the reflection of your eyes.*

– Why are there so many enlightened Masters in India?

– *Red bananas grow in Kerala. We don't ask why, we simply enjoy the fact."*

– Can we have several gurus?

– *A single guru is more than sufficient for you to manoeuvre... Why would you want several?*

– How can one become like you?

– *There are two possible ways: become like a child, or go mad!*

– Does a guru sometimes get angry?

– *That happens!*

– When is that?

– *When his anger can bring about something good. But people don't believe it... And the occasion rarely presents itself.*

– Guruji, I would like to find God.

– *Have you really nothing better to search for?! This idea is all to your credit... But what matters, is the intensity of your desire to find God.*

– I would like to enter into silence for a long time, do you think I can?

– *A long period of silence isn't necessary. An intense silence is quite beneficial enough. The time factor isn't important. Be active in society. Do good to the people around you.*

– What is the difference between the spirit and consciousness?

– *The spirit is consciousness. These are just two different words. The spirit is the religious term. Consciousness is the scientific name.*

– Are we contained within the soul, or is it the soul that is contained within ourselves?

– *What do you yourself think?*

– I don't know... I am confused...

– *Who is confused?*

– I am confused about that too!

– You are the only doctor qualified to deal with nuts like us!

– *I thought I was in heaven with angels, and you tell me I'm in a psychiatric hospital! That's all right if there is so much laughter and joy in psychiatric hospitals, it's absolutely Okay!*

– Does one have to go to the doctor's or can one simply count on the guru's grace?

– *Both are all right. But I wouldn't like to take the bread out of the doctors'mouths! However, you should continue to put your faith in consciousness which builds and rebuilds everything.*

– There are people who have access to you more easily. Are they more blessed?

– *Absolutely not. Don't put other people between us. You are here and I am here. That's all.*

– The colour black is considered unlucky. Is it true?

– *Not at all. All colours are beautiful.*

– Do ghosts exist?

– *I've not seen ghosts. But if you ask me if Shiva exists, I will say yes.*

– Why is there always a yellow seat?

– *What does that change? Don't attach any importance to external things. Each substance has its own vibration. But you are much more powerful than anything else. Don't be afraid. Don't live like a mouse. Live like Krishna. Show humility and authority.*

– Why is energy both positive and negative?

– *Energy can only circulate if there are two poles. The flow of energy is dynamic. Dynamism needs a direction. Duality is in the nature of energy."*

– How do you keep your energy level so high?

– *Hmm? I keep watching you all.*

– How do you know what our wishes are?

– That's a professional secret...! But I think you can guess how, can't you?

– Why do we ask you for your opinion when we have an important decision to take?

– I have no idea.

– When we doubt, we turn to you. When you yourself have a question, who do you turn to?

– To you!

– Why was I created if, eventually, I am destined to disappear?

– To disappear and be recreated... Wake up: nothing dies here on earth.

– Guruji, does the mind never rest?

– Isn't it resting just now? I am here, with you, which is why it is resting. Feel that you are always with me.

– How can one attain salvation during one's life on earth?

– You are sitting in the right place!

– I can't abandon myself as easily and as often as I would like to. I find that very soon I am distracted...

– You would like everything to be quick and easy. Forget about abandoning yourself.

– I've an obsessive mind. What can I do about it?

– Give it to me.

– What career would you advise me to go in for?

– The choice is yours, the blessing is mine.

– What do you think about the fact of giving life to a child?

– The choice is yours, the blessing is mine.

– Can't one have both?

– The lack of choice is a blessing. If you have both, you are very lucky.

– What do you say to someone who has persistent problems?

– Be patient.

– How can I convince people of the benefits you've brought me?

– Don't try too hard to please people. Behave with dignity.

– What is really funny?

– Your own mind.

– Can you explain this: 'I am not the doer'?

– When you find yourself very busy, you will understand. Someone who is indolent cannot understand. Only people who are dynamic, active and absorbed in what they are doing can be aware of it.

– Is destruction part of nature?

– According to you? Doesn't God understand economic principles? What do you think?

– Who and what do we live for?

– Live for the world. If that's not enough, live for the people you love. And if that is still not enough, live for me. I need a lot of help to do my work – to bring a smile to peoples' faces...

– I want you always to be by my side.

– You have no choice! Once you have learned how to live, it's difficult to forget! It's impossible to get away from the Art of Living; you are hooked!

Gurudev stays silent for quite a while, and then says, *"Don't take questions too seriously. All these remarks are meant to make you smile. Celebrate, sing, dance, be as wise as children... The aim of each answer is to produce a 'Yes', a 'Yeah' or an 'Oh, really?' in your mind. Any answer which would fail to evoke these in your mind is not an answer. So just say 'Yeah' to all the questions, and take it that you have answered them...! Give your question up to me and you will realise that you are inside the answer itself.*

Some questions can only find their answer in silence. When you wonder: 'Who am I?' the only relevant answer is silence. Every other way of answering must be set aside, including: 'I am nothing', or 'I am the cosmic Self', or 'I am the Self'. Just bear in mind the question: 'Who am I?' The rest is just thoughts. Thoughts can never be complete, only silence is complete.

We see so many people die. We see so much suffering and we remain unmoved. Why? Because there is no silence. We are wrapped up in our own little desires, attractions and aversions. The mind is full of its own noise; it is incapable of hearing the music of existence. Silence is the music of this existence. Silence is the secret of existence.

Are you all here? Perhaps. Nothing is sure. Your mind is perhaps somewhere else even if you are sitting here."

♦

In September 2002, Gurudev Sri Sri Ravi Shankar gave a message to the world, entitled 'The Promise':

"If I had to promise you something, what would it be?

I can't promise that you would always be comfortable

because comfort brings boredom and discomfort.

I can't promise that all your desires will be fulfilled

because desires, whether fulfilled or unfulfilled, bring frustration.

I can't promise that there will always be good times

because it is the tough times that make us appreciate joy.

I can't promise you that you will be rich or famous or powerful

because they can all be pathways to misery.

I can't promise that we will always be together,

because it is separation that makes togetherness so wonderful.

Yet if you are willing to walk with me,

if you are willing to value love over everything else,

I promise that yours will be the richest and most fulfilling life possible,

I promise your life will be an eternal celebration,

I promise you I will cherish you more than a king cherishes his crown,

and I shall love you more than a mother loves her newborn child.

If you are willing to walk into my arms,

if you are willing to live in my heart,

You will find the one you have always been waiting for...

You will meet yourself in my arms...

I promise."

He will not be back in the West for some time. The seeds have been sown. If you wish to meet him you will have to travel to India to see him.

The Art of Living

&

The International Association for Human Values

Transforming Lives...

The Founder

Gurudev Sri Sri Ravi Shankar

Gurudev Sri Sri Ravi Shankar is a universally revered spiritual and humanitarian leader. His vision of a violence-free, stress-free society through the reawakening of human values has inspired millions to broaden their spheres of responsibility and work towards the betterment of the world. Born in 1956 in southern India, Gurudev was often found deep in meditation as a child. At the age of four, he astonished his teachers by reciting the Bhagwad Gita, an ancient Sanskrit scripture. He has always had the unique gift of presenting the deepest truths in the simplest of words.

Gurudev established The Art of Living, an educational and humanitarian Non-Governmental Organisation that works in special consultative status with the Economic and Social Council (ECOSOC) of the United Nations in 1981. Present in over 156 countries, it formulates and implements lasting solutions to conflicts and issues faced by individuals, communities and nations. In 1997, he founded the International Association for Human Values (IAHV) to foster human values and lead sustainable development projects. Gurudev has reached out to more than 300 million people worldwide through personal interactions, public events, teachings, The Art of Living workshops and humanitarian initiatives. He has brought to the masses ancient practices which were traditionally kept exclusive, and has designed many self development techniques which can easily be integrated into daily life to calm the mind and instill confidence and enthusiasm. One of Gurudev's most unique offerings to the world is the Sudarshan Kriya, a powerful breathing technique that facilitates physical, mental, emotional and social well-being.

Numerous awards have been bestowed upon Gurudev Sri Sri Ravi Shankar which includes Padma Vibhushan (India's second highest civilian award) and the highest civilian awards from Paraguay, Mongolia and Colombia. Gurudev has addressed several international forums, including the United Nations Millennium World Peace Summit (2000), World Economic Forum (2001, 2003), World Summit On Ethics In Sports at FIFA Headquarters, Zurich (2014, 2016), UNESCO (2015), Parliaments of France, Britain, Norway (2016) and others.

Gurudev has played a key role in conflict resolution across the world including Colombia, Kashmir, Iraq, Ivory Coast, Naxal inhabited regions of India, and many other places.

Follow Sri Sri on:

Twitter - @srisri

Facebook - www.facebook.com/SriSriRaviShankar

Website - www.srisri.org

YouTube - www.youtube.com/srisri

Instagram - www.instagram.com/srisriravishankar

LinkedIn - www.linkedin.com/in/srisriravishankar

The Art of Living

In Service Around The World

Founded in 1981 by Gurudev Sri Sri Ravi Shankar, The Art of Living is engaged in stress-elimination programs and service initiatives. The organization operates globally in 156 countries with one of the largest volunteer bases in the world and has touched the lives of over 370 million people.

The organisation works in special consultative status with the Economic and Social Council (ECOSOC) of the United Nations, participating in a variety of committees and activities related to health and conflict resolution.

In 1997, Gurudev Sri Sri Ravi Shankar also founded the International Association for Human Values (IAHV) to coordinate sustainable development projects, nurture human values and coordinate conflict resolution in association with The Art of Living. In India, Africa and South America, the two sister organizations' volunteers are spearheading sustainable growth in rural communities, and have already reached out to 40,212 villages.

The Art of Living movement has spread peace and transformation across communities through diverse humanitarian projects.

- Conflict Resolution
- Alleviating pain in War Zones
- Relieving trauma in Post Terror Attacks
- Disaster Relief
- Environment
- Education
- Empowerment of Women
- Prisoner Rehabilitation
- Rural Transformation

The Art of Living Programs

The Art of Living programs are guided by Gurudev Sri Sri Ravi Shankar's philosophy of peace: "Unless we have a stress-free mind and a violence-free society, we cannot achieve world peace." To help individuals get rid of stress and experience inner peace, The Art of Living offers stress-elimination programs which include breathing techniques, meditation and yoga. They cater to every age group - children, youth, adults and every section of society – rural communities, governments, corporate houses, etc. These programs have helped millions around the world to overcome stress, depression and violent tendencies. Emphasizing holistic living and personal self-development, the programs facilitate the complete blossoming of an individual's full potential. The cornerstone of all our workshops is the Sudarshan Kriya, a unique and potent breathing practice.

Introductory Programs:

- **The Happiness Program (Age 18+):**
  The 3-day program equips participants with practical knowledge and techniques to unlock their deepest potential and bring fullness to life.
- **Sahaj Samadhi Meditation (Age 18+):**
  Meditation technique that deeply relaxes the mind and rejuvenates the system.
- **ART Excel (Age 8-13):**
  Introduce your children to spirituality, nurture human values, inculcate self-discipline, and develop their personality to be healthy and well-rounded.
- **YES (Age 14-18):**
  Dynamic and innovative educational program for both high school and college students.
- **Prajñā Yoga (Age 5-18):**
  Helps children tap into the inherent intuitive abilities of the mind.

For more information please visit: www.artofliving.org

International Centres

INDIA
21st km, Kanakapura Road, Udayapura,
Bangalore - 560 082, Karnataka
Telephone: 0091 - 80-67262626 / 27 / 28
Email: info@srisripublications.com

GERMANY
Bad Antogast 1, 77728 Oppenau,
Baden-Württemberg
Telephone: 0049 - 7804-973-90
Email: info@artofliving.de

CANADA
13 Infinity Road, St. Mathieu du Parc,
Quebec G0X 1N0
Telephone: 001 - 819-532-3328
Email: artdevivre@artofliving.org

USA
639 Whispering Hills Rd,
Boone, NC 28607
Telephone: 001 - 828-263-4910
Email: info@artoflivingretreatcenter.org

www.srisriravishankar.org
www.artofliving.org
www.iahv.org

